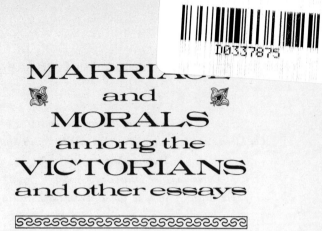

MARRIAGE
🌺 and 🌺
MORALS
among the
VICTORIANS
and other essays

〜〜〜〜〜〜〜〜〜〜〜〜〜〜〜〜〜〜〜

ALSO BY GERTRUDE HIMMELFARB

The Idea of Poverty (1984)
On Liberty and Liberalism: The Case of John Stuart Mill (1974)
Victorian Minds (1968)
Darwin and the Darwinian Revolution (1959)
Lord Acton: A Study in Conscience and Politics (1952)

EDITOR OF

John Stuart Mill, *On Liberty* (1974)
John Stuart Mill, *Essays on Politics and Culture* (1962)
T. R. Malthus, *On Population* (1960)
Lord Acton, *Essays on Freedom and Power* (1948)

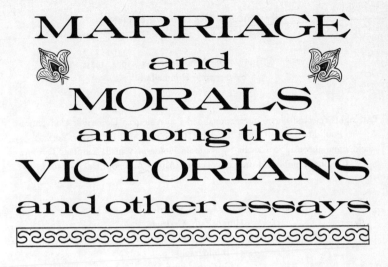

MARRIAGE and MORALS among the VICTORIANS and other essays

by

GERTRUDE HIMMELFARB

Vintage Books
A Division of Random House
New York

First Vintage Books Edition, August 1987

Copyright © 1975, 1978, 1981, 1982, 1983, 1984, 1985, 1986
by Gertrude Himmelfarb

Library of Congress Cataloging-in-Publication Data
Himmelfarb, Gertrude.
Marriage and morals among the Victorians, and other essays.
Bibliography: p.
Includes index.
1. Great Britain—Moral conditions.
2. Great Britain—Intellectual life—19th century.
3. Social history—19th century.
I. Title.
[HN400.M6H56 1987] 306'.0942 86–40476
ISBN 0–394–75290–2 (pbk.)

Grateful acknowledgment is made to the following magazines, who printed
the original versions of the following essays:
The American Scholar: "Social Darwinism, Sociobiology, and the Two Cultures,"
"Bentham versus Blackstone," and "Michael Oakeshott:
The Conservative Disposition."
Commentary: "A Genealogy of Morals: From Clapham to Bloomsbury."
The Journal of British Studies: "Bentham's Utopia."
The New Criterion: "Marriage and Morals Among the Victorians"
and "Who Now Reads Macaulay?"
The New Republic: "Godwin's Utopia," "Disraeli: The Tory Imagination,"
and "The Webbs: The Religion of Socialism."

Display Typography by Sandra Josephson

Manufactured in the United States of America
10 9 8 7 6 5 4 3 2 1

For Rebecca and Anne

Contents

Introduction

In the preface to the first volume of his magisterial *History of the English People in the Nineteenth Century*, which appeared just before the First World War, Elie Halévy remarked on the audacity of a foreigner presuming to write about England. The Frenchman had to learn what even the most uneducated Englishman knew instinctively. But to compensate for that deficiency, he brought to his subject a "valuable capacity for wonder." Where the English historian H. T. Buckle, writing the *History of Civilization in England* half a century earlier, simply assumed that all other forms of civilization were deviations from the norm—that is, from England—a French historian like himself could appreciate how unique English civilization was. What the native took for granted, what was so familiar to him as to be part of his "intellectual and moral nature," was for the foreigner a cause for astonishment and explanation.

An American historian today has even more reason to apologize. Apart from the obvious disability of not being a Halévy, the American is still further removed, temporally, geographically, culturally, and socially, from nineteenth-century England. And the difficulty is increased if the subject of inquiry is not the polity and society of that unique civilization but the "intellectual and moral nature" that made it unique. Yet here too one may find virtue in necessity. For distance puts into sharper focus those ideas and beliefs, morals and manners, which made for a culture so different from our own. Now, more than ever, we have much to wonder at and even more to explain.

From this perspective, too, the perimeters of the "nineteenth century" appear remarkably elastic. Again we may be emboldened by Halévy, who took as a crucial event, in his first volume on "England in 1815," the Wesleyan movement initiated three-quarters of a century earlier, and who devoted the whole of his last volume to the period preceding the outbreak of the war in 1914. Or we may cite the example of that admirable journal, *Nineteenth Century*, which started publication in 1877 and in 1901 changed its name to *Nineteenth Century and After*. The conventional explanation is that the title *Twentieth Century* had been patented by an unscrupulous entrepreneur who hoped to sell it to the journal at an exorbitant price, which the editor indignantly refused to pay. I should like to think that the editor had a secret fondness for the original title (and for the age it evoked) and was not averse to the amended version. In any case, it was in that form that the magazine continued to flourish until 1951, when it finally emerged as *The Twentieth Century*.

It is in this spirit that the present volume takes its bearings from the nineteenth century even when it ventures outside it. One excursion brings us back to the time of the American Revolution, when Jeremy Bentham launched his attack on Blackstone and the English Constitution; but since Bentham and Benthamism survived well into the nineteenth century, it requires no great boldness of imagination to claim him for that century. Another essay brings us forward into our own time with one of the most influential conservative philosophers of the twentieth century, Michael Oakeshott, whose mode of thought, it has been said, recalls an earlier, more spacious and civilized time. Other essays, such as that tracing the "genealogy of morals" from Clapham to

Bloomsbury, or the "two cultures" from Social Darwinism to Sociobiology, span the centuries, permitting the nineteenth to serve as a foil (or, it may be, a corrective) to the twentieth.

If I have taken some liberties with chronology, I have taken fewer with nationality. The subject of this book is unashamedly England. ("Britain" or "Great Britain," while technically correct, does not capture the spirit of an age that saw the publication of Bulwer-Lytton's *England and the English,* Macaulay's *History of England,* and Buckle's *History of Civilization in England.*) Yet I have allowed myself some fleeting views from abroad. In "Bentham versus Blackstone," Bentham stands in contrast to the American Founding Fathers, as well as to the English tradition represented by Blackstone. "A Genealogy of Morals" opens and closes with Nietzsche (and, of course, takes its title from him). And "The Victorian Trinity" starts with Voltaire, moves on to the Young Hegelians and Marx, and, once again, comes to rest with Nietzsche. In these instances the effect is to emphasize the uniqueness of English thinkers by confronting them with their peers on the Continent and overseas.

To the historian of ideas, the insularity of England in the nineteenth century is a standing challenge. One is constantly tempted to bring England into Europe, to demonstrate the influence of Kant on Coleridge, Goethe on Carlyle, Feuerbach on Eliot, Comte on Beatrice Webb, Nietzsche on Shaw. But in each case the foreign ideas were so thoroughly domesticated, so completely assimilated (coopted, we would now say) that the very word "influence" seems inappropriate. Like the Common Market today, the common market of ideas in the nineteenth century (whose capital in the 1840s was Paris) had only a peripheral effect on England. More often the attempt to bridge the cultures was as unavailing as the perennial schemes for a "chunnel" linking France and England. Yet it is important to retain the perspective of foreign cultures, if only to appreciate the distinctiveness of the English, and to overcome the schizophrenia that besets anyone who tries to deal seriously with the intellectual history of both England and Europe.

In most volumes of essays, the author is hard put to find a unifying theme. In this case I am embarrassed to discover how often—how obsessively, some might say—I have dwelt on the same theme. In part this may be attributed to the fact that all but one of the essays reprinted here, as well as that not previously published, were written within the past decade, and most of them within the past four years. (Some have been substantially rewritten and expanded for the present volume, although not for the purpose of eliciting a common theme.) But it also reflects a sense of the "intellectual and moral nature" of nineteenth-century England which goes back to my first book, on Lord Acton, and which is not far from the center of my other books.

The words "morals" and "morality," conspicuous in the titles of the first three essays and cropping up again and again in the texts of the others, convey a range of meanings. In the most formal sense, they refer to the "moral philosophy" of G. E. Moore (in the second essay), of Henry Sidgwick (in the third), or of Michael Oakeshott (in the last). But more often they have a less formal, more existential connotation, something like the "moral imagination" described by Lionel Trilling, an imagination that penetrates all aspects of life—mind, literature, politics, social affairs, and, of course, personal conduct. I myself have been much influenced by Trilling, especially by his most provocative volume of essays, *The Liberal Imagination;* it is in one of those essays, "Manners, Morals, and the Novel," that the concept of the "moral imagination" appears. I was all the more delighted, therefore, to come across that expression in one of my other favorite writers, Edmund Burke, and in precisely the same sense, as applying to the public and the private, the highest reaches of mind and the commonplaces of everyday life. In his *Reflections on the Revolution in France,* Burke condemned the revolutionaries for violating the "moral imagination" of mankind:

But now all is to be changed. All the pleasing illusions, which made power gentle, and obedience liberal, which harmonized the different shadows of life, and which, by a bland assimilation, incorporated into politics the sentiments which beautify and soften private society, are to be dissolved by this new conquering empire of light and reason. All the decent drapery of life is to be rudely torn off. All the super-added ideas, furnished from the wardrobe of a moral imagination, which the heart owns, and the understanding ratifies, as necessary to cover the defects of our own naked shivering nature, and to raise it to dignity in our own estimation, are to be exploded as a ridiculous, absurd, and antiquated fashion.

Within a decade of Burke's prophecy his worst fears were realized in two of the most remarkable "utopias" of modern times, one utterly anarchic, the other utterly repressive, but both equally dedicated to the "new conquering empire of light and reason." Neither the utopian imagination of a Godwin nor that of a Bentham prevailed against the moral imagination of the Victorians, an imagination that treasured the complexity of heart and mind and that sought, by aesthetic means as well as ethical, to adorn and enhance rather than destroy the "decent drapery of life." At its most trivial this took the form of piano legs sheathed in pantaloons and human legs christened "limbs," a *Family Shakespeare* purged of indelicacies and the works of male and female authors chastely residing on separate shelves, and all the other proprieties of Mrs. Grundy and hypocrisies of Mr. Pecksniff. But these follies were ridiculed by the Victorians themselves; indeed, it is their satires that call our attention to them. And they were ridiculed most of all by those who were most solicitous of morality in its larger sense.

From the perspective of our own time, we can better appreciate Victorian morality "properly understood": the morality that dignifies and civilizes human beings, removing us from our natural brutish state and covering, as Burke said, our "naked shivering nature." Today more than ever, we have reason to be wary of the kind of "civilization" celebrated by Bloomsbury, which dismissed conventional morality as "a ridiculous, absurd, and antiquated fashion." And we have even more reason to be apprehensive of the "new civilization" of the Webbs, that latter-day Benthamite utopia which would have abolished all those ridiculous, absurd, and antiquated institutions that made England the model of a liberal polity and society.

Gertrude Himmelfarb
April 1985

MARRIAGE

and

MORALS

among the

VICTORIANS

and other essays

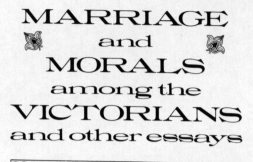

1

Marriage and Morals among the Victorians

When Lytton Strachey was asked to propose a toast to his *Eminent Victorians,* he quoted an eminent Victorian biographer: "When I hear men called 'judicious,' I suspect them; but when I hear them called 'judicious and venerable,' I know they are scoundrels." Strachey amended this to describe his own credo: "When I hear people called 'Victorians,' I suspect them. But when I hear them called 'Eminent Victorians,' I write their lives."[1]

Strachey wrote their lives to expose them, to reveal the private selves behind the public façades, the private vices that belied their public virtues. His book, published toward the end of the First World War, was his personal declaration of war (he refused to serve in his country's war) against the Victorian pieties and hypocrisies, as he saw them, which still governed society—and which also governed the writing of biography, those multi-volume tomes that told everything about their subjects except the essential truth. A later generation, further removed from the Victorians and still more removed from the Victorian mode of biography, has learned to be wary of the "essential" truth conveyed by the Strachey technique: the derisory physical detail (Thomas Arnold's legs, which were "shorter than they should have been"); the revealing *mîse-en-scène* (the open Bible next to the open brandy bottle on General Gordon's table); the list of peculiar names ("St. Bega, St. Adamnan, St. Gundleus, St. Guthlake, Brother Drithelm . . .") which made a mockery not only of the *Lives of the Saints* but of the very idea of sainthood.[2] We are now as apt to be suspicious of Strachey's *Eminent Victorians* as he was of the eminent Victorians themselves.

For all his irreverence, however, Strachey did the Victorians the honor of dealing with those aspects of their lives that made them eminent; it was their moral earnestness, their military heroism, their social service, their religious piety that he ridiculed. And his ridicule was so patent that the reader knew it for that, knew that the public persona was being measured against the private, and by that standard found wanting. More recently it has become the fashion to dwell on the private lives of historical figures, not to illuminate or even to expose their public lives but to discover some essential truth that is essentially private, and that is as essentially true for a public or historical person as for an ordinary, private person. If the eminent continue to be the subject of study, it is because they are so eminently accessible; they have left so much more evidence about their lives, public and private, than the "anonymous masses." The biographer may not even have any conscious animus against the eminent, any desire to condemn or ridicule them. Yet they are inevitably diminished when that which is peculiarly great about them, which made them public figures in their time and historic personages for us, is ignored.

A case study in the new mode of inquiry is *Parallel Lives: Five Victorian Marriages,* by Phyllis Rose. The title itself is suggestive. Plutarch's *Parallel Lives of the Greeks and Romans,* the author reminds us, was meant to instruct the reader about the "perils and pitfalls of public life"; the present volume is meant to do the same about domestic life.[3] These five Victorian marriages, however, hardly typify the domestic life of the Victorians. They are, indeed, the most unrepresentative couples one can imagine, both because of their eminence and because of their peculiarities. The five are the Carlyles, the Ruskins, the Mills, the Dickenses, and George Eliot and George Henry Lewes. To anyone having the least acquaintance with Victorian literature, these couples are notorious for the "irregularity"—that wonderful Victorian word —of their relationships. Two pairs (the Carlyles and Ruskins) never consummated their marriage; one (Eliot and Lewes) lived together without benefit of marriage; another (the Mills) had a long-standing, intimate (if platonic, as they insisted) relationship while she was married to another man; and the fifth (the Dickenses) separated when he fell in love with another woman. These particular subjects were chosen, we are told, for their variety and narrative interest, which makes one wonder why there is no example of that other deviant variety not uncommon at the time, the homosexual. Or, for that matter, that still more common (but less commonly written about) variety, the properly married, sexually compatible, conventionally devoted couple who might even qualify as interesting (the Darwins come to mind).

The stories of these five couples are familiar enough; each has been the subject of long and detailed study. What is novel is the theme uniting them. Marriage—or "parallel lives," as Rose prefers, to emphasize the separateness of the partners—is presented as a political experience, indeed, "the primary political experience in which most of us engage as adults." Like any political experience it involves power, the management and balance of power determining the "priority of desires" of the two partners. A marriage is sustained so long as there is a mutual understanding of the terms of the balance of power and mutual gains to be derived from it; it fails when the terms are violated or are no longer satisfactory, when "the weaker member feels exploited or the stronger feels unrewarded for his or her strength." Love is the mask used to "disguise transactions involving power"; it is the "ideological bone thrown to women to distract their attention from the powerlessness of their lives." It may momentarily "inhibit the process of power negotiation," thus promoting the "illusion of equality so characteristic of lovers." If this inhibition comes from within, it is "one of life's graces and blessings." But if, as is often the case, it comes from without, if it is "culturally induced" or desired more by one sex than by the other, it is a "mask for exploitation."[4]

It is a powerful thesis (the pun is irresistible), powerfully stated, with some interesting turns to redeem it from banality. Divorce, we are told, so far from ameliorating or correcting the inequities of marriage, compounds them—which does not mean, Rose hastens to add, that she would like less divorce, only less marriage. "Bad enough to choose once in a lifetime whom to live with; to go on choosing, to reaffirm one's choice day after day, as one must when it is culturally possible to divorce, is really asking a lot of people." It was better in the old days, when indissoluble unions were combined with "a great deal of civilized behavior—in other words, secrecy, even lying—for the sake of harmony." Or better yet, the way of the future: "frankly personal unions entered into personally, with carefully articulated and individualized pledges of fidelity, if any."[5]

In view of the boldness of the thesis, one may be surprised that it appears (intrudes, an unsympathetic reader might say) only occasionally in the course of the book. Yet it is precisely its boldness that makes it relatively unintrusive. If every kind of marriage—regardless of the peculiarities of character, circumstance, sentiment, or sexual disposition—is a form of "sexual politics," it is enough to record the manifold ways in which these "imaginative projections and arrangements of power" reveal themselves.[6] No judgment is called for because all such arrangements are equally political. Thus sexless marriages can be tolerantly described as "examples of flexibility rather than of abnormality."[7] And sympathy can be extended impartially to everyone unwittingly caught up in these power relationships, the exploited and the exploiters being alike victims of an institution more powerful than they, which oppressed them even as they oppressed their mates.

There is another reason why the thesis is more prominent in the prologue than in the rest of the book and in some chapters more than in others, and that is that it is so often irrelevant to the case in point. If it appears hardly at all in the account of the Ruskins, it is because the only kind of power that is at issue here is sexual potency, in which Ruskin was sadly lacking—and this is not, presumably, what the author has in mind when she speaks of marriage as a "projection" of power. Ruskin did not even choose to use what legal power he had to prevent his wife from leaving him, or, later, to contest the annulment. Since there is no evidence of this kind of "political" power, the author makes the most of the conspicuous failure of sexual power. Ruskin's impotence thus becomes the occasion for generalizations about the sex life of the Victorians.

Ruskin's was a notorious case in his own time and continues to fascinate biographers. And for good reason—it is not often that the subject of a biography provides so many titillating details about his intimate life. In a letter to his lawyer, Ruskin explained that he did not consummate his marriage on his wedding night because he was repelled by the sight of his wife's body. There was something wrong with it, he felt; it was not as he had imagined it; it was "not formed to excite passion."[8] One theory has it that he was especially repelled by her pubic hair and possibly by her breasts, his image of the female body having come from the highly idealized, de-sexualized nudes he was familiar with in paintings and statues. This would also explain his later attraction to little girls not marred by the unsightly evidence of maturity. Rose is intrigued by this explanation: it offers proof of the "radical innocence" of the Victorians, and, better yet, of the power of art over experience. Unfortunately, she adds, it was probably not true, Ruskin having told his parents that he had seen pictures of "naked bawds" while at Oxford.[9] (And were those painted nudes—by Raphael or Rubens, for example—as asexual and immature as this theory supposes?)

Whatever the source of Ruskin's impotence (presumably paintings and statues were the least of it), Rose is less interested in what was peculiar about Ruskin's wedding night than in what was typical about it, the light it sheds on "Victorian sexuality." And what was typical was the ignorance and inexperience that made the Victorian wedding night a "barbaric trial" for at least the woman, and sometimes the man as well. That experience was all the worse because sexual relations, having been utterly forbidden before marriage, became an absolute requirement after marriage—a certain prescription for impotence and frigidity. While the Ruskins were not a representative couple, their plight was "probably less extraordinary and eccentric than one might think at first."[10] Were it not for a footnote at this point, one might let this statement pass for the speculation it frankly is. But the note itself, raising the expectation of proof, only makes the generalization more dubious, for it cites a similar and even more unsubstantiated speculation concerning an equally unrepresentative and thoroughly un-Victorian figure, the American poet Delmore Schwartz.

The question of proof is almost irrelevant, however, for the thesis is so comprehensive it can accommodate itself to any form of sexual or domestic behavior, any symptoms of normality or abnormality, any kind of adjustment or maladjustment, any evidence of frigidity or fertility. If marriage itself is anomalous, if the legal commitment itself taints any relationship, then any of its manifestations must be equally anomalous. The footnote about Delmore Schwartz, for example, goes on to explain that even now, when premarital sex is the rule rather than the exception, there may be "wedding night trauma," although of a different kind. "Can society's sudden approval quench one's private pleasures as society's disapproval did before?"[11] It is not clear what is meant by "society's sudden approval," if indeed premarital sex is so prevalent and acceptable. But one takes the point: a permissive society creates its own traumas—and not only, one may add, on the wedding night but also in that supposedly voluntary, spontaneous, premarital period unfettered by legal bonds.

If some Victorians were rendered impotent by the prevailing sexual code and marital fetters, others, brought up under that same code and bound by the same ties, were evidently sexually stimulated to a degree that could not be contained within marriage. Charles Dickens was one such. After twenty-two years of marriage and ten children, Dickens moved out of his home, arranged for a legal separation from his wife, and entered into a long-standing affair with the actress Ellen Ternan. The situation was one that might be expected to evoke the sympathy of a commentator who takes so dim a view of marriage, who thinks "personal unions" more meaningful than legal ones, and, in the absence of such an enlightened alternative, recommends marriage combined with "a great deal of civilized behavior"—i.e., clandestine affairs.[12]

Dickens was twenty-four when he married, his wife twenty-one. Within nine months of their wedding, their first child was born and his first successful book published. Thereafter he sired as many books as children, each book taking him further away from a wife who was ineffectual even in the household, still more in the literary and social world (to say nothing of the private, creative world) inhabited by England's premier novelist. It was an all-too-familiar, and not peculiarly Victorian, situation, and Dickens handled it in the all-too-familiar way, with protestations of innocence and professions of outrage that he should be so maligned as to be accused of having an affair. Rose admits that Dickens's life after the separation was far happier than it had been before, and confesses some sympathy for his "flailing against middle age and domesticity," for "living as though no one had ever lived before." She nevertheless chastises him for his "ungentlemanly behavior" (as a Victorian would put it), and presents

him as a "fine example of how not to end a marriage."[13] The
rebuke is worthy of a good Victorian, but it comes oddly from
an opponent of marriage and a proponent of sexual liberty. One
wonders whether she would have been so severe on a wife who
exhibited such "unladylike behavior."

Another kind of double standard is evident in the discussion
of the Mills. Here the wife was not the pathetic, vulnerable
partner but the aggressive, dominant one. Rose does not conceal
her distaste for Harriet Taylor, later Harriet Mill, who manipu-
lated both of her husbands with as fine a disregard for their
sensibilities as for the conventions, whose domestic bullying was
matched only by her intellectual arrogance, and whose self-
esteem was as inordinate as Mill's uxoriousness. It was she who
read and approved of those extraordinary passages in Mill's *Autobiography* in which he praises her as superior to himself intellectually, emotionally, and aesthetically, her mind the "same perfect
instrument" in penetrating into the "highest regions of speculation" as into the "smallest practical concerns of daily life." Shelley was but a child "in thought and intellect" compared with her;
Carlyle could only be interpreted "by one greatly the superior
to us both—who was more a poet than he, and more a thinker
than I"; Coleridge and the German poets and philosophers were
an amalgam of truth and error, whereas in her, "I could not, as
I had done in those others, detect any mixture of error"; his own
father had no equal among men and "but one among women."
After that it comes almost as an anticlimax to find Mill endowing
her with "excellencies" so unique that "the highest poetry, philosophy, oratory, or art, seemed trivial by the side of her, and
equal only to expressing some small part of her mind."[14] Nor is
it surprising to find him altering crucial passages in his *Principles
of Political Economy,* against his own judgment and in spite of the
logic of the argument of the book, "even if there were no other
reason than the certainty I feel that I never should long continue
of an opinion different from yours on a subject which you have
fully considered."[15]

This record of self-deception and self-abasement is, at first sight, disconcerting. "How splendid it would be," Rose observes ruefully, "if we could find in the Mills' marriage what they hoped we would find, an exemplary model." Instead, we find a reversal of the patriarchal model: "A female autocrat replaced the usual male."[16] This was much the view of Mill's friends, one of whom described him as in a "state of subjection" to his wife (an ironic play on the title of Mill's famous essay, "The Subjection of Women"). But unlike his friends who thought this a violation of the natural order of things, and unlike later commentators who think it a violation of his own principle of the "perfect equality" of the sexes, Rose makes of it a higher principle, a more advanced form of equality. Mill must have been aware, she argues, that by claiming to be his wife's inferior he was "altering the usual allocation of power between the sexes." It was precisely because this "great experiment," the attempt to create "a true marriage of equals," was so unusual that it required unusual measures. Unwittingly echoing Orwell's *Animal Farm,* in which some pigs are more equal than others, Rose explains that "for Harriet to be anywhere near equal she had to be 'more than equal.'" "Think of it," she suggests, "as a domestic case of affirmative action. To achieve equality, more power had to go to Harriet, in compensation for the inequality of their conditions."[17]

It is curious to find, in this insistently political interpretation of marriage, so little concern for the actual political ideas (or, for that matter, ideas of any kind) of the individuals. Was there a correlation between liberalism and marital liberality? Between radicalism and sexual liberation? Between conservatism and domestic authoritarianism? Even within the limited scope of this book, in the lives and minds of these five couples, there is matter enough for speculation, if not for generalization. Ruskin, Dickens, Mill, Eliot, Carlyle—they were all people of strong political convictions. Yet only in the case of Carlyle does politics come to the fore, and then only in terms of a single incident, the famous Eyre case.

Edward Eyre was the colonial governor of Jamaica in 1865 when a riot resulted in the death or torture of dozens of white settlers. In suppressing the riot (which Eyre declared to be a rebellion), government troops killed almost a hundred blacks, court-martialed and executed hundreds more, and flogged and tortured still others. When news of the event reached England, it provoked a heated controversy that went on for years in the press and Parliament and that was not quelled by the appointment of a Royal Commission or by the dismissal of Eyre. In this account, the two sides in the controversy appear as a line-up of "two hockey teams ranged for the face-off." Opposing Eyre were the "liberals and scientific progressives": Mill, Darwin, Huxley, Spencer, Lewes; defending him were the "romantic authoritarians": Carlyle, Dickens, Tennyson, Tyndall, Kingsley.[18] To a knowledgeable reader, the names themselves suggest the inadequacy of these labels. But Rose sees the affair as symptomatic of all the "great democratic movements" of the century—"emancipation, nationalism, universal suffrage, women's rights, even trade unionism"—in each of which progressives sought a redistribution of power while authoritarians regarded the status quo as "divinely ordained."[19] Since marriage is also a matter of the distribution of power, political authoritarianism is said to have a natural affinity with patriarchy and domestic tyranny.

It is an intriguing idea, or would be if there were any serious attempt to demonstrate the correlation between sex and politics. Were trade unionists, for example, less tyrannical, as husbands, fathers, and lovers, than non–trade unionists? Or the supporters of Italian independence than those opposed or indifferent to it? Or little-Englanders than imperialists? Or, to be more specific, Gladstone than Disraeli? Is the correlation even true of the subjects of this book? Was Eliot being patriarchal when she opposed female suffrage, as she did? Or Ruskin when he permitted his wife to leave and gave her an uncontested annulment? Or Carlyle when he married so strong-minded a woman and made no attempt to curb her tongue and pen—indeed, urged her to read and write, and not casually but seriously?

And what of Jane Carlyle herself, who, in spite of her husband's encouragement, did not do any serious writing but did have trenchant opinions and was in the habit of expressing them incisively? She, it appears, was as vehement a supporter of Eyre as he was, and she evidently came to this position on her own. At a dinner party, in the absence of her husband, she found herself engaged in conversation with an irate man who would have liked to see Eyre, as she reported it, "cut into small pieces and eaten raw." He told her that women might patronize Eyre, because they were naturally cruel, but that no man would stand up for him. "I hope Mr. Carlyle does," she retorted. "I haven't had an opportunity of asking him; but I should be surprised and grieved if I found him sentimentalising over a pack of black brutes!"[20] This is hardly the kind of "progressive" sentiment Rose might be expected to approve of. Yet it is Jane Carlyle who emerges, only a few pages after this quotation, as the principal "heroine" of the book, and this in the closing sentences where the statement carries the largest weight.

> Feisty Jane went down fighting, demanding equal time, and writing about it all in marvelous prose which just might outlast her husband's. Because of her, the Carlyles' marriage seems, in the strange afterlife which literature grants, to be also a marriage of equals, where equality consists—as perhaps it must, in an imperfect time such as hers, or ours—in perpetual resistance, perpetual rebellion.[21]

"Feisty Jane"! Few men today would dare write so condescendingly of a woman.* Or, again condescendingly, to make so

---

*Or to first-name the women but not the men, as is done throughout this book. It is odd to find so ardent a feminist consistently speaking of Jane and Carlyle, Effie and Ruskin, Harriet and Mill, Catherine and Dickens. Only George Eliot is spared, perhaps because of the masculinity of her pseudonym.

little of Jane Carlyle's opinions (as in the Eyre case) while making so much of her husband's. Or to credit her with qualities she patently did not have while denying others she did have. Yes, she wrote marvelous prose—but better than his? Are her letters, witty and entertaining as they are, likely to outlast his essays and histories? And the "equality" that consists in "perpetual resistance, perpetual rebellion"—does that really describe a woman who devoted herself tirelessly to her husband's needs and comforts, who ingeniously, selflessly protected him from the intrusions of servants, workmen, and visitors, from the noises of the street and the crowing of the cocks, who put up with his crotchets and rages, with his sexual impotence and, finally, with his attachment to Lady Ashburton, which was as close as he could get to having an affair? Confronted with less cause for grievance, Effie Ruskin did in fact resist and rebel, to the point of leaving her husband, marrying another man (her husband's friend), and proceeding to have the children she had always desired. Jane Carlyle took out her misery and resentment in acidulous conversation, correspondence, and (when the Ashburton episode was at its worst) a diary which she left for Carlyle to find after her death. There is a good deal to admire in Jane Carlyle, but it is not the "equality" that comes from resistance and rebellion. It is, rather, a love and devotion that transcended all the difficulties and frustrations of her life. Only in this last sense, the Victorian sense of the word, does she truly qualify as a "heroine."

The more obvious heroine and hero of the book are George Eliot and George Henry Lewes, whose "devotion, stability, and equality grew outside the bounds of legal marriage."[22] To be sure, this was a matter of necessity rather than preference. When George Eliot—Marian Evans as she then was—met Lewes, he was married, the father of three children, and unable to get a divorce because he had condoned his wife's affair with his friend Thornton Hunt. (Hunt, with whom Mrs. Lewes had another three children, was himself married to another woman.) It was a rather free and easy circle in which Lewes moved. But there was nothing free and easy about Marian Evans or about her relationship with him. For twenty-four years until his death, they lived together as monogamously as the most proper Victorian couple, with the small exception that they were not legally married.[23]

It is the fact that they were not legally married that makes them Rose's "favorite couple," the happiest couple she knows "outside of fantasy literature."[24] Because of their ostracism from society, she explains, they were totally drawn in upon each other, totally occupied with the books they had in lieu of children, totally united in purpose and interests. This was possible only because they were spared the "burdens of respectability"—being nice to each other's friends, giving dinner parties, having weekend guests, appearing together in public. "Treated as sinful lovers, they remained lovers." They did not have to waste their energies "wishing themselves more free"; they had only to enjoy their freedom in solitude, devoting themselves to each other and to their work.[25]

This is as extraordinary a vision of marital (or extramarital) bliss as it is of human freedom. To think it liberating not to have children or friends, to shun society and public life, is a remarkable message to draw from this relationship. But it is the author's message, not her subjects'. When Eliot professed to be well rid of the "petty worldly torments" of society and the chatter of "frivolous women,"[26] or when she pretended not to mind when Lewes failed in his attempt to get a divorce abroad, she was obviously trying to put the best face on a situation that she found most distasteful. And she was not nearly as reclusive as is made out here. She broke with some friends, but retained others and made many new ones; she went to concerts and the opera, dined out and had dinner guests, and held regular Saturday evening or Sunday afternoon "at homes." So far from not being "received in society," she was received in the highest society, including nobility and royalty. If she was ostracized by some, she was lionized by many others. And if Lewes often went to parties without her, it was because she chose not to go, not because she was uninvited. (In fact, it was Lewes who objected to her attending meetings without him.)[27]

Nor did Eliot enjoy the freedom of not being married. That freedom was more onerous to her than any of the "burdens of respectability" of which she is presumed to have been happily relieved. Indeed, she voluntarily assumed the stigmata of respectability. She publicly referred to Lewes as her "husband" and to herself as his "wife," signed her letters "Marian Lewes," asked her friends to address her as "Mrs. Lewes," and had the satisfaction of having the real Mrs. Lewes do just that. (As if to reinforce that surname, she also took his first name as her pseudonym.) These are not the actions of a woman cherishing her independence, rebelling against law and convention, resisting the bonds of matrimony. And when those bonds were dissolved with the death of Lewes, she took the first opportunity to unburden herself of her freedom. A year and a half after his death she married John Cross. That legal marriage shocked her friends as much as had her earlier non-marriage—because of the discrepancy in age (she was sixty, he forty), because he was her intellectual inferior as well as her junior, and because of the marriage itself with all its trappings (the preparation of clothes as for a trousseau, the formal wedding in church, the honeymoon). The intellectual partnership that may serve to explain and justify her relationship with Lewes can hardly be invoked in the case of Cross. What Cross did provide, however, was what was so important to her: a total, unequivocal commitment, the kind she had been fortunate enough to have from Lewes despite the fact that they were not married, and which was now all the more compelling because it had the sanction of society and of the law.

It is of Eliot, but implicitly of all her subjects, that Rose puts the question:

What makes a marriage valid? its endorsement by church or state? or the commitment of the people involved? That was the question her behavior posed, and her radical stance was calculated to undermine morality as it had been known and to re-establish it on a more serious, a more existential, basis.[28]

In fact, Eliot's behavior—and Mill's and Dickens's and Ruskin's and Carlyle's—was calculated to do just the opposite: to strengthen "morality as it had been known" and to reestablish it on a more serious, a more *philosophical* basis.

In each case the violation of conventional morality was made to appear the exception that proved the rule. Mill and Harriet Taylor did not deliberately choose to defy convention; they did so reluctantly and regretfully, only because she happened to be married to another man. When her husband died, they delayed their marriage for almost two years in order to observe a proper period of mourning. And when they did get married, Mill was absurdly anxious about the perfect legality of the ceremony. He had happened to sign the marriage register "J. S. Mill," which was the form he used in writing, and when the clerk told him that his full name was required, he squeezed in the missing letters. A year later, haunted by the thought that his signature had been faulty, he wrote his wife a formal letter suggesting that they go through a church ceremony "so that hereafter no shadow of a doubt on the subject can ever arise." For once his wife was more sensible than he, and prevailed upon him not to take a step that would expose them to ridicule. But he carefully kept that letter among his effects as a written record of his intentions.[29]

Nor did Dickens flaunt his affair with Ellen Ternan; indeed, he publicly denied it. Even after his separation from his wife (which was itself conducted with a scrupulous regard for convention), he did not openly live with Ternan, and his relationship with her, so far as is known, was monogamous. So too Ruskin and Carlyle. Their sexual problems were not of their choosing, and insofar as they were capable of it, they tried to maintain the fiction of normality and conventionality. In the case of the Carlyles, they did succeed in maintaining it, at tremendous emotional cost. When they died, they left behind them confessions of harrowing misery and guilt—tributes to a marriage that was as sacred to them as it was painful.

For all these Victorians, perhaps for all the eminent Victorians, morality was not an "existential" condition independent of, let alone opposed to, convention and law. On the contrary, they firmly believed morality to be existentially rooted in social conventions and legal institutions. They might seek to reform these conventions and institutions, to make marriage and divorce more equitable and humane, but they did not presume to transcend or negate them. They did not want to remove marriage and divorce from the jurisdiction of the state (from the church perhaps, but not the state), or to make them, as Rose would like, entirely a matter of the private, personal "commitment of the people involved."[30] If individuals did find themselves, as a result of circumstance, passion, or compulsion, in some illicit or abnormal situation, this was regarded as an unfortunate aberration, to be normalized and legalized if possible, and, failing that, to be concealed (as in the case of Dickens) or domesticated (as with Eliot). It was out of respect for convention and law that they sought to observe at least the forms of propriety, the spirit, if not the letter, of the law. And those who did deviate from the norm, for whatever reason, did so knowing they would pay the price. Like the "fastidious assassin" in Camus' *The Rebel,* who deliberately gave up his own life when he took the tyrant's life, so the Victorians (or at least the most eminent of them) insisted upon paying for their indiscretions. Agonizing over their dilemma, they tormented themselves, one has the impression, more than they enjoyed themselves. And when society proved to be less censorious than they expected, they projected upon society their own guilt. As often as not, their ostracism was self-imposed; they were their own worst critics.

So much may be deduced from the personal lives of these eminent Victorians. But there is another kind of evidence that is pertinent, indeed essential, in understanding them. These were, after all, no ordinary Victorians; they were eminent Victorians, and eminent by virtue of their ideas. And preeminent among their ideas, infusing their novels and essays, their social criticism and art criticism, were ideas about morality. It was this tension between their public and private lives, between their professions of belief and personal conduct, that Strachey exploited so effectively, if disingenuously. By confining herself largely to the domestic sphere, Rose forfeits that sense of tension, and with it a good measure of understanding.

On one of the few occasions when Rose does venture upon ideas, the results are unfortunate. Eliot, we are briefly told, abandoned the evangelicalism of her youth in favor of a "Christianity without faith, emphasizing *caritas,* good works and acts of loving kindness, instead of belief."[31] This might well describe a fashionable young lady of the time smitten by a mild case of religious malaise, but it hardly does justice to Eliot's religious crisis or to her strenuous effort to find other sources of spiritual and moral certitude. Nor is the description of her personal dilemma more satisfactory.

> She believed in duty and self-sacrifice. But where did duty lie? In pleasing family and friends by conforming to conventional codes of behavior, or in standing with the man she had willed into central importance in her life? And what was to be sacrificed, "that which is the deepest and gravest joy in human experience," or the greatest good life offers after that, friendship and the esteem of others?[32]

"Standing" with her man or "pleasing" her family and friends —was that how Eliot understood her alternatives? Was that the meaning of her "Christianity without faith," her creed of "duty and self-sacrifice"? Eliot, after all, was not only Lewes's lover. She was also the translator of Spinoza, Goethe, and the young Hegelians, Strauss and Feuerbach; and for a time (although with reservations) she was a disciple of Comte. A notably strong-minded woman, she had especially strong views on the subject of morality. Long after she lost faith in Evangelicalism, she retained the deepest respect not only for religion but also for religious conformity, and precisely because she saw them as having the most intimate relationship with morality. With or without faith, she once explained, the mere attendance at church or chapel signified a "recognition of a binding belief or spiritual law, which is to lift us into willing obedience, and save us from the slavery of unregulated passion or impulse."[33] Whatever agony she experienced in translating that creed into practice, in justifying her "irregular" relationship with Lewes, she was never dismissive of "conventional codes of behavior." Her moral dilemma is interesting precisely because she took convention itself seriously as a moral duty rather than as the banal chore of "pleasing family and friends."

In different ways each of the others went through a similar spiritual and intellectual crisis. Ruskin, like Eliot, reared as an Evangelical, rebelled against its sectarianism and proceeded to make a religion first of art and then of socialism. Mill, reared as a utilitarian, rebelled against its sterile rationality and sought a new morality in a "purely human religion, which sometimes calls itself the Religion of Humanity and sometimes that of Duty."[34] Carlyle, reared as a Calvinist, rebelled against its theological dogmas and made a religion of work: *"Laborare est Orare."*[35] Dickens is the only one who does not quite fit this pattern, his rebellion having an emotional rather than religious or philosophical source—the memory of that "very small and not-over-particularly-taken-care-of boy" that haunts some of his novels.[36] But even he gave that grievance a moral dimension when he attacked utilitarianism, materialism, laissez-faireism, and the do-goodism of "telescopic philanthropists" who were more interested in the natives of Borrioboola-Gha than in their own children. The symbols of "hearth and home" represented his alternative to those immoral, inhuman doctrines—which was why his own departure from his own hearth and home took on all the weight of a moral crisis.

If these eminent Victorians agonized so over the irregularities and improprieties of their personal lives, it was because they were so anxious about morality itself. And not because there was any actual breakdown of morality in their own time: mid-Victorian England was more moral, more proper, more law-abiding than any other society in recent history. What made morality problematic, for the future if not the present, was the breakdown of the religious consensus. When Eliot was asked how morality could subsist in the absence of religious faith, she replied that God was "inconceivable," immortality "unbelievable," and Duty nonetheless "peremptory and absolute."[37]* This is the clue to the Victorian obsession with morality. Feeling guilty about the loss of their religious faith, suspecting that that loss might expose them to the temptations of immorality and the perils of nihilism, anticipating the Nietzschean dictum that if God does not exist everything is permitted, they were determined to make of morality a substitute for religion—to make of it, indeed, a form of religion. And having forfeited the sanctions of religion, they were thrown back all the more on the sanctions of convention and law. Whatever legal reforms or social changes they sought were designed to strengthen those sanctions, to give them greater moral authority and legitimacy by purging them of whatever might appear to be unjust or inhumane.

This was the common denominator, the common faith, of these Victorians. The duty to be moral, they believed (or wanted desperately to believe), was not God-given but man-made, and it was all the more "peremptory and absolute" for that. If there

---

*An American friend of Bertrand Russell, on being shown the Fellows' Garden at Trinity, said: "Oh yes! This is where George Eliot told F. W. H. Myers that there is no God, and yet we must be good; and Myers decided that there is a God, and yet we need not be good." It is a clever story but should not be taken too literally, at least in respect to Myers.[38]

is any message to be found in these Victorian marriages, it is
not in the realm of "sexual politics," in the struggle for domina-
tion or liberation, equality or individuality, but in the realm of
morality, the struggle to preserve the sanctity of marriage, as
of all moral institutions, even when the form and substance were
wanting.

2

A Genealogy of Morals: From Clapham to Bloomsbury

"For the Englishman," Nietzsche wrote in 1889, "morality is not yet a problem." The English thought that religion was no longer needed as a "guarantee of morality," that morality could be known "intuitively." But that illusion was itself a reflection of the persistent strength and depth among them of the Christian "ascendancy." Forgetting the religious origin of their morality, they also forgot the "highly conditional nature of its right to exist."[1] If Christianity should ever lose that ascendancy, Nietzsche implied, morality would be deprived of even that tenuous hold on reality and would then truly become a "problem."

A generation later morality was very much a problem, and for precisely the reasons Nietzsche foresaw. It was not a problem, to be sure, for the mass of Englishmen. But then Nietzsche was not thinking of the mass, the "slave class," who mindlessly observed the moral rules and conventions sanctified by time. He was thinking of the "priestly aristocracy," or its modern equivalent, the "ruling caste" of philosophers, scholars, and aesthetes—what Coleridge and Mill had called the national "clerisy" and what more recently has gone under the name of the "intellectual aristocracy."[2] Noel Annan, who has written the classic study of that intellectual aristocracy, required ten genealogical charts to trace the lineage of some of its central characters.[3] But it would require something like a three-dimensional chart to show their literary, philosophic, philanthropic, and political relationships, as well as those of blood and marriage. And it would require nothing less than a history of modern England to draw out all the implications of that tangled web. Yet the line of intellectual and spiritual development, the genealogy of morals, is fairly simple and straightforward. Indeed, it is very much as Nietzsche predicted.

It took one century for that genealogy to work itself out, a century encapsulated in the opening sentence of an essay by E. M. Forster: "Hannah More was the godmother of my great-aunt."[4] In good aristocratic fashion, Forster did not deign to identify his characters. He did quote some gems from Hannah More: "Going to the opera, like getting drunk, is a sin that carries its own punishment with it, and that a very severe one"; and "He who is taught arithmetic on a Sunday when a boy, will, when a man, open his shop on a Sunday."[5] But he did not bother to explain that More was a leading figure in the "moral reformation" movement of the late-eighteenth and early-nineteenth centuries, the campaign to reform rich and poor alike by persuading the rich to give up their dissipations (the opera) and the poor theirs (drink). Nor did he explain that More's strictures against the teaching of arithmetic on Sunday did not apply to the teaching of reading; she was, in fact, a vigorous advocate of Sunday Schools (she personally founded and subsidized several such schools), which played an important part in the advance of literacy among the poor.

Hannah More was not only the godmother of Forster's great-aunt, Marianne Thornton; she was a friend and associate of his great-grandfather, Henry Thornton. Banker, philanthropist, and Member of Parliament, Thornton is principally known as one of the founders of the "Clapham Sect," the influential group of Evangelicals whose most notable public achievement was the abolition of the slave trade. (He was, in fact, responsible for the name of the group, since it was his home in Clapham, shared for some years by William Wilberforce, that served as its headquarters and attracted other Evangelicals to that remote part of London.) In another essay, Forster assigned to Thornton "two claims on the notice of posterity": an essay on paper credit, which had the distinction of being reissued more than a century later with an introduction by Friedrich Hayek, and a best-selling volume, *Family Prayers,* which continued to provide royalties for the family even into Forster's own time.[6] The conjunction of the two works seems to make of Clapham an unholy union of commerce and piety. Only at the very end of the essay did Forster consider the possibility that posterity might also remember his great-grandfather as the man who helped free the slaves. But this fact, belatedly noted, was somewhat discounted by the observation that while it was a great work, it "now needs all doing over again," for Thornton, although acutely aware of the evils of slavery, was totally insensitive to the evils of "commercialism."[7]

Had Lytton Strachey been writing of the Clapham Sect, he would have been frankly contemptuous of those high-minded Evangelicals who drew their spiritual sustenance from prayer, their material sustenance from commerce, and their moral sustenance from philanthropy. That was not at all Forster's tone. He was tolerant, even respectful of his ancestors, making it clear that so far from being bigoted or hypocritical, they were intelligent, cultivated, urbane, humane, their religiosity expressing itself more in moral conduct and good works than in theological dogma or rituals. But he did not conceal his own sense of remoteness from them, and this in spite of his childhood memories of Clapham and his considerable knowledge of the family history. His biography of Marianne Thornton is a period piece, charming but slight, as if any serious work might have obliged him to be more critical.[8] Read in the context of his own life and work, it only serves to accentuate the enormous distance between the Clapham of his forebears and the Cambridge and Bloomsbury that were his own natural habitats.

At one point, introducing another prominent member of the

Clapham Sect, Forster asked, "Who on earth was Zachary Macaulay?" to which he replied, "Mr. R. C. Trevelyan's great-grandfather."[9] It was a typical Forster (and Bloomsbury) ploy: to reduce the sublime, so to speak, to the ridiculous, the Clapham worthy to the Bloomsbury acolyte. R. C. Trevelyan (Bob Trevy, as he appears in the memoirs of his Bloomsbury friends) was a minor poet and playwright—"amusing but vague to a degree," Lytton Strachey described him.[10] Zachary Macaulay would surely have preferred to be identified as the great-grandfather of G. M. Trevelyan, Regius Professor of History at Cambridge, or, better yet, as the father of Thomas B. Macaulay, one of England's greatest historians.

Thomas Macaulay was not only the historian-laureate of Victorian England; he was a perfect specimen of the second-generation Evangelical. Lacking the religious fervor of his father, he cherished the moral and civic values that he knew to be the bequest of that Evangelical heritage. When he criticized Bentham's utilitarianism, it was on the ground that such a philosophy could not satisfy the moral instincts of men, the need for an "ought" that was not identical with the "is," a sense of obligation that was not the same as self-interest. Christianity provided that additional element, he explained, because it held out the prospect of an "infinite happiness thereafter" in compensation for whatever sacrifice of happiness was required in the pursuit of duty on earth. "This is practical philosophy. . . . A man is told to do something which otherwise he would not do, and is furnished with a new motive for doing it."[11] It was, to be sure, a "practical philosophy" based upon a much attenuated religion. But even in that form, as a kind of evangelized utilitarianism, it was far removed from the secularized utilitarianism of the Benthamites —and still further removed from the later philosophy of Bloomsbury, which provided no ground, either in utility or in religion, for doing anything save what one wanted to do.

A similar intellectual and moral lineage can be traced in other families that were in a direct line of descent from Clapham to

Bloomsbury. James Stephen, a passionate Evangelical and dedicated abolitionist, moved to Clapham to be close to the sect and married into it when he took as his second wife Wilberforce's widowed sister. Like the Macaulays, each generation of Stephens witnessed a successive diminution of religious faith. Leslie Stephen, the grandson of James and the father of four of Bloomsbury's charter members, was so far gone in disbelief as to call himself an agnostic. But like most agnostics of that late-Victorian generation, he believed irreligion to be entirely compatible with the most rigorous and conventional morality. His credo was simple: "I now believe in nothing, but I do not the less believe in morality etc., etc. I mean to live and die like a gentleman if possible."[12] His *Science of Ethics* was one of many attempts to base ethics upon evolution and altruism upon egoism, and it was no more successful than the others. But the impulse behind it was clear: to provide a "scientific" basis for a moral code that made the good of others more compelling than the good of oneself. If that secular moral code, the code of a "gentleman," separated him from the Clapham of his grandfather, it separated him still more from the Bloomsbury of his children.

Not all the members of Bloomsbury traced their descent from Clapham. But most of them were related to that "intellectual aristocracy" which, by the end of the century, included some of the most notable Victorian names: Macaulay, Trevelyan, Tennyson, Wilberforce, Thornton, Stephen, Strachey, Fry, Wedgwood, Darwin, Huxley, Arnold, Thackeray, Booth.* And those who were not related by blood or marriage developed even closer ties in the still more exclusive aristocracy spawned by Cambridge. All of the men later identified with Bloomsbury (with the exception of Duncan Grant) had been at Cambridge, and most of them had belonged to that most coveted and select society, the Apostles. Since membership in the Apostles was a lifetime affair, the

*There are conspicuous omissions in this aristocracy—Mill, Carlyle, Ruskin, Eliot, Newman—those who, for one reason or another (sexual, marital, or clerical), left no progeny.

few undergraduates ("embryos") fortunate enough to receive that distinction had the privilege of associating with the "angels" of previous generations. Thus Lytton Strachey, Leonard Woolf, Maynard Keynes, and Saxon Sydney-Turner found themselves, in the Saturday evening meetings of the society, engaged in discussion with G. E. Moore, Bertrand Russell, Roger Fry, E. M. Forster, Desmond MacCarthy, and others who were to become lifelong friends. (Clive Bell was one of the few Bloomsbury men who was not an Apostle, and he felt the slight all his life.) In a sense Bloomsbury was to be another kind of select society, a continuation of university life in the more bohemian environs of London, close to the center of literary and artistic life and far from the respectable, conventional homes of their parents.

If "Victorianism," in the familiar sense of that word, antedated the reign of Queen Victoria (a good case can be made for locating its origins in the Evangelicalism of the early decades of the century), it did not long survive the death of the queen. It was a nice accident of history that Edward VII, that very un-Victorian Prince of Wales, should have ascended the throne in January 1901, thus inaugurating a new century as well as a new era. Three years later Leslie Stephen died, and shortly afterward his children moved from the family house in Kensington to the then unfashionable Bloomsbury. It was to be, Virginia was determined, the beginning of a new life. "Everything was going to be new; everything was going to be different. Everything was on trial."[13]

By the end of the decade (and of Edward's reign), Bloomsbury had become the home, or home away from home, for Leslie Stephen's children, Vanessa, Virginia, and Adrian (the older brother Thoby having died a few years earlier), Clive Bell (married to Vanessa), Maynard Keynes, Lytton Strachey, Duncan Grant, Desmond MacCarthy, Roger Fry, and Saxon Sydney-Turner; Leonard Woolf joined his old Cambridge friends when he returned from India in 1911 (and married Virginia the following year). This was the hard core of Bloomsbury. As with all such

groups there was a circle of "fellow-travellers" or "sympathiz-
ers," which included E. M. Forster, James Strachey (Lytton's
brother and the translator of Freud), R. C. Trevelyan, Francis
Birrell, and others who drifted in and out of the Bloomsbury
orbit. And as with all such groups, there were those among them
who insisted that they were too varied to constitute a group. The
disclaimer is disingenuous; no one has suggested that they were
homogeneous or monolithic.[14] But they did have a good deal in
common, and they did think of themselves, and others thought
of them, as "Bloomsbury." They were, in fact, more organized
than most such groups, gathering regularly before the war at
Thursday soirées in Bloomsbury (Saturday evenings being reserved for the Apostles at Cambridge), and during the twenties
and thirties meeting as a "Memoir Club" for the express purpose
of reminiscing about themselves. (At one time the painters among
them met on Fridays and another group on Tuesdays for the
reading of plays.)

If the "Bloomsberries" (again, their term) did not review one
another's books quite as consistently and effusively as their enemies
claimed, they certainly had more opportunities than most to do so.
In the twenties Leonard Woolf became literary editor of the
Nation (after it had been reorganized financially by Keynes), while
Desmond MacCarthy was literary editor of the *New Statesman*
and, later, of *Life and Letters,* as well as literary critic of the *Sunday
Times.* And it is not many such groups that can boast their own
publishing house, the Hogarth Press, which even had its own
printing press. Nor was it only the literary branch of Bloomsbury
that was so well connected. Roger Fry's first Post-Impressionist
exhibit of 1910 had been exclusively French, but his second, two
years later, was more cosmopolitan; of the nine English painters,
three were pure Bloomsbury—Vanessa Bell, Duncan Grant, and
Fry himself—and the non-Bloomsbury painter, Wyndham Lewis,
was represented by a portrait of Lytton Strachey. Clive Bell, who
was later to protest that they were not a group, suggested to Fry in
1917 that he paint a "great historical group portrait of Blooms-

bury." Fry himself did not paint such a portrait, but Vanessa started to do one of "Old Bloomsbury," the original members. Although that picture was never finished, she later painted one which included the younger generation, with portraits of the deceased members in the background.[15]

Bloomsbury was, in fact, as much a group (or circle or coterie) as Clapham was a "sect." And it performed something of the same function, setting the tone and agenda for the cultural "vanguard" of the nation. Where Clapham had inspired a moral and spiritual reformation, Bloomsbury sought to effect a moral and spiritual liberation—a liberation from Clapham itself and from those vestiges of Evangelicalism and Victorianism that still persisted in the early twentieth century. If Bloomsbury was not much concerned with religion, of the Evangelical or any other variety, it was because its parent generation had already abandoned conventional religion. What had not been abandoned by that older generation, however, was a moral and social ethic that was as compelling as the religious ethic of Clapham. The late Victorians were as philanthropic-minded as the early Evangelicals, but lacking the religious imperative for philanthropy, they made of it a science and a profession. Instead of founding Sunday Schools, they instituted a system of compulsory day schools; instead of improving the morals and manners of the poor, they improved their housing and working conditions; instead of engaging in family prayers, they observed the moral proprieties that had become a surrogate for religious pieties.*

It was against the whole of this late-Victorian ethos, the public and the private, that Bloomsbury rebelled. "How does one come

---

*There were, of course, mavericks among the late Victorians: Oscar Wilde, Max Beerbohm, Aubrey Beardsley, Arthur Symons, and the other *fin de siècle* "aesthetes" and "decadents." But they never had anything like the influence of Bloomsbury. And Bloomsbury itself felt no connection with them.

by one's morality?" Virginia Woolf asked. "Surely by reading the poets."[16] It was an answer that would have appalled her father, who suspected poetry of being a prescription for immorality, an invitation to be "morbid" and "unmanly," to indulge one's private emotions and fancies at the expense of one's personal and public duties.[17] In invoking poetry as a source of "morality," Virginia was claiming for aesthetics that absolute, peremptory quality her father had assigned to ethics. And in making the novel a species of poetry, as she tried to do, she was removing it from the domain of social reality where it might have intimations of social morality. The true novel, Virginia Woolf maintained, was held together not by a story or plot but by the emotions of the author. "She is a poet," Forster said of her, "who wants to write something as near to a novel as possible."[18]

As Virginia Woolf made a "morality" of poetry, so Roger Fry and Clive Bell made a "religion" of art. "Art is a religion. It is an expression of and a means to states of mind as holy as any that men are capable of experiencing." It was, moreover, the distinctively modern form of religion. "It is towards art that modern minds turn, not only for the most perfect expression of transcendent emotion, but for an inspiration by which to live."[19] That "inspiration" was entirely private and personal, not a way to live in society but a way to live with oneself, with one's own feelings and sensibilities. True art was autonomous: "completely self-consistent, self-supporting and self-contained—constructions which do not stand for something else, but appear to have ultimate value and in that sense to be real."[20]

When Virginia Woolf made her famous pronouncement, "In or about December, 1910, human character changed,"[21] she may have chosen that date because of the Post-Impressionist exhibit of that time which had so altered the artistic sensibilities of the generation. But her more immediate frame of reference was literary—the passage from the "social realism," as we would now say, of the Edwardian writers (H. G. Wells, Arnold Bennett, John Galsworthy) to the "impressionism" of the Georgians

(E. M. Forster, D. H. Lawrence, Lytton Strachey, James Joyce, and, of course, herself). For the former, the novel was inseparable from the external reality; it was incomplete without an account of the social and physical milieu. For the latter, it was self-sufficient, a thing-in-itself; its world was what the author chose to make of it.

If the modern novel was, in this sense, free, unconstrained by reality, so was the modern author. The "human character" that changed in December, 1910 was the character of the artist, not of the common man. Ordinary people were bound, as they had always been, by the habits and customs devised for "timid natures who dare not allow their souls free play." But writers and artists could no longer be so circumscribed; they had to be free to follow the "vast variety and turmoil of human impulses." Their own characters were as autonomous as the characters they created. To look upon them as ordinary people, to place them "under an obligation to others," to put them in the position of "living for others, not for ourselves," was to violate their nature and endanger their calling.[22]

This was the Bloomsbury credo: living for "ourselves." Not, significantly, for "oneself." The Bloomsberries were not Nietzscheans, "proud solitaries . . . hard, strict, continent, heroic," each drawing upon his own inner resources to resist the conventions and illusions of his culture.[23] They derived their strength and independence from each other. If they recognized no obligations to "others," to society at large, they did recognize (in their own perverse fashion) a loyalty to each other. Like the Apostles who professed to find only themselves "real" and referred to everyone else as "phenomena,"[24] the Bloomsberries extended their affections only to their intimates; for the rest of the world they had at best an amused tolerance, at worst (and more often) an undisguised contempt. It was because they were so conspicuously a group that they were able to found an "adversary culture" strong enough to challenge the bourgeois culture. And it was for this reason too that they were spared the solipsism that would other-wise have been their individual fates.

The philosophical rationale of Bloomsbury derived from G. E. Moore. For Virginia the move to Bloomsbury in 1904 was the beginning of a new life. For most of the men in the group —her brother Thoby, her future husband Leonard Woolf, her future brother-in-law Clive Bell, her friends Lytton Strachey, Maynard Keynes, and Desmond MacCarthy—the beginning came in Cambridge several months earlier with the publication of Moore's *Principia Ethica*. "I date from October 1903," Strachey wrote Moore at the time, "the beginning of the Age of Reason."[25] Keynes, in retrospect, was even more rhapsodic. "It was exciting, exhilarating, the beginning of a renaissance, the opening of a new heaven on a new earth, we were the forerunners of a new dispensation, we were not afraid of anything."[26]*

The author of that new dispensation was only a few years older than his disciples. Keynes was twenty and Strachey twenty-three when the *Principia* appeared; Moore himself, having earlier dis-cussed many of the ideas of the book with the Apostles, was all of twenty-eight when he started to write it and not quite thirty when it was published. For these young men the *Principia* was a manifesto of liberation, a release from the old morality and, they suspected, from all morality. The heart of the book, as they read it, was the last chapter, "The Ideal," where Moore argued that the fundamental truth of moral philosophy involved "states of consciousness" (not, as traditional moral philosophy had it, of conscience), and that the highest states of consciousness were "the pleasures of human intercourse and the enjoyment of beautiful objects." These were the only "goods in themselves," desirable

*Again and again one hears that triumphal acclaim of the new. Thus Vanessa Bell: "A great new freedom seemed about to come." Or Leonard Woolf: "We were out to construct something new. . . . We were in the van of the builders of a new society which should be free, rational, civilized."[27]

"purely for their own sakes"; they included *"all* the greatest, and *by far* the greatest, goods we can imagine."[28] (The italics are Moore's.) If Bloomsbury had any philosophy, it was this: a total commitment to "personal affections" and "aesthetic enjoyments." This was not, to be sure, the whole of Moore's philosophy. But it was the part that appealed to the Cambridge undergraduates and Apostles who later made up Bloomsbury. Even Virginia Woolf, who had no taste for philosophy, read the *Principia* in 1908, persevering in spite of great difficulties; according to Leonard Woolf, Moore was the only philosopher to have influenced her. (The *Principia* appears in the novel she started to write in 1909, *The Voyage Out,* where the reader is expected to recognize the work by its familiar dark brown binding.)*

In a memoir read to the surviving members of Bloomsbury many years later, Keynes spoke movingly of Moore's effect upon them. They accepted, he explained, Moore's "religion" while discarding his "morals." "Indeed, in our opinion, one of the greatest advantages of his religion, was that it made morals unnecessary—meaning by 'religion' one's attitude towards oneself and the ultimate and by 'morals' one's attitude towards the outside world and the intermediate."[29] What they did not accept was the feeble concession to conventional morality in the penultimate chapter of the *Principia,* where Moore suggested that in those cases where one was unable to foresee the long-term consequences of any particular mode of conduct, one should observe the existing rules of morality. This, Keynes insisted, violated the most important principle of Bloomsbury.

> We repudiated entirely customary morals, conventions and traditional wisdom. We were, that is to say, in the strict sense of the term, immoralists. The consequences of being found out had, of

---

*While Moore himself was not a "member" of Bloomsbury (he did not attend Virginia's Thursday evenings, although his work was often discussed there), he remained a presence in the lives of Keynes, Woolf, Bell, and the others. Long after they left Cambridge, they continued to see each other at meetings of the Apostles and at the reading parties organized by Moore.

course, to be considered for what they were worth. But we recognised no moral obligation on us, no inner sanction, to conform or to obey. Before heaven we claimed to be our own judge in our own case.[30]

What Bloomsbury took from Moore was a philosophy that sanctioned, if not immorality, as Keynes said, then at the very least amorality. For the "states of consciousness" that were at the heart of this philosophy had nothing to do with conduct or consequences. "Being good" was the objective, not "doing good." And being good meant being in those heightened states of consciousness, those "timeless, passionate states of contemplation and communion," which were conducive to "love, beauty and truth"—not virtue. And even love, beauty, and truth were carefully delineated so as to remove any taint of utility or morality. Useless knowledge was deemed preferable to useful, corporeal beauty to mental qualities, present and immediately realizable goods to remote or indirect ones. Thus, Keynes recalled, Bloomsbury "lived entirely in present experience," repudiating not only the idea of "duty" but any kind of "social action," and not only social action but the "life of action generally," a life that might entail such disagreeable pursuits as "power, politics, success, wealth, ambition."[31]

Writing thirty-five years after the delivery of the "new dispensation," when he himself, having engaged very successfully in a life of action, had achieved a fair measure of the goods of that life, Keynes was able to be wry and even critical about some aspects of the Bloomsbury creed. It was based, he came to realize, upon too rational and utopian a view of human nature; it did not appreciate how thin and precarious the crust of civilization was, how dependent men were upon "customary morals, conventions and traditional wisdom."[32] That judgment, made in the fall of 1938, on the eve of the Second World War, did not require great insight or boldness. More remarkable is the fact that even at that time and in his mature age, Keynes should have taken the occasion to reaffirm the essential tenets of the creed. Whatever its faults, he found it still "nearer the truth than any other that I know, with less irrelevant extraneous matter and nothing to be ashamed of." In retrospect he was confident that "this religion of ours was a very good one to grow up under." And not only to grow up under but to live with, for it was still, he went on to say, "my religion under the surface." Nor did he shrink from the implication of that "religion": "I remain, and always will remain, an immoralist."[33]*

In one sense Keynes is the most interesting of the group, because he defied at least one of its precepts. He not only lived a "life of action"; he did so in the most bourgeois and materialistic of professions. If it was partly accident that originally drew him to economics, it was talent and ambition that kept him there. Yet even while pursuing that sordid occupation, at Cambridge and at the Treasury, he made it clear that he regarded economics as a separate and altogether inferior sphere of life and that he personally deplored any emphasis on economic motives or criteria. Bertrand Russell recalled that while Keynes "escaped into the great world," he did so with the air of a "bishop *in partibus*"; when he ventured forth into the mundane world of economics or politics, "he left his soul at home."[35]†

*Keynes did not claim that Moore was an "immoralist"; what he did say was that Bloomsbury found in Moore's philosophy the rationale for immoralism. This interpretation of Moore was not peculiar to Bloomsbury. Beatrice Webb deplored the influence of the *Principia* on Bertrand Russell and some of the young Fabians. "I never can see anything in it, except a metaphysical justification for doing what you like and what other people disapprove of!"[34]

†Leonard Woolf also ventured into the "great world." He was an active member of the Fabian Society, served on parliamentary commissions, and was deeply involved in Labour Party politics. (He once even sought a seat in Parliament.) But then Woolf was never regarded as a full-fledged member of the clan. In his novel *The Wise Virgins,* a *roman à clef* written while he was courting Virginia, one character complains, "You talk and you talk and you talk—no blood in you! You never *do* anything." When his friend asks why

In fact, something of the "soul" of Bloomsbury penetrated even into Keynes's economic theories. There is a discernible affinity between the Bloomsbury ethos, which put a premium on immediate and present satisfactions, and Keynesian economics, which is based entirely on the short run and precludes any long-term judgments. (Keynes's famous remark, "In the long run we are all dead," also has an obvious connection with his homosexuality—what Schumpeter delicately referred to as his "childless vision.")[38] The same ethos is reflected in the Keynesian doctrine that consumption rather than saving is the source of economic growth—indeed, that thrift is economically and socially harmful. In *The Economic Consequences of the Peace,* written long before *The General Theory,* Keynes ridiculed the "virtue" of saving. The capitalists, he said, deluded the working classes into thinking that their interests were best served by saving rather than consuming. This delusion was part of the age-old Puritan fallacy.

> The duty of "saving" became nine-tenths of virtue and the growth of the cake the object of true religion. There grew round the non-consumption of the cake all those instincts of puritanism which in other ages has withdrawn itself from the world and has neglected the arts of production as well as those of enjoyment. And so the cake increased; but to what end was not clearly contemplated. Individuals would be exhorted not so much to abstain as to defer, and to cultivate the pleasures of security and anticipation. Saving was for old age or for your children; but this was only in theory,—the virtue of the cake was that it was never to be consumed, neither by you nor by your children after you.[39]

In his public life as well, Keynes kept faith with Bloomsbury. Although he was much criticized by his friends for not resigning

---

he thinks it important to do things, he replies, "Why? Because I'm a Jew, I tell you—I'm a Jew."[36] No one in that circle ever forgot that Woolf was a Jew, least of all Virginia (although she was very grateful to him and, in her way, loved him). Years later, she recalled, "How I hated marrying a Jew— how I hated their nasal voices, and their oriental jewellery, and their noses and their wattles."[37]

from the Treasury in protest against the First World War, he managed to oppose the war in his own way, and perhaps more effectively than he might have done had he retired to private life. He used his official position to promote the view that military conscription and food rationing were both unnecessary and impractical, and that Britain's resources were inadequate for a serious full-scale war. And he intervened on behalf of friends who sought to be relieved of military service by pleading conscientious objection. He himself, like most of the Bloomsbury men, applied for exemption on that ground and withdrew his application only when he decided to continue at the Treasury and thus was automatically exempt.[40] Whatever discretion he exercised in public, within the group he made no secret of his hostility to the war. When the proposals for peace talks broke down late in 1917, he wrote to Duncan Grant: "I work for a government I despise for ends I think criminal."[41] Nor did he think better of the British government or its allies at the Versailles Conference. *The Economic Consequences of the Peace,* published in 1920, had something of the same tone and character as Strachey's *Eminent Victorians,* which had appeared the previous year; Lloyd George, Wilson, and Clemenceau were made out to be as hypocritical and venal as Cardinal Manning, Dr. Arnold, and General Gordon.

The First World War, which took so heavy a toll among just that class represented by Bloomsbury (and which is so movingly described in Robert Graves's *Good-bye to All That*), left Bloomsbury itself with no casualties. The only ones to come anywhere near the front lines were Desmond MacCarthy, who was with the Red Cross in the first winter of the war, and David Garnett, who served briefly with a Friends' ambulance unit. The rest were either excused from military service for medical reasons or were conscientious objectors assigned to farm labor. Grant and Garnett, for example, spent the last years of the war at Charleston, a farm in Sussex rented by the Bells. Only four miles from the home of the Woolfs, Charleston became the wartime center of the clan —"Bloomsbury-by-the-Sea," Quentin Bell dubbed it.[42]

Even in its opposition to the war, Bloomsbury distinguished itself from other conscientious objectors—indeed, gave as much offense to them as to the supporters of the war. It was not pacifism that inspired Bloomsbury; its objections were not to war in general but to this war. And to this war not on specific political grounds but rather on social grounds, so to speak, because of disaffection from the society and the country at large. Duncan Grant explained to his father, a major in the army, why the war seemed to him to be a crime against "civilization." He was, he confessed, "unpatriotic," as most artists were. "I began to see that one's enemies were not vague masses of foreign people, but the mass of people in one's own country and the mass of people in the enemy country, and that one's friends were people of true ideas that one might and did meet in every country one visited."[43]

This contempt for the masses, as well as for the bourgeoisie, is dramatically illustrated in the familiar anecdote about Strachey's appearance at the tribunal considering his request for exemption from military service. Before an audience packed with friends and relatives, Strachey slowly inflated an air cushion, carefully seated himself upon it (he claimed to have piles), and adjusted a travelling rug over his knees, before finally deigning to address himself to the questions of the tribunal. One question proved irresistible. Asked what he would do if he saw a German soldier trying to rape his sister, he solemnly looked at each of his sisters in turn and replied, in his high-pitched voice, "I should try and interpose my own body."[44] Even if one discounts this episode as Strachey at his most outrageous, it is harder to discount the delight with which his friends received this quip, or the comment of Quentin Bell, a true son of Bloomsbury, that Strachey's attitude was "at once intelligent and irreverent."[45]

If there were fewer such episodes after the war, it was because Bloomsbury chose to épater les bourgeois in other ways. But the basic attitude toward public affairs persisted, a combination of irreverence, indifference, and aristocratic disdain. In 1938, about the same time that Keynes was preparing his memoir, Forster wrote an essay that perfectly captured the Bloomsbury spirit. "I do not," the essay opened, "believe in Belief." What is more, he did not regret his lack of belief; indeed, he disliked and distrusted belief. His law-givers were not Moses or St. Paul but Erasmus and Montaigne; his temple stood not on Mount Moriah but in that Elysian Field "where even the immoral are admitted"; his motto was: "Lord, I disbelieve—help thou my unbelief." But pressed for his own belief, he would oblige by invoking "personal relationships," the only good and solid thing in a world full of violence and cruelty. This was the one article of faith he could unequivocally affirm: "I certainly can proclaim that I believe in personal relationships."[46]

It was in this essay, written after the rise of Communism and Nazism and under the shadow of war, that Forster made the much-quoted statement: "If I had to choose between betraying my country and betraying my friend, I hope I should have the guts to betray my country."[47] For Forster and his friends that choice did not take guts; it was only another way of asserting the primacy of "personal relationships" they had always prided themselves on and the contempt for public affairs that was really a contempt for the public. Nor did it take guts to give only "two cheers for Democracy." "Two cheers are quite enough," Forster insisted, "there is no occasion to give three. Only Love the Beloved Republic deserves that."[48] The two cheers were for the variety and criticism stimulated by democracy, which, in turn, nurtured the true aristocracy—"not an aristocracy of power, based upon rank and influence, but an aristocracy of the sensitive, the considerate and the plucky." It might have been Bloomsbury Forster was alluding to when he described an aristocracy whose members have a "secret understanding when they meet," and who represent "the true human condition, the one permanent victory of our queer race over cruelty and chaos."[49]

Forster's two cheers for democracy were not rousing cheers; they were more like a well-mannered "Hear, hear." They were intended on the one hand as a rebuke to those who were inclined to give democracy no cheers at all—to the Communists, who cared little for criticism or variety and wanted only to impose their own version of a Beloved Republic under the aegis of the Party. But they were also a rebuke to those who were so misguided as to give three cheers to democracy, not realizing that the best part of democracy, its saving remnant, was the aristocracy that was not beholden to it, an aristocracy whose ultimate loyalty was to "Love the Beloved Republic," and who would betray, if need be, their country but not their friends (still less their lovers).*

"Love the Beloved Republic"—that motto is a cruel parody of Bloomsbury. Only recently have we discovered how large a part love played among its members and what form it took. It is fitting, as Hilton Kramer has pointed out, that so much of the attention given them should focus upon their private lives rather than their work.[54] For in spite of their enormous productivity, the fact is that, with the exception of Keynes and Virginia Woolf, their memoirs, letters, and diaries have proved more memorable than their novels, biographies, essays, and paintings. Indeed, it is

---

*An earlier version of the "two cheers" theme was Forster's statement, to a congress of writers in Paris in 1935, that he was "a bourgeois who adheres to the British constitution, adheres to it rather than supports it."[50] That lecture also suggests that Forster was not as immune from the "virus" of communism as Keynes supposed all of Bloomsbury to be.[51] To a group that included many Communists, Forster explained that while he himself was not a Communist, he might have been had he been "a younger and a braver man," for in communism he could see hope; although it did many evil things, "I know that it intends good."[52] (He went on to devote the bulk of his speech to the "Fabio-Fascism" that was menacing England, the major example of which was the censorship of a homosexual novel, *Boy*.) Although his tolerance for communism disappeared in later years, his distrust of democracy did not. He was convinced that a second World War, however necessary, would inevitably bring totalitarianism with it. "Sensitive people," he wrote just after Munich, knew what the politicians did not: "that if Fascism wins we are done for, and that we must become Fascist to win."[53]

hard to see how they could have written and painted as much as they did in view of the enormous amount of time and effort that went into all those memoirs, letters, and diaries, to say nothing of the extraordinary amount of psychic energy that went into their complicated personal lives. (Virginia Woolf herself left five volumes of diaries and six of letters.) If they were so absorbed with themselves—how many such groups could sustain a Memoir Club over the period of two decades?—it is little wonder that others have shared that interest. Nor is it surprising that they should be exposed to the kind of biographical scrutiny that Strachey made fashionable, and that their public lives, their work, should be seen as a reflection of their private lives. Thus *Eminent Victorians* is thought to be more an expression of the personality of the author than of his ostensible subjects. And Virginia Woolf's novels, when they are not serving as the text for a "feminist" message, are ransacked for autobiographical allusions and revelations.[55]

It is ironic that people who prided themselves on their honesty and candor, especially in regard to their much-vaunted "personal affections"—in contrast, as they thought, to Victorian hypocrisy and duplicity—should have succeeded for so long in concealing the truth about those personal affections. Even so perceptive and psychoanalytic-minded a critic as Lionel Trilling was able to write a full-length study of Forster in 1943 without realizing that he was a homosexual. Nor did Roy Harrod, in his biography of Keynes published in 1951 (the definitive biography, as it seemed at the time and as it remained for more than thirty years), see fit to mention Keynes's homosexuality—a deliberate suppression, since Harrod was a friend of Keynes and was perfectly well aware of his sexual proclivities and activities. Nor did Leonard Woolf, in a five-volume autobiography that was entirely candid about his wife's mental breakdowns, give any indication of the frenetic sexual affairs of everyone around him. Nor was James Strachey, Lytton's younger brother, more forthcoming; it is especially ironic that the disciple, translator, and popularizer of Freud should have forbidden access to Lytton's papers for more than thirty years after Lytton's death, and that he raised innumerable objections to the biography in which they were finally used. (He did, however, intervene to preserve Keynes's letters to Strachey when Keynes's brother threatened to destroy them.)

As late as 1968, Quentin Bell, the son of Clive and Vanessa Bell, published a book on Bloomsbury in which he admittedly "suppressed a good deal that I know and much more at which I can guess." He could hardly claim that such information would be damaging to those who were long since dead (only Leonard Woolf and Duncan Grant were then still alive). Instead, he offered an explanation worthy of the most proper Victorian: "This is, primarily, a study in the history of ideas, and although the *moeurs* of Bloomsbury have to be considered and will in a general way be described, I am not required nor am I inclined to act as Clio's chambermaid, to sniff into commodes or under beds, to open love-letters or to scrutinise diaries."[56] That explanation is especially incongruous in the case of people who made an art form of letters and diaries, and who were themselves not at all averse to sniffing into commodes and under beds.

It is now apparent that what was being suppressed was not the fact of homosexuality itself; that was far too commonplace to qualify as a revelation, let alone to warrant suppression. The true revelation, which first emerged in Michael Holroyd's two-volume biography of Lytton Strachey in 1967–68 and which has since been confirmed in a host of memoirs and biographies (of which the most notable is the first volume of Robert Skidelsky's biography of Keynes, published in 1983), is the compulsive and promiscuous nature of that homosexuality. Bloomsbury itself marvelled at the "permutations and combinations" of which it was capable. In 1907, for example, Strachey discovered that his lover (and cousin) Duncan Grant was also having an affair with Arthur Hobhouse, who, in turn, was having an affair with Keynes. The following year Strachey was even more distressed to learn that Grant was now having an affair with Keynes as well.

He apprised Leonard Woolf, then in Ceylon, of this latest development: "Dieu! It's a mad mixture; are you shocked? We do rather permeate and combine. I've never been in love with Maynard and I've never copulated with Hobbes [Hobhouse], but at the moment I can't think of any more exceptions."[57] Thirty years later Keynes recalled that period as "a succession of permutations of short sharp superficial 'intrigues.' "[58]

The wit who described Bloomsbury as a place where "all the couples were triangles and lived in squares" did not do justice to them;[59] some more polygonal figure would be required to describe those "couples." Vanessa Stephen, for example, was regarded by the others as the most solid and stable of them all—"monolithic," they called her, a "solid feminine integrity," one historian has described her.[60] In 1907 Vanessa married Clive Bell, in part, as she recognized, to console her for the loss of her beloved brother Thoby who had been Clive's friend. (She had earlier rejected Clive and agreed to marry him two days after Thoby's death.) Four years later, with the tacit acquiescence of her husband, who had been having a series of affairs, including one with Molly MacCarthy, Desmond's wife, Vanessa started an affair with Roger Fry. The *ménage à trois* had lasted two years when Roger complained to Clive that Vanessa was transferring her affections to Duncan Grant, who had suddenly (and, unhappily for Vanessa, only temporarily) acquired a taste for heterosexuality. (Duncan had earlier been her brother Adrian's lover as well as Strachey's and Keynes's.)

The following year Vanessa gave birth to Angelica. Although everyone in the circle knew that Duncan was the father, the child was registered under the name of Bell and was brought up to think of him as her father. (This was partly for the benefit of Clive's parents, who helped support them.) By the time Angelica herself was married to David ("Bunny") Garnett, she knew the identity of her real father. What she did not then know was that her husband had been her father's (Duncan's) lover and had tried, for once unsuccessfully, to have an affair with her mother as well

—this about the time when she was conceived. Out of pique and jealousy, Garnett had written to Strachey, on the day of her birth: "I think of marrying it; when she is twenty, I shall be forty-six —will it be scandalous?"[61] He eventually did just that, his time-table off by only a couple of years. He even managed to make his first sexual overtures to her in a car, with Duncan in the back seat and in sight of his invalid wife who was watching for their arrival from her window. Although Duncan and Vanessa were somewhat disturbed by the thought of the marriage of their daughter to their old and great friend, they were not sufficiently so to try seriously to prevent it; they were far more distressed at not being invited to the wedding.

"The world is damned queer—it really is. But people won't recognize the immensity of its queerness."[62] We are only now beginning to recognize how "queer" that world was—not only homosexual but androgynous, near-incestuous, and polymor-phously promiscuous. If the biographer or historian of Blooms-bury is obliged to take this seriously, it is because his characters did, because they made a morality (or "religion," as Keynes put it) of "personal affections" as well as of "aesthetic enjoyments." Indeed, the two were of a piece, the "new dispensation" inaugu-rating an ethic of modernism, so to speak, together with the aesthetic of modernism.

The "Higher Sodomy," as they called it, seemed to them to be not only a higher form of sexuality but a higher form of morality. In sex as in art they prided themselves on being autono-mous and self-contained, free to experiment and express them-selves without inhibition or guilt. The exalted sense of autonomy and liberty, the cultivation of consciousness and feeling, the elevation of the self and the denigration of society, the emphasis upon immediate gratification, all contributed to the narcissism and egoism, the perversity and promiscuity, that Keynes himself recognized to be a form of immorality. If this was a vulgarization of Moore, it was one to which Moore was susceptible and which

Bloomsbury exploited. Strachey once explained to Keynes the difficulty of converting the world to "Moorism":

> Our great stumbling-block in the business of introducing the world to Moorism is our horror of half-measures. We can't be content with telling the truth—we must tell the whole truth; and the whole truth is the Devil. Voltaire abolished Christianity by believing in god. It's madness of us to dream of making dowagers understand that feelings are good, when we say in the same breath that the best ones are sodomitical.[63]

They had, in fact, too much contempt for the "dowagers" of this world to try to convert them. Instead, they themselves chose to live with that "whole truth."

Perhaps in a hundred years, Strachey speculated, when their letters were finally published, everyone would be converted. Now that those letters, and so much else as well, are being published, we can begin to take the measure of their "truth."* We can also, finally, begin to discard the myths that they circulated about themselves and that have been perpetuated by their admirers. These myths have a long history and come to us on good authority: from Leonard Woolf before the First World War proclaiming themselves "the builders of a new society which should be free, rational, civilized";[65] to Virginia Woolf a decade later assuring a friend that Bloomsbury's view of life was by no means "corrupt or sinister or merely intellectual" but rather "ascetic and austere indeed";[66] to Forster in the midst of the Second World War commemorating Strachey for his "wit and

---

*Virginia Woolf's letters and diaries make especially painful reading. Clever, perceptive, often scintillating, they are also unremittingly snobbish (her contempt for the middle classes was matched only by her disgust with the working classes), anti-Semitic, malicious, and even cruel (toward servants, most notably). These traits spill over into her literary judgments, as in her comments on Joyce's *Ulysses:* "An illiterate, underbred book it seems to me; the book of a self taught working man, and we all know how distressing they are, how egotistic, insistent, raw, striking, and ultimately nauseating." Her husband, who rarely permitted any sexual comments to appear in his edition of her diaries, evidently found nothing objectionable in this entry.[64]

aristocratic good manners," his implacable "pursuit of truth," his belief in "fidelity between human beings" and "constant affection";[67] to Quentin Bell praising his parents' generation for seeking "a life of rational and pacific freedom," of "reason, charity and good sense";[68] to the historian describing Bloomsbury's mission as carrying forward "the highest and most spiritual ideals of the past into a century which has paid scant attention to the things of the spirit";[69] to the distinguished biographer Leon Edel, who takes his title, *A House of Lions,* from Virginia's comparison of Bloomsbury with the lions' house at the zoo where "all the animals are dangerous, rather suspicious of each other, and full of fascination and mystery," and who transforms that lions' house into an eminently "humanistic world," where they were all bound together by a chain of love and sex happily freed of "Victorian guilt and shame";[70] to all the others who continue to pay tribute to the brave new world of Bloomsbury, a world devoted to beauty, truth, and love.

Against that view the few dissenting voices have seemed churlish and priggish. Keynes's memoir had been provoked by an earlier paper by David Garnett recalling the bitter hostility of D. H. Lawrence to the Cambridge-Bloomsbury group. Garnett quoted a letter Lawrence had written him in 1915:

> To hear these young people talk really fills me with black fury: they talk endlessly, but endlessly—and never, never a good thing said. They are cased each in a hard little shell of his own and out of this they talk words. There is never for one second any outgoing of feeling and no reverence, not a crumb or grain of reverence. I cannot stand it. I will not have people like this—I had rather be alone. They made me dream of a beetle that bites like a scorpion. But I killed it—a very large beetle. I scotched it and it ran off—but I came on it again, and killed it. It is this horror of little swarming selves I can't stand.[71]

To Garnett the issue was simple: Lawrence was jealous of Garnett's friends and vexed by a rationalism so at odds with his

own faith in intuition and instinct. Keynes took a more complicated view of the matter, seeing Lawrence as simultaneously
repelled and attracted by a "civilization" that was alien to him.
But Keynes, while affirming his own commitment to that civilization, went on to concede a measure of justice in Lawrence's
attack. Bloomsbury's civilization, he admitted, was a thin veneer
beneath which seethed the reality of "vulgar passions." Its rationalism was a disguise for cynicism, and its irreverence and libertinism were a form of "intellectual *chic.*"[72]

Reviewing Keynes's memoir after its posthumous publication,
F. R. Leavis saw it as an unwitting confirmation of Lawrence's
views. Even at that late stage of his life, Leavis found, Keynes
still did not appreciate the full enormity of the "Cambridge-
Bloomsbury ethos." He still took it seriously, not realizing that
its gravest flaw lay in its being "inimical to the development of
any real seriousness." The articulateness and sophistication he
admired were a form of callowness, conceit, and complacency,
a symptom of arrested development and undergraduate im-
maturity. In place of Lawrence's image of a large hideous beetle,
Leavis invoked what he took to be its equivalent: the figure of
Lytton Strachey. "Let it be remembered that the 'civilization'
celebrated by Keynes produced Lytton Strachey, and that the
literary world dominated by that 'civilization' made Lytton Strachey a living Master and a prevailing influence." And then, as if
to point up still more the heinousness of that fact, he asked: "Can
we imagine Sidgwick or Leslie Stephen or Maitland being influenced by, or interested in, the equivalent of Lytton Strachey?
By what steps, and by the operation of what causes, did so great
a change come over Cambridge in so comparatively short a
time?"[73]

Leavis wrote that review long before Holroyd's biography of
Strachey gave us the full measure of the man, and before a host
of other biographies and autobiographies gave us the full measure
of Bloomsbury. We can now appreciate that Strachey, so far
from being an anomaly in Bloomsbury, was, as Leavis implied,

its essence. And we can also appreciate the contrast between the generation of Strachey and that of his elders—those late Victorians whom Strachey, and Bloomsbury, so mercilessly derided.

We may also better appreciate the force of Nietzsche's warning: that the late-Victorian Englishmen for whom "morality is not yet a problem" would give way to a post-Victorian generation for whom morality would be not only problematic but nonexistent. For what Nietzsche saw, and what Leavis did not, was the precariousness of that late-Victorian morality, a morality that was all the more admirable, perhaps, because it tried to maintain itself without the sanctions and consolations of religion, but that was too impoverished, too far removed from its original inspiration, to transmit itself to the next generation.

The Victorian Trinity: Religion, Science, Morality

During one period of his life Voltaire made a point of concluding his letters with the motto "Ecrasez l'infame," often abbreviated as "Ecr. linf." Sometimes this salutation stood in place of a signature, which led one censor to observe that "M. Ecrlinf doesn't write badly."[1] Historians debate whether the infamy to be destroyed was Christianity, the Church, or religion in general. But there is little doubt that their fate was intertwined, that when the entrails of the last priest would have been strangled in the entrails of the last king, as little would be left of orthodox religion as of legitimate royalty.

Religion, however, unlike royalty, proved to be remarkably resilient, so that later generations of dissidents had to confront the old enemy with new tactics. In Germany, the Young Hegelians proceeded first to de-historicize Christ by making him the mythical embodiment of the consciousness of the early Christians; then to de-mythicize him by exposing him as the symbol of the false consciousness of the Christians; then to de-spiritualize him by restoring that "alienated" consciousness to man himself. *Homo homini Deus est*— "Man is the God of Man"; surely one could go no further than Feuerbach did in liberating man from God than by making a God of man.[2] Marx, of course, did go further, by "unmasking" not only the "sacred form" of alienation—religion

—but "human self-alienation in its secular forms"—social exploitation.[3] And Nietzsche went further still, unmasking, both in society and in man, the morality that was the ultimate bequest of religion, the "priestly system of valuations" that had transformed good into bad, strength into weakness, punishment into justice, will into conscience, "autonomous man" into "moral man."[4]

That, however, was on the Continent. And only against that background can one appreciate how very different the intellectual climate was in England. It took a Frenchman to coin the memorable phrase, "the miracle of modern England," to call attention to England's good fortune in having been spared the political and social revolutions that convulsed the countries of Europe[5]—and, he might have added, the religious and intellectual revolutions as well. While European thinkers were waging a life-and-death struggle against religion, culminating in the triumphant (if premature) announcement of the "death of God," Englishmen were engaged in niggling quarrels, as they seemed by comparison, over the legal status of Catholics, Dissenters, and Jews, with a few audacious souls calling for the disestablishment (though not the abolition) of the Church of England. There were small groups of "unbelievers," as they were called: Owenites, rationalists, secularists, Positivists, agnostics, even atheists of a primitive variety. The most serious challenge to religion, however, came not from philosophy but from science, and from Darwinism especially. It was *The Origin of Species* that precipitated the "war of science and religion," a war that was as confused, complicated, and ambiguous—indeed, as unwarlike—as any that has ever been fought.[6]

The most bellicose incident in the war occurred at the annual meeting of the British Association for the Advancement of Science in 1860. Accounts of that meeting are generally confined to the memorable exchange between Bishop Wilberforce and T. H. Huxley, when Wilberforce was imprudent enough to put the provocative question: Was it from his grandfather or grandmother that Huxley claimed descent from a monkey? "The Lord hath delivered him into my hands," Huxley whispered to his neighbor. And this is just how historians have reported it, with Huxley delivering the coup de grâce.

> I asserted—and I repeat—that a man has no reason to be ashamed of having an ape for his grandfather. If there were a ancestor whom I should feel shame in recalling, it would rather be a *man,* a man of restless and versatile intellect, who, not content with an equivocal success in his own sphere of activity, plunges into scientific questions with which he has no real acquaintance, only to obscure them by an aimless rhetoric, and distract the attention of his hearers from the real point at issue by eloquent digressions and skilled appeals to religious prejudice.[7]

If Wilberforce, as Huxley claimed, obscured the real issue of Darwinism, Huxley's retort has distracted attention from some of the more interesting circumstances of that event. The meeting opened with a paper by an American, John William Draper, defending Darwin and applying what he took to be the lesson of Darwinism to society. Just as the progression of species was determined by immutable law, so, he argued, was the intellectual progression of mankind. (He was later to expand this thesis in his *History of the Conflict Between Religion and Science,* which traced the progress of thought from religious barbarism to scientific enlightenment.) Although Huxley was privately contemptuous of this paper, he chose not to comment on it publicly, leaving the floor to others: an economist who disputed Darwin's theory on religious grounds, a clergyman who did the same, and a defender of Darwinism who provided a mathematical demonstration of it complete with diagrams on the blackboard. ("Let this point A be man, and let that point B be the monkey"—monkey unfortunately pronounced "mawnkey," which provoked shouts of "mawnkey" from the audience.)[8]

It was then that Wilberforce made the speech that provoked

Huxley's rebuttal, after which the debate (if it can be called that) resumed. An Oxford don disputed the idea of evolution by pointing out that Homer had lived three thousand years ago and his like had not been seen since; a young naturalist accused Darwin's critics of resorting to fraud to discredit him (he himself has been sent a specimen of wheat ostensibly from an Egyptian mummy, which turned out to be made of French chocolate); Darwin's old commander on the *Beagle,* holding up an immense Bible, adjured the audience to follow divine revelation rather than human conjecture; and a distinguished botanist explained why he himself had been converted to the new theory. During most of these proceedings the students in the audience, with a nice impartiality, shouted down speakers on both sides, while a crowd of women waved their handkerchiefs in support of the bishop. One woman fainted and had to be carried out, overcome, perhaps, more by the heat in the crowded room than by the excitement.

The episode is full of curiosities. What were seven hundred people doing at a meeting of the Zoological Section of the British Association for the Advancement of Science? Why was the opening paper on a subject of intellectual history, and by a not quite reputable American historian? Why did an economist, a mathematician, a naval officer, and assorted scientists and clergymen feel competent to discuss a scientific theory of some complexity that had been published only the year before? How did it come about that an Anglican bishop played so prominent a part in the debate? What were so many students doing in Oxford during vacation time, what were so many women doing there at any time, and what were they all doing at a scientific meeting? Why were the proceedings so lacking in the gravity, even punditry, one might expect in a learned society? An adequate account of this affair would go far toward explicating not only the popular reaction to Darwinism but the role and social status of science in Victorian England, at a time when science was widely diffused and heatedly engaged, and when it was so accessible to laymen that it could be readily exposed to popular judgment and dispute.

In the conventional telling of it, the episode appears as the opening battle in the "war" between science and religion, enlightenment and obscurantism. But it can as well serve to illustrate the anomalies and complications that make that metaphor peculiarly inappropriate. It was, in fact, less a major battle than a disorderly skirmish between two motley bands, some of the combatants having more in common with their enemies than with their allies, and very little in common with the familiar stereotypes of the Scientist and the Cleric. Huxley, for example, was no more respectful of Draper who was a Darwinist than of Wilberforce who was not. And Wilberforce himself was not the scientific illiterate and religious bigot he has been made out to be. He had taken a First in mathematics at Oxford, had twice served as vice-president of the British Association, and was on the Council of the Geological Society. Although not a professional scientist (a concept almost anachronistic for that time), he was sufficiently well regarded in scientific circles to be asked to review the *Origin* in the *Quarterly Review,* and sufficiently aware of his own limitations to call upon Richard Owen for assistance. (Owen, a reputable zoologist, was one of Darwin's staunchest critics, although he himself held to an evolutionary theory of sorts.) The review, which appeared only a few days after the meeting of the British Association, was sufficiently cogent to give even Darwin pause. "It is uncommonly clever," he wrote a friend. "It picks out with skill all the most conjectural parts, and brings forward well all the difficulties."[9]

Nor does the British Association fit the stereotype of a scientific establishment at odds with a religious establishment. Its leaders were predominantly Anglican, many were ordained or the sons of clerics, and most were of the liberal Anglican or Broad Church party. The definitive history of the association aptly characterizes them as a "scientific clerisy," echoing the "national clerisy" described by Coleridge in his book *On the Constitution of Church and State.*[10] (By a nice coincidence the book was published in 1830, only a year before the founding of the British Association.) Just as Coleridge's clerisy, although primarily religious and humanistic, included men of science among those who were to give intellectual and moral direction to the nation, so the scientific clerisy included men of impeccable religious credentials. The founding fathers of the British Association would not have quarreled with Coleridge's conception of religion as "the centre of gravity in a realm," still less with his assertion that "science, and especially moral science, will lead to religion and remain blended with it."[11] In associating themselves for the "advancement of science," they did not mean to challenge the preeminence of religion; for them the advancement of science could only contribute to the advancement of religion—"properly understood," as Tocqueville would have said.*

After the British Association meeting there did emerge something like a pro-Darwinian party and an anti-Darwinian one. But they did not neatly correspond to the science-religion antithesis. If many in the anti-Darwinian camp were there because they believed the theory to be inimical to religion, others were there simply because they believed it to be scientifically untrue or unproved. Similarly, the pro-Darwinian camp included those

*The analogy with Coleridge illuminates an interesting feature of the British Association. Coleridge had distinguished between the "fountain heads of the humanities," who presided over the national clerisy and were charged with cultivating and elevating the intellectual life of the nation, and the larger body of clerisy, who were distributed throughout the country and provided each locality with its "resident guide, guardian, and instructor."[12] The same distinction appears in the British Association, where the leadership was vested in the distinguished "gentlemen of science," while the rank and file was made up of men of lesser status and renown—a lesser clerisy, so to speak.[13] And just as Coleridge insisted that the clerisy be distributed throughout the nation, so the association made the conscious decision to become a truly national organization (unlike the Royal Society of London), in token of which its annual meetings were to be held not in the metropolis but in provincial centers. Thus the first conference was in York, with subsequent meetings at Oxford, Cambridge, Edinburgh, Dublin, Bristol, Liverpool, and so on.

who were persuaded of it on scientific grounds, as well as those (like Draper) who exploited it as part of their own war against religion—and still others who welcomed it as an ally of religion, who saw it, indeed, as a higher form of religion. The latter response was not, as one might think, an afterthought, a valiant attempt to make the best of a bad situation. It was the spontaneous, honest reaction of such men as Charles Kingsley, an Anglican minister and amateur naturalist, who found himself confirmed in his faith by his reading of the *Origin*. "It is just as noble a conception of the Deity," he wrote Darwin, "to believe that He created primal forms capable of self-development into all forms needful *pro tempore* and *pro loco*, as to believe that He required a fresh act of intervention to supply the *lacunas* which He himself had made."[14]

Essays and Reviews, published only a few months after the *Origin* and provoking almost as much controversy, cited Darwinism as proof of "the grand principle of the self-evolving powers of nature" and thus the most certain "evidence of Christianity."[15] It was at the memorable meeting of the British Association that another contributor to *Essays and Reviews*, Frederick Temple (then headmaster of Rugby, later Bishop of Exeter, and later still Bishop of London), delivered a sermon criticizing the theologian's habit of dwelling upon the weaknesses or inadequacies of science rather than upon its strengths, as if theology started where science ended. The book of science and the book of revelation, he reminded his audience, were by the same author, and the power of God was more clearly exhibited in the laws of nature than in miraculous interference with those laws.[16] While Darwin himself was not entirely comfortable with a teleological interpretation of his theory (although he himself sometimes lapsed into such an interpretation), others were, and they had no trouble identifying the natural teleology of evolution with the natural theology of Christianity—the doctrine that God operated through law and design. The American botanist Asa Gray was one of Darwin's earliest and most enthusiastic converts; as Huxley was his "bull-dog" in England, so Gray was in America. Gray also happened to be a deeply religious man who was persuaded of the validity of Darwinism as much on theological grounds as on scientific ones.

> The important thing to do is to develop aright evolutionary teleology, and to present the argument for design from the exquisite adaptations in such a way as to make it tell on both sides; with Christian men, that they may be satisfied with, and perchance may learn to admire, Divine works effected step by step, if need be, in a system of nature; and the antitheistic people, to show that without the implication of a superintending wisdom nothing is made out, and nothing credible.[17]

It was not only religious liberals and "natural theologians" who found Darwinism congenial. Some Calvinists welcomed it precisely because they saw it as a vindication of the God of chance rather than of a God of design. The Darwinian image of nature seemed to them to correspond to a providential order that was spontaneous and unpredictable, in which grace was arbitrarily bestowed upon the elect, and the divine will, so far from being an assurance of benevolence, was more often productive of human tragedy—just as the survival of the fittest unhappily required the suffering and death of the unfit. One American theologian, a professor holding the chair of "The Harmony of Science and Revelation," suggested that Darwinism was to natural science as Calvinism was to theology: a foe to sentimentalism and optimism, a check on the reign of law and the rule of reason.[18]*

---

*Carried to its extreme, the idea that Darwinism was compatible with religion ends up in the paradox that Darwinism was most congenial to orthodox theologians and least congenial to liberal ones. This is the thesis of James R. Moore, who distinguishes between "Darwinians" for whom the theory was entirely consistent with orthodox theology, and "Darwinists" who had to "reconstruct" their theology to accommodate it. "Christian Darwinism was a phenomenon of orthodoxy, Christian Darwinisticism, on the whole, an expression of liberalism. The correlation between Darwinism and orthodoxy was not inverse but direct."[19]

If earlier in the century science and religion did not neatly align themselves as the forces of light and darkness, still less did they do so later in the century. As the initial shock of Darwinism wore off and it became more widely accepted as a scientific theory, its implications for religion, social theory, and moral philosophy became more questionable. Indeed, science in general became more problematic when a host of theories rushed in to occupy the middle ground between science and religion. The half-dozen figures who are the subjects of Frank Miller Turner's *Between Science and Religion* exemplify some of the varieties of belief and disbelief, of pseudo-scientific and pseudo-religious theories, entertained by some eminent late-Victorians.[20]

Alfred Russel Wallace is now remembered only as the co-founder of the theory of natural selection, not a small achievement in itself but by no means the whole of his accomplishments. The breadth of his interests and his standing in the scientific community are attested to by the variety of medals he received from scientific societies, honorary degrees from universities (valued all the more because he himself had not attended a university), and the coveted Order of Merit. George Romanes, whose name today memorializes a distinguished series of lectures, was a founder of the Physiological Society, honorary secretary of the Linnaean Society, a member of the Royal Society, and a friend and professional associate of Darwin. James Ward, better known in his time than in ours, was a physiologist and psychologist—the father, it has been said, of modern British psychology. Henry Sidgwick was a distinguished philosopher who resigned his fellowship at Trinity College, Cambridge, when he discovered that he could not in good conscience subscribe to the Apostles' Creed, and who was thereupon appointed to a lifetime lectureship in Moral Sciences. Frederic Myers (like Matthew Arnold) was an inspector of schools as well as a man of letters, and (unlike Arnold) a founder of the Society for Psychical Research, a leader of the International Congress of Experimental Psychology, and one of the first to introduce Freud to an English audience. Samuel Butler was the oddest of the lot, least respected in his time and best known today, although not for the polemics against both science and religion which occupied so much of his time and which earn him his place in this company.

It might seem an intellectual curiosity that men as distinguished as these should have been among the most ardent devotees of psychic research, spiritualism, telepathy, mesmerism, clairvoyance, and the like—and not as eccentricities, aberrations, or sentimental lapses brought on by the death of a beloved wife or child, but as serious philosophical enterprises.* When Sidgwick joined with Wallace, Myers, and others to found the Society for Psychical Research in 1882, they did so not in defiance of the authority of science but to carry out scientifically a mission they thought had been shamefully neglected by science.

> We believed unreservedly in the methods of modern science, and were prepared to accept submissively her reasoned conclusions, when sustained by the agreement of experts; but we were not prepared to bow with equal docility to the mere prejudices of scientific men. And it appeared to us that there was an important body of evidence—tending *prima facie* to establish the independence of soul or spirit—which modern science had simply left on one side with ignorant contempt; and that in so leaving it she had been untrue to her professed method, and had arrived prematurely at her negative conclusions.[21]

That scientific mission brought the society a sympathetic and respectful hearing from William James, Arthur Balfour, Henri Bergson, Carl Jung, and scores of others. While many were obviously predisposed to believe in spiritualist manifestations, others were simply indisposed to disbelieve them out of hand. But it was more than a question of keeping an open, skeptical,

---

*There were good precedents for such intellectual "curiosities": Bruno's and Campanella's attraction to demonic magic and the occult; Newton's interest in alchemy, biblical prophecy, and apocalyptic revelation; Bacon's relationship to the Hermetic, Cabalist, and Rosicrucian traditions; the Enlightenment's fascination with mesmerism.

scientific mind. If they sought objective, material, empirical evidence for the existence of the soul or spirit, it was because they were prepared to recognize the reality of something they were willing to call "soul" or "spirit," something they believed science had rejected out of hand. They also recognized the ambiguity of their enterprise: the attempt to validate religious concepts by scientific means, to seek material evidence for the immaterial, objective evidence for the subjective, phenomenal evidence for the noumenal.

"I had at first great repugnance," Myers later explained, "to studying the phenomena alleged by Spiritualists;—to reentering by the scullery window the Heavenly mansion out of which I had been kicked through the front door."[22] Like the others he was acutely aware of how credulous his activities seemed to scientists and how vulgar to the religious, but he was willing to risk their contempt because the Heavenly mansion to which he so desperately sought readmission was nothing other than the habitation of the immortal soul. And the proof of immortality was worth that small ignominy. It is curious that the man who today is remembered, if remembered at all, for his walk with George Eliot in the Fellows' Garden at Trinity when Eliot made her famous pronouncement about God, Immortality, and Duty, did not at all accept the terms of her aphorism.[23] For him what was "peremptory and absolute" was not Duty but Immortality; so far from being "unbelievable," Immortality was the one essential tenet that made God conceivable and man's existence tolerable. And this tenet, the most important dogma of Christianity, depended on the kind of proof that only psychic research could provide. "In consequence of the new evidence," Myers predicted, "all reasonable men, a century hence, will believe the Resurrection of Christ, whereas, in default of the new evidence, no reasonable man, a century hence, would have believed it."[24]

Myers, however, was the only one of this group to give priority to immortality and to value it for its own sake. For most of the others immortality was the prerequisite of morality, and the spiritual nature of man the precondition of his moral nature. "Duty is to me," Sidgwick wrote, "as real a thing as the physical world, though it is not apprehended in the same way; but all my apparent knowledge of duty falls into chaos if my belief in the moral government of the world is conceived to be withdrawn."[25] His personal universe did in fact fall into chaos, and he experienced a "mental crisis" not unlike that of John Stuart Mill. Mill's crisis was a loss of faith in utilitarianism. If that philosophy could not nourish his own mind and imagination, if it could not provide for his own happiness, how could he devote his life to it as a public philosophy, a means of assuring "the greatest happiness of the greatest number"? For Sidgwick the crisis was a loss of faith in spirituality. If there was no proof of the reality of the soul, how could he himself live in that bereft condition, and how could he, as a professor of ethics, teach a discipline that lacked the essential basis for any moral philosophy? Sidgwick overcame that crisis (as perhaps Mill did his) by an act of will, the will to believe, which permitted him to resume his studies on the assumption that such proof would eventually be forthcoming. But while Sidgwick had to be content to live and philosophize without the certainty he had sought, he had no doubt that science too lacked the certainty it professed to have. And science's failure was the more serious because it consigned man to a state of moral chaos, a world destitute not only of certitude but of the spiritual faith that could alone sustain a moral life.

In different ways the others came to similar conclusions. "If we cannot have omniscience," Ward remarked, "then what we want is a philosophy that shall justify faith—justify it in the only way in which it can be justified, by giving it room."[26] "Giving it room" meant rejecting the mechanistic concept of mind congenial to science in favor of a philosophy of mind that was empirical, subjective, evolutionary, teleological; for only such a philosophy could account for human beings who were capable of being free, hence moral. Romanes came to this view later in life and somewhat reluctantly. His first book, *A Candid Examina-*

tion of Theism, was in fact a candid, if troubled, profession of agnosticism: "I am not ashamed to confess that with this virtual negation of God the universe to me has lost its soul of loveli-ness."[27] He went on to find, however, that scientific dogmas were as vulnerable as religious ones, and, finally, that agnosticism itself was dubious. In his last books he reverted to something like theism when he posited a "Superconscious," a transcendent mind the nature of which man could not know but the existence of which he had to assume if the universe was to be meaningful and if it was to recover even a semblance of its former "loveliness."

The most thoroughgoing skeptic was Butler, whose disbelief in religion, orthodox science, and conventional morality was compounded by an intense hostility toward those of his contem-poraries with whom he became personally or polemically in-volved. It is not easy to sympathize with so irascible a man, but there is a poignant note in his remark that a "loss of faith in the general right-mindedness and clear-headedness of one's age is a much more serious thing than loss of faith in a personal Deity."[28] Yet even he could not abide that total loss of religious faith. "We have tried to get rid of faith altogether as involving uncertainty, and, behold, when our faith was dead, our reason was dead also."[29] The "reason" he finally embraced was the idea of inher-ited experience, a Lamarckian form of adaptation and evolution. And that, in turn, was grounded in the sense of "something still more incomprehensible," an "Unknown God" who gave the universe a divine quality and who gave man the possibility, if not the certainty, of immortality.[30]

It is especially ironic that the co-founder of the theory of natural selection should have been so zealous in the pursuit of alien gods—phrenology, mesmerism ("animal magnetism," as it was sometimes called), spiritualism—and that all of these should have been intimately related to his other great passion, socialism. It is also interesting that Wallace's agnosticism came about as a result not of his scientific studies, still less of his discovery of evolution, but of his earlier reading of Thomas Paine, David Strauss, and Robert Owen. From the beginning, his religious dissent carried with it a large measure of social dissent. He was appalled by a doctrine of predestination that arbitrarily disposed of men in the afterlife with no regard for their virtues or vices in this life, and by a society that arbitrarily disposed of them in this life with no regard for their merits or needs. In Owenism he found the model for a more equitable society, and in science (in which category he included phrenology, mesmerism, and spiritualism) for a more just moral order—in this world as in the next, both worlds being predicated on the assumption that man was a spiritual being.*

This was Wallace's quarrel with Darwin. Natural selection, Wallace maintained, functioned up to a point, making of man a very superior animal. But beyond that point man's evolution depended upon his unique qualities: a brain that was larger than that of the most developed animal, and a spirit that was qualitatively distinctive. Long before Wallace came to the theory of natural selection, before he had even begun his scientific investigations, he had discovered in phrenology the cranial evidence, as he saw it, of those mental and moral faculties—Veneration, Firmness, Conscientiousness, Hope, Wonder, Ideality, Wit, Imitation—which were uniquely human and gave promise of evolution toward an even higher human nature. Spiritualism and mesmerism were different ways of achieving the same ends, spiritualism by establishing the autonomy and immortality of the human spirit, and mesmerism by activating the magnetic forces that were, as the prospectus of the mesmerist journal put it, "a

---

*Owen himself was a spiritualist, as was his son Robert Dale Owen. The connection between spiritualism and socialism was recognized in an early history of spiritualism: "There appears to be some natural affinity between Socialism of a certain type and Spiritualism. The vision of a new heaven will perhaps be most gladly received by those whose eyes have been opened to the vision of a new earth, the dwelling-place of righteousness. It is certain that many Socialists have been spiritualists."[31]

mighty engine for man's regeneration, vast in its power and unlimited in its application, rivalling in morals the effects of steam in mechanics."[32] Finally, the spirituality of man pointed to a higher spirituality still, a "Supreme Intelligence," Wallace called it, that guided the development of the human being, just as man himself guided the development of so many animal and vegetable species.[33]*

What Wallace and the others were so strenuously dissenting from, according to Turner, was "scientific naturalism": the belief in nature as the only reality, in man as entirely comprehended within nature, and in the scientific method as the only means of achieving truth. That belief was shared by a group as diverse as the dissenters themselves, including such scientists, philosophers, and men of letters as T. H. Huxley, John Tyndall, Herbert Spencer, W. K. Clifford, Francis Galton, Frederic Harrison, John Morley, and G. H. Lewes. The most distinguished and influential of this group was Huxley, who is said to have subscribed to a "dogmatic science" that was entirely "sufficient for the expression, explanation, and guidance of human life."[35]

But it is only if Huxley is presented as a foil to the other group that he can be cast in this role, for any serious treatment of him in his own right would make it obvious how ill suited he was to play the part of the dogmatic scientist. Even in the early years

---

*It seems odd that Wallace, a confirmed socialist and committed to the idea of man's unique spirituality, should have been tolerant of slavery, not only in Brazil and the Malay Archipelago where he personally encountered it, but also in the United States. Whereas Darwin, who was neither a socialist nor a spiritualist, was opposed to slavery in principle and an ardent partisan of the North in the Civil War, Wallace openly sympathized with the South. Lewis Feuer, who has called attention to this paradox, has suggested that in opposing slavery so vehemently Darwin was perhaps deliberately taking a moral position at odds with his own theory of natural selection and the survival of the fittest, which left open the possibility that slaves were less fit. Wallace, on the other hand, like his mentor Robert Owen, could view slavery as a benevolent institution that would eventually be eliminated as society continued to evolve and as cooperation replaced competition.[34]

of Darwinism, when he battled for the cause as if it were indeed a war between the forces of light and darkness, he did so in a spirit very different from that of John William Draper, for example, who initiated that famous debate at the British Association meeting. Huxley's combative instinct, to be sure, was irrepressible, and his rhetoric even more so. "Extinguished theologians," he wrote in a review of the *Origin,* "lie about the cradle of every science as the strangled snakes beside that of Hercules; and history records that whenever science and orthodoxy have been fairly opposed, the latter has been forced to retire from the list, bleeding and crushed if not annihilated, scotched, if not slain."[36] But even then it was the Darwinian "hypothesis," as he consistently referred to it, that he defended so militantly, and he did not hesitate to point out one of the main weaknesses of that hypothesis: the fact that "as the evidence stands, it is not absolutely proven that a group of animals, having all the characters exhibited by species in Nature, has ever been originated by selection, whether artificial or natural."[37] He had made the same point in an earlier review when he said that at that stage of the inquiry (that is, on the basis of the *Origin* itself), it was impossible to "affirm absolutely either the truth or falsity" of the hypothesis. All one could do was to approach it in the state of mind described by Goethe as *"Thätige Skepsis"*—active doubt.[38]

Huxley himself was shortly obliged to draw upon all the resources of his skeptical faculty. To Charles Kingsley's condolences upon the death of his young son, Huxley replied that he had no need of the consolation of immortality, because he was convinced that moral retribution was meted out in this world. He neither believed nor disbelieved in immortality, he explained, because he knew of no proof or disproof of it. But he had no *a priori* objection to it. "It is not half so wonderful as the conservation of force, or the indestructibility of matter. Whoso clearly appreciates all that is implied in the falling of a stone can have no difficulty about any doctrine simply on account of its marvellousness."[39] Three years later he returned to the subject, this time admitting that from the point of view of a Christian he might rightly be regarded as an "atheist and infidel." Yet he himself had "the greatest possible antipathy to all the atheistic and infidel school," and no objections in principle to religious dogmas. How could he, who believed in the immortality of matter and force and in a present state of rewards and punishments, object on *a priori* grounds to the immortality of the soul or to a future state of rewards and punishments? "Give me a scintilla of evidence," he told Kingsley, "and I am ready to jump at them."[40]

Unlike Wallace, Myers, or Sidgwick, Huxley did not find that "scintilla of evidence" in spiritualism any more than in Christianity, and he was condemned to remain in a state of *"Thätige Skepsis."* In 1869, he coined the term "agnosticism" to characterize that state of doubt. As a founder and active member of the Metaphysical Society, he explained, he was incessantly bombarded by "isms" of one or another variety, until in self-defense he invented an "ism" for himself. The word was meant to suggest the antithesis of the "gnostic" in the early Church, who professed to know so much about the very things of which Huxley professed to be ignorant.[41]

If Huxley's exposition of agnosticism was philosophically jejune, it was partly because the doctrine itself was insubstantial, being little more than the assertion that some things were not known, perhaps because they were unknowable. But such as it was, the doctrine cut both ways. For the most part Huxley directed his agnosticism against theologians who claimed the authority of revelation for miracles and the supernatural. But he also turned it against Positivists who invoked the authority of science for their Religion of Humanity, and against atheists who announced with certainty the untruth of propositions that were only unproved. After the term "agnosticism" had been in vogue for fifteen years and had become sufficiently well established to have spawned, among other things, an *Agnostic Annual,* Huxley wrote in that journal, only half facetiously: "If a General Council of the Church Agnostic were held, very likely I should be condemned as a heretic." His own heretical view of agnosticism required him to be equally skeptical of "popular theology," which assumed the truth of the supernatural, and of "popular anti-theology," which denied the truth of anything but material reality. "On the whole," he confessed, "the 'bosh' of heterodoxy [anti-theology] is more offensive to me than that of orthodoxy, because heterodoxy professes to be guided by reason and science, and orthodoxy does not."[42]

As Huxley repudiated atheism, so he also repudiated material-ism, and for the same reasons. Turner cites an essay in Huxley's *Man's Place in Nature* as typical of a scientific faith that "simply excluded all those facets of human nature that did not fit into the preconceived pattern of physical nature."[43] But even that essay, written at the height of the Darwinian controversy (it was deliv-ered as a lecture in January, 1862, and published later that year), was not as dogmatic as Turner intimates. Applying the Darwinian hypothesis to the descent of man, Huxley illustrated the relation-ship of man and the apes by means of a detailed comparison of their physical structures. But he was careful to point out that there was no "intermediate link" bridging the gap between man and the ape, and that, for all their similarities, there were also great and significant differences. Even if it should turn out that some structural difference was the cause of the faculty of speech that accounted for much of the divergence between the two species, the divergence itself was "immeasurable and practically infinite."[44]

No one is more strongly convinced than I am of the vastness of the gulf between civilized man and the brutes; or is more certain that whether *from* them or not, he is assuredly not *of* them. No one is less disposed to think lightly of the present dignity, or despairingly of the future hopes, of the only consciously intelli-gent denizen of this world.[45]

Throughout his career Huxley repeatedly confronted the charge of materialism and as often denied it. And not because he was reluctant to face up to the implications of his position; he was hardly one to shun controversy or cater to conventional opinion. As early as 1861, when he delivered his first talk on the relations of man and the ape and was duly criticized for being materialistic and reductivist, he protested to a friend: "I wish not to be in any way confounded with the cynics who delight in degrading man, or with the common run of materialists, who think mind is any the lower for being a function of matter. I dislike them even more than I do the pietists."[46] A quarter of a century later he was still defending himself against the same charge, this time from the spiritualists. His own view was that materialism was "untenable and destined to extinction"—just as untenable, indeed, as spiritualism, which was "little better than materialism turned upside down." If he were obliged to choose between materialism and idealism, he would elect for the latter, but he would have nothing to do with the "effete mythology of spiritualism." Unlike the materialists, he refused to reject as unverifiable everything beyond the bounds of science. However devoted he was to science, he recognized that a great many very familiar and extremely important phenomena lay outside the "legitimate limits" of science—most notably, the phenomena of consciousness.[47]

It is ironic that Huxley's *Man's Place in Nature* should be cited as evidence of a scientific creed that reduced all of human nature to physical nature. For that volume, in the very edition quoted by Turner, has an introduction by Oliver Lodge protesting against just this view of Huxley. The protest carries all the more weight, coming as it does from a distinguished physicist who was also an ardent spiritualist—a worthy companion of Myers, Sidgwick, and Wallace. Lodge quotes an essay by Huxley discussing Berkeley's refutation of the materialist thesis that all phenomena are resolvable into matter and motion. Even if this were so, Berkeley reasoned, matter and motion are themselves known to us only as "forms of consciousness," which in turn presuppose a "thinking mind." Declaring that argument to be "irrefragable,"

Huxley concluded that as between "absolute materialism" and "absolute idealism," the latter was preferable.[48]

It is also ironic to find attributed to Wallace and Sidgwick the view that "the evolution of society toward material civilization furnished no guarantee for the ethical correctness of either the process or the end toward which it moved,"[49] as if this idea were peculiar to those who rejected scientific naturalism. Yet no one stated that position more cogently or passionately than Huxley himself in his famous lecture on "Evolution and Ethics" in 1893 (a lecture delivered in the series sponsored by another of Turner's protagonists, Romanes, and upon Romanes's personal invitation). It was then that Huxley argued that evolution, or "the cosmic process," was diametrically opposed to the "ethical process," that morality consisted not in following the precepts of nature but in defying them, that civilized man was committed to an ideal of the good which might be the converse of the idea of the fittest, and that to enjoy the advantages of society, man had to curb his individualistic, competitive, aggressive spirit.[50] That ethical process, he had written earlier, needed all the support it could get, from Judaism and Christianity as well as other sources. It was for this reason, because of the Bible's strong appeal to the ethical sense, that he was convinced that "the human race is not yet, possibly may never be, in a position to dispense with it."[51]

The final irony is to have the old stereotypes, of an enlightened science and a bigoted religion, replaced by new ones: a "scientific naturalism" that was dogmatic, narrow-minded, jealous of its newly acquired authority, lacking social vision and emotional depth; and a "spiritualism" that was imaginative, open-minded, compassionate, receptive to new forms of consciousness and speculation. One sympathizes with the attempt to respect the metaphysical and moral passions that gave rise to spiritualism, mesmerism, and phrenology—but not by setting up a straw man in the form of a sterile and mechanical "scientific naturalism." This is not to say that there were not scientists of the kind Turner describes, who seized upon Darwinism as an invitation to revive an older materialistic, mechanistic, reductivist philosophy. But the best of that generation of late Victorians, including most of those identified by Turner, did not conform to that stereotype.

It was not only Huxley who had subtle and complicated views of the relationship of science and society, nature and morality, Darwinism and Social Darwinism. Darwin himself was extremely wary of converting a scientific doctrine into a social ethic and was most uncomfortable when others did so. Even Herbert Spencer, the most simplistic and "scientistic" of them all—the original (and perhaps the only) Social Darwinist—was sufficiently respectful of religion to place at the head of his *First Principles* the "Unknowable," a term he equated with the "First Cause," the "Infinite," the "Absolute," the "Unconditioned," and which he took to be the common premise, the common denominator, of religion and science. So too Frederic Harrison, who was so intoxicated with the idea of a "Religion of Humanity" that he knew of no better way to legitimize that religion than by identifying it with science. In fact a good number of these scientific naturalists belonged, together with the spiritualists, in that anomalous region located "between science and religion."

From the height of his own atheistic nihilism, Nietzsche looked down at the pathetic flounderings of the "English flatheads":

> They have got rid of the Christian God and now feel obliged to cling all the more firmly to Christian morality: that is *English* consistency, let us not blame it on little bluestockings à la Eliot. In England, in response to every little emancipation from theology one has to reassert one's position in a fear-inspiring manner as a moral fanatic. That is the penance one pays there.[52]

The situation was, in fact, worse (from Nietzsche's point of view) than he thought. For not only did the English have to rehabilitate themselves, after their feeble attempts at emancipation from theology, by asserting themselves as "moral fanatics"; they also had to rehabilitate themselves theologically. If they were bold enough to cast off the Christian God, they felt obliged to pay homage to some kind of God—in part because they sensed what Nietzsche knew so well, that there was no security for morality without some kind of divinity: "Christian morality is a command: its origin is transcendental; it is beyond all criticism, all right to criticize; it possesses truth only if God is truth—it stands or falls with the belief in God."[53] And truth itself, as Nietzsche also knew, stands and falls with faith in God. Thus it was that those who had been evicted from the "heavenly mansion" tried to find their way back, as Myers said, through the scullery window, and that those who could not believe in the orthodox God found themselves believing all the more in an "Unknowable," a "Superconscious," a "World Soul," a "Supreme Intelligence," an "Unknown God"—or, as in the case of some of the scientific naturalists, a "Humanity" (as in the "Religion of Humanity") that had to bear all the metaphysical and moral burdens of that Unknown God.

The question, however, remains: Why did English intellectuals take that course? Why were they so resistant to atheism and nihilism, so hostile to anything that resembled an apocalyptic mode of thought? It cannot have been because of a failure of imagination or a failure of nerve; they were imaginative and bold enough in their own fashion and for their own purposes. Nor were they so parochial, so insulated, as to be unaware of what was being thought and said on the Continent. Coleridge was much influenced by Kant; Carlyle by Fichte and Goethe; George Eliot and G. H. Lewes by Strauss, Feuerbach, and Comte; Mill and Harrison by Saint-Simon and Comte; Benjamin Jowett, T. H. Green, Bernard Bosanquet, and F. H. Bradley by Hegel; the Webbs, Shaw, and H. M. Hyndman by Marx; Shaw and Walter Pater by Nietzsche. But Coleridge and Carlyle created philosophies so distinctively their own that they, rather than their mentors, became major intellectual influences in their own right. Eliot, having translated the Young Hegelians, proceeded to transmute their "radical humanism" into a "peremptory"—and not unconventional—morality. The English Comteans made a point of renouncing the "excesses," as they thought them, of the master, while the English Hegelians so anglicized Hegel that they properly became known as the "Oxford School." Those who read Marx became not Marxists but Fabians and Social Democrats, thus incurring Marx's wrath and contempt. And the few who read Nietzsche did so almost frivolously, playing with his ideas as if they were characters on a stage.*

Nietzsche thought he understood why the English were so un-Nietzschean. They had all the virtues that made for mediocrity: they were Puritanical, moralistic, pious, industrious. "It was a masterpiece of *English* instinct to make the Sabbath so holy and so boring that the English begin unconsciously to lust again for their work- and week-day."[55] A nation so devoted to the mundane was incapable of serious thinking; "they are no philosophical race, these Englishmen." The most famous of the English philosophers either attacked the philosophical spirit, as Bacon did, or, like Hobbes, Hume, and Locke, debased the very idea of philosophy. "It is characteristic of such an unphilosophical race that it clings firmly to Christianity: they *need* its discipline to become 'moralized' and somewhat humanized."[56] Instead of philosophy, they sought out the kind of morality that was congenial to mediocre minds and mediocre spirits—hence the repute of those eminently mediocre Englishmen, Darwin and Mill.

It is interesting that Darwin, even more than Mill, was Nietzsche's bête noire. One might think that the idea of the struggle for existence and survival of the fittest would be congenial to him, that he would welcome it as an antidote to a liberalism that

---

*About the same time that he wrote *Man and Superman,* Shaw recommended that the actor Forbes-Robertson follow up his great success as Hamlet by playing Richard III. "All Nietzsche," Shaw told him, "is in the lines

> Conscience is but a word that cowards use
> Devised at first to keep the strong in awe.
> Our strong arms be our conscience, swords our law![54]

was rational and peaceful, and to a socialism that extolled compassion and cooperation. Instead, he saw in Darwinism yet another manifestation of the "herd instinct." The "fittest" who survived in the Darwinian universe were not those who were closest to perfection but those who were most skilled in self-preservation and adaptation; not those exceptional individuals capable of triumphing by sheer strength of will but those species where the majority endured and perpetuated themselves by means of prudence, patience, cunning, self-control, and other so-called "virtues." Natural selection, like Christianity, had the effect of making the weak prevail over the strong, the "good" over the "evil," the welfare of the many over the will of the superior few.[57]

The utilitarians shared the same "herd instinct." Under the guise of a new "scientific morality," Nietzsche saw them smuggling in that "old English vice" of cant and "moral Tartuffery." That a nation of former Puritans should try to make a science of morality was itself a sign of bad conscience. "Isn't a moral philosopher the opposite of a Puritan? Namely, insofar as he is a thinker who considers morality questionable, as calling for question marks, in short as a problem? Should moralizing not be—immoral?" Yet the English persisted in being moralists and, what is more, in seeking a peculiarly "English morality" that would be scientific. Utilitarianism professed to be "right" because it promoted both the happiness of the individual and that of the "greatest number," thus reconciling egoism and the general welfare. But that was an impossible ideal, for it failed to realize "that what is fair for one *cannot* by any means for that reason alone also be fair for others; that the demand of one morality for all is detrimental for the higher men; in short, that there is an order of rank between man and man, hence also between morality and morality."[58]

Nietzsche's indictment of Darwinism and utilitarianism could have been extended to positivism and spiritualism as well, for in each case the attempt to create a scientific morality carried with it the assumption that such a morality would be democratic, would apply equally to everyone, and would serve everyone's interests equally. Just as it was impossible for the Victorians to contemplate a form of moral philosophy that made morality itself problematic, that seriously considered the possibility of a morality that was "immoral," so they also found it impossible to contemplate a moral philosophy that distinguished between "morality and morality": the morality of an individual as distinct from that of society as a whole, or of an elite as distinct from the mass. This was perhaps the secret behind the English obsession with morality. It was not only that they clung to moral certitudes when religious certitudes failed them, so that they made a religion of morality; they also made a social ethic of individual morality.

In a society that accepted inequality as a fact of life—an inequality that manifested itself in every detail of life, in speech and dress as much as work and wealth—morality appeared to be the one good that was available to all, that established their common humanity and their common nationality, that, as Nietzsche said, "moralized" and "humanized" them.[59] There is something in Nietzsche's perception that this egalitarian morality was a variation on the Golden Rule: "What is right for one is fair for another"; "Do not unto others what you would not have them do unto you." This, he said, was the *"niaserie anglaise,"* the English folly that passed as morality, the desire to base all human intercourse on mutual service, reciprocity, and equivalence, as if all people were essentially the same and all actions could be balanced out against one another.[60] He might have added that it was this "English morality" that had been transmitted from the early Methodists to the Evangelicals and so to the late Victorians, who sometimes secularized and even "scienticized" it, but never discarded it.

To try to explain why English intellectuals so readily assumed the role of a "clerisy" and undertook to expound and disseminate that ethic would be to rehearse the entire history of the English polity and society, a polity and society that were consistently more open and mobile, and at the same time more stable, than those on the Continent. Perhaps for the same reasons that England was spared a revolution, it was also spared a class of alienated intellectuals—of "real" philosophers, Nietzsche would have said, willing to think radically, apocalyptically, about morality and religion, capable of genuine atheism and a true "transvaluation of all values." The Englishman who was closest in temperament to Nietzsche, most Germanic in his rhetoric and most demonic in his thought, was Carlyle—which is perhaps why Nietzsche was so hard on him. It was typical, he said, of the English, the "nation of consummate cant," to consider Carlyle the most honest of thinkers when he was in fact the most dishonest. For Carlyle was "an English atheist who wants to be honoured for *not* being one."[61]

In his own terms, of course, Carlyle was not an atheist—and precisely because he was a moralist. Nor was Huxley, who repudiated not only atheism but any "scientific naturalism" that presumed to derive a moral philosophy from nature rather than from man. Nor was Frederic Harrison, who took "positive science" to be the ultimate, absolute sanction for altruism. Nor was the spiritualist, or phrenologist, or mesmerist, who sought in the interstices of religion and science for that validation of man's spirit that he could find neither in orthodox religion nor in orthodox science.

❧ 4 ❧

Social
Darwinism,
Sociobiology,
and the
Two Cultures

〜〜〜〜〜〜〜〜〜

When the centenary of *The Origin of Species* was celebrated in 1959, it was a truly celebratory occasion, most commentators professing entire satisfaction with Darwin's theory.* Little more than two decades later, the centenary of the death of Charles Darwin produced some discordant, if respectful, voices. In that short period, developments in genetics, paleontology, embryology, molecular biology, and other sciences, some of which did not even exist in Darwin's time, had not only transformed the theory but made it problematic in ways that Darwin could not have anticipated and would not have recognized. And if Darwinism has come a long way from its origins, the social theories derived from Darwinism have had an even more curious evolution. It is a situation another eminent Victorian, Lord Acton, would have appreciated. "Ideas," Acton wrote, "have a radiation and development, an ancestry and posterity of their

*My own book published at the time, *Darwin and the Darwinian Revolution*, was one of the few to suggest that there were flaws in the logic of Darwin's argument and extra-scientific reasons for its acceptance. Shortly before publication, I was introduced to Julian Huxley by a friend who remarked that I was writing a book on Darwin that would put his theory in a new light. "New," Huxley protested. "There is nothing new to say about it. Everything that needs saying has already been said. The theory is incontrovertible."

own, in which men play the part of godfathers and godmothers more than that of legitimate parents."[1]

The most familiar form of Social Darwinism is that espoused not by Darwin but by Herbert Spencer: the idea that natural selection functions, or should function, the same way in society as in nature; that the struggle for existence is the precondition for the emergence of the socially fit as for the biologically fit; and that the best society is one that approximates a state of nature, that is least regulated, least governed, least controlled by extraneous forces or purposes—a laissez-faire society, in short.

This view of Social Darwinism is unsatisfactory on several counts. In equating a laissez-faire society with a Hobbesian state of nature, it suggests that the laws of the marketplace are nothing more than the laws of the jungle, and that the ethos of a commercial society is a barely veiled legitimization (sublimation, in the more sophisticated version of this theory) of violence. Nor is the alternative genealogy more satisfactory—that which derives Social Darwinism not from Hobbes but from Malthus. It is no accident, it is often said, that Darwin was inspired by that classic of laissez-faire, *An Essay on the Principle of Population.* But in one sense it was an accident, and an ironic one, for Malthus's *Essay* contains an explicit denial of the theory of evolution. Refuting Smith's theory of progress as well as Godwin's theory of perfectibility, Malthus insisted that both were belied not only by the law of population but also by that law of nature which assured the fixity of species. Just as no amount of artificial breeding could produce a carnation the size of a cabbage, or a sheep with a head so small as to be "evanescent," so no amount of social reform could alter the natural condition of man.[2] Darwin did, to be sure, take his clue from the *Essay,* but it was only by turning Malthus on his head that he derived a theory of evolution from the Malthusian struggle for existence.

It is also curious that Darwinism should have appeared on the scene at precisely the time when laissez-faire had lost its original force. Even in the supposed heyday of laissez-faire, as Lionel Robbins and others have demonstrated, the doctrine was never as rigid and dogmatic as it is often made out to be. Certainly by the time Darwinism established itself as the dominant scientific theory—the new orthodoxy, Huxley ruefully admitted—England had accommodated itself to a pragmatic, conciliatory, reformist temper far removed from the ideological rigors of a Malthus or a Ricardo. Only in America, where Darwinism entered under the auspices of Herbert Spencer, did it take a laissez-faire form. In England, by yet another irony of intellectual history, Darwinism was invoked in support of eugenics, a system of controlled breeding designed to promote "national efficiency" —the very antithesis of laissez-faire.

If Darwinism, in England at any rate, did not inspire any upsurge of Social Darwinism in the familiar sense, neither did it inspire the religious crisis of faith often attributed to it. Long before Darwin, religious orthodoxy had been subverted by one intellectual current after another: by rationalism, naturalism, utilitarianism, biblical criticism, and a host of evolutionary theories dating back at least to Erasmus Darwin. Indeed, theories of evolution were becoming so commonplace in Darwin's own time that his great fear was not that his theory would be attacked but that it would be anticipated by someone else (as, indeed, it very nearly was). In this intellectual atmosphere, the effect of *The Origin of Species* was not so much to produce a crisis of religious faith as to confirm and dramatize that crisis.

There was, however, a profound crisis produced by Darwinism, and it was one that struck at the heart of Victorian England. If the Victorians had no dogmatic social ideology, no binding religious faith, they did have a compelling, almost obsessive faith in morality. As revelation, ritual, and religious authority failed them, they clung all the more firmly to the most categorical of all imperatives: an inner law, a sense of rectitude inherent in man which was presumed to be a sufficient guide to private and public behavior, and which could be violated only at the risk of inviting a retribution as certain as any devised by church or state. In 1862 a prominent literary critic observed that "many of the most daring sceptics in matters of theology have been strict and even fanatical in their conformity to the established ethics." The poet Arthur Hugh Clough was a prime example: "Even when he doubted in theology most, he was firm and orthodox in his creed as to what is moral, noble and manly."[3]

Those eminent Victorians who no longer believed in God believed all the more in man. They deified man, not, like Feuerbach, to "de-alienate" him, or, like Marx, to "socialize" him, but, like Comte, to moralize him. Their "Religion of Humanity" had only one dogma: that man was capable, by virtue of his distinctively human nature, of every higher impulse, every moral and spiritual quality, which had formerly been thought to require the inspiration and sanction of religion. This was the function of the "clerisy" that Coleridge, and John Stuart Mill after him, made so much of: to propagate and transmit this secular faith to future generations for whom the conventional religious creeds would have become so attenuated as to be, finally, vitiated.

When George Eliot was asked to define her idea of duty, she said that it was the "recognition of something to be lived for beyond the mere satisfaction of self, which is to the moral life what the addition of a great central ganglion is to animal life."[4] What Darwinism did was to imperil that moral faith by making the "great central ganglion" of animal life the nerve center of human life as well. This was the traumatic effect of Darwinism: it did not so much displace God by man as displace man by nature, moral man by amoral nature. Malthusianism had earlier been accused of de-moralizing man, making him a creature of primitive biological needs, needs for sex and food that were beyond rational or moral control. But Darwinism de-moralized him further, by making him a creature of nature who had evolved, slowly and painfully, from the animal world, but who still bore the traces of his origins and was still subject to that process of evolution, the struggle for survival, which had made him what he was.

The Origin of Species, as contemporaries immediately recognized, contained within it the seeds of *The Descent of Man* published a dozen years later; and *The Descent of Man,* as was also recognized at the time, was exactly what its title said: an account of the *descent* of man—not, as some commentators would have it, the *ascent* of man. The book was, literally, reductivist, designed to demonstrate that the intellectual and spiritual faculties of human beings differed only in degree, not in kind, from those of animals. Thus language was interpreted as a more sophisticated form of animal cries and gestures. The moral sense (which John Stuart Mill had characterized as a uniquely human trait) became only another form of the "sociability" exhibited by animals. And the religious impulse, the sense of reverence and devotion, was said to be akin to the emotion displayed by Darwin's dog after Darwin had returned from his travels—in confirmation of which he quoted a German professor who had written that "a dog looks on his master as on a god."[5]

While some moralists rejected Darwinism out of hand, and others (Mill, for example) chose to belittle or ignore it, a few adopted the strategy devised earlier by Tennyson. Appalled by a nature "red in tooth and claw," Tennyson looked to evolution as the instrument for the redemption of man, the means by which man would rise above nature, would, as the famous lines went, "Move upward, working out the beast, / And let the ape and tiger die."[6] Still others professed to find in nature a providential order that was as moral as the divine providence it replaced. This was the tactic adopted at first by T. H. Huxley, when he spurned the consolation of immortality on the ground that the real world was as moral as the supposedly immortal world. "The wicked does *not* flourish, nor is the righteous punished. . . . The absolute justice of the system of things is as clear to me as any scientific fact. The gravitation of sin to sorrow is as certain as that of the earth to the sun."[7] Huxley reaffirmed that creed a quarter of a century later in his lecture "Science and Morals." "The safety of morality lies neither in the adoption of this or that philosophical speculation, or this or that theological creed, but in a real and living belief in that fixed order of nature which sends social disorganisation upon the track of immorality, as surely as it sends physical disease after physical trespasses."[8]

One suspects that by this time Huxley was desperately reasserting a faith he no longer believed, for only two years later he reversed himself and became the principal witness for the prosecution. Arguing against Spencer's version of Social Darwinism— the view that the struggle for existence was as essential to progress in society as in nature—Huxley pointed out that even in nature Darwinism did not preclude occasional regression, and that in human society the assurance of eventual progress did not justify the suffering and sacrifice of one generation for the sake of another. In any event nature was no guide to morality. "From the point of view of the moralist the animal world is on about the same level as a gladiator's show."[9]

Having started this train of thought, Huxley could not let it go. During the last half-dozen years of his life he was as dogged in exposing the moral limitations of Darwinism as he had earlier been—indeed, as he still was—in defending its scientific validity. The most dramatic statement of his position appeared in his famous Romanes Lecture of 1893, "Evolution and Ethics," which might more properly have been called "Evolution versus Ethics." Had Huxley had before him the text of his earlier letter assuring Kingsley that "the wicked does *not* flourish, nor is the righteous punished," he could not now have repudiated that doctrine more precisely and deliberately. "If there is a generalization from the facts of human life which has the assent of thoughtful men in every age and country, it is that the violator of ethical rules constantly escapes the punishment which he deserves; that the wicked flourishes like a green bay tree, while the righteous begs his bread; that the sins of the father are visited upon the children."[10] His conclusion was equally stark. The evolutionary or "cosmic process," the process of struggle and selection which had made the world what it was, had resulted in the survival of the "fittest" but not of the "best." The ethical process was precisely the opposite.

> Social progress means a checking of the cosmic process at every step and the substitution for it of another, which may be called the ethical process; the end of which is not the survival of those who may happen to be the fittest . . . but of those who are ethically the best. . . . The ethical progress of society depends, not in imitating the cosmic process, still less in running away from it, but in combating it.[11]

Under the terms of the Romanes lectureship, Huxley was enjoined from any discussion of politics. But he could not resist one reference to the "fanatical individualism" that sought to apply the principles of nature to society.[12] Nor could he be prevented, the following year, from publishing a "Prolegomena" to his lecture in which he made it clear that his objection was not only to the "fanatical individualist" like Herbert Spencer, but also to the "administrator," the socialist or eugenicist, who would take it upon himself to create an "earthly paradise, a true garden of Eden." That "pigeon-fanciers' polity," Huxley suspected, was unattainable, but if it were attainable it would be a despotism as ruthless as any known to man, for it would require a vigilant battle against the instinct of self-assertion that was part of man's animal nature.[13]

The effect, indeed the intention, of the "Prolegomena" was to enhance the paradox inherent in the lecture. The ethical process was required to counteract the evolutionary one, to restrain the combative instincts of man in the interests of society and morality. But to the degree to which the ethical process succeeded in that purpose, in impeding the operation of natural selection, it was debilitating to society and a deterrent to progress. It was this tragic paradox that made Huxley pronounce his lecture "a very orthodox discourse on the text, 'Satan, the Prince of this world.' "[14]

Long before Huxley had come to that Manichaean conclusion, another kind of dualism had been advanced by the man who is often described as the co-discoverer of the theory of natural selection, Alfred Russel Wallace. When Huxley first read Darwin's theory, he said to himself, "How extremely stupid not to have thought of that!"[15] But one man had in fact thought of it and had even written a brief account of it. Wallace's place in the history of Darwinism has been a subject of much controversy. To what extent did he in fact anticipate Darwin's theory? Can his brief essay claim priority over the treatise Darwin had been working on for many years? Was there, as has been charged, a "conspiracy and cover-up" on the part of the scientific establishment to deprive Wallace of his just claim to fame?[16] It is a dramatic story that all too easily lends itself to a spurious melodrama. It has also had the unfortunate effect of diverting us from what may be a more significant part of the story. For Wallace not only had the distinction of being the first Darwinist; he was also the first renegade Darwinist.

Even before Darwin had published his *Descent of Man,* Wallace was refuting it by arguing that evolution could not account for the physical development of man's brain, still less for his moral capacity. In these respects man was unique, not part of the animal kingdom, not a product of the struggle for existence and natural selection. Wallace cited physiological and anthropological evidence in support of his contention, but he also had good political reasons to take the position he did. Long before he had become a scientist, he had been a socialist, and he remained that while he pursued his other passions: entomology chiefly, but also phrenology, spiritualism, and mesmerism. Where Huxley was initially attracted to the theory of evolution because it placed man firmly in the world of nature and made of him an "anthropoid ape," Wallace was attracted to it because it gave promise of elevating man above the world of nature and establishing his uniqueness and his superiority over the ape. Eventually both felt obliged to separate man from the evolutionary process: Huxley because he became convinced that man, in spite of his animal nature, had the ethical duty to restrain, even suppress that nature; Wallace because he was convinced that man's nature was qualitatively different from that of the animal, that man was naturally social, moral, cooperative, pacific—a natural socialist, in fact. From quite different perspectives, then, and for quite different reasons, Huxley and Wallace arrived at much the same point: a radical disjunction between nature and man, science and morality.

For Huxley, and for Wallace too, that disjunction was a measure of desperation, a strenuous attempt to keep Darwinism from being tainted by Social Darwinism, to preserve the scientific integrity of the theory without permitting it to encroach upon the domains of ethics and society. But there were other Victorians who had no need of such strategies: those like Herbert Spencer who found no moral dilemma in Social Darwinism, and those like Matthew Arnold who were so firmly ensconced in a pre-Darwinian universe that the problem never arose.

Arnold, one suspects—and this is not said derisively—had a mind so fine that no idea so gross as Darwinism could violate it. Long before the *Origin,* in a poem ironically entitled "In Harmony with Nature," he had disposed of the illusion that there could be any such harmony.

> . . . Man hath all which Nature hath, but more,
> And in that *more* lie all his hopes of good.
> Nature is cruel; man is sick of blood:
> Nature is stubborn; man would fain adore:
> Nature is fickle; man hath need of rest:
>
> . . . .
>
> Man must begin, know this, where Nature ends;
> Nature and man can never be fast friends.[17]

In 1882, delivering the Rede Lecture at Cambridge, Arnold made it the occasion for an impassioned defense of humanistic education against those, like his good friend Huxley, who had been urging a predominantly scientific curriculum. Against Huxley's argument that "natural knowledge," scientific knowledge, was the basis of modern life and therefore essential for the mass of the people, Arnold insisted that it was precisely the masses who urgently required a humanistic education, an education that was not utilitarian in any vulgar sense but that did serve the practical purpose of elevating the spirit above the mundane circumstances of life by satisfying "our need for conduct, our need for beauty." The greatest of scientists might not require that stimulus. Darwin, he recalled, had confessed that he had no feeling for religion or poetry; science and the domestic affections were enough for him. But the Darwins of the world, Arnold suspected, were few. Most people needed art and poetry, religion and philosophy—"the best that has been thought and uttered in the world"—for the realization of their true humanity.[18]

That Rede Lecture was in 1882, the year, as it happened, of Darwin's death. In 1959, at the time of another Darwinian anniversary, C. P. Snow delivered another Rede Lecture to quite the opposite effect. This was the famous lecture on "The Two Cultures." Had Snow known of Arnold's lecture—he gave no indication that he did—he could not have controverted it more boldly. Decrying what he took to be the gulf separating the scientific and humanistic cultures, he made no secret of the fact that he held the "literary intellectuals" responsible for it. Parochial in their interests and complacent in their ignorance, they were guilty of an "intellectual Luddism" that was stultifying and disastrous, for it prevented any serious attempt to solve the most critical problem of the time: the growing disparity between the rich countries and the poor. That disparity could only be reduced by a new industrial revolution that would do for the poor nations what the old industrial revolution had done for the poor people

of England. But a new industrial revolution required a commitment to the new scientific revolution that was then taking place,
unbeknownst to the literary intellectuals.[19]

However deplorable the tone of the ensuing controversy, one
cannot but be impressed by the passion generated by it in America
as well as in England, suggesting that Snow had hit a deep and
sensitive nerve. Everything that could be said about that lecture
has assuredly been said—except perhaps to comment on what
Snow did *not* say. In all his talk about scientific revolutions he
never mentioned that earlier and at least as momentous a revolution, Darwinism. This was all the more remarkable because he
delivered his lecture at the very time the centenary of *The Origin
of Species* was being celebrated (and celebrated especially at his
own college, which had also been Darwin's). When Snow
wanted to illustrate the ignorance of science on the part of the
literary intellectuals, he cited their inability to define the second
law of thermodynamics—the equivalent in literary terms, he said,
of never having read a play by Shakespeare. He later regretted
that example. He thought it sounded comic, was too easily paro-
died; he would have done better to take as his example molecular
biology.[20] But even then, Snow did not choose the theory of
evolution as his example—perhaps because he realized that literary intellectuals knew something of that theory, knew enough to
be skeptical of its application to social and political affairs, knew
not only something of the difficulty of applying it, but of the
ambiguous, even dangerous, effects of its application.

If Snow paid no heed either to Darwin or to Arnold, it was
perhaps because his own intellectual universe was curiously pre-
Victorian. Whatever else one may say about the intellectual
habits of the Victorians—their penchant for large categories and
bold antitheses: man and nature, morality and science, reason and
faith—one cannot charge them (although they have, of course,
been so charged) with complacency or undue optimism. On the
contrary, some of the most eminent, and certainly the most
interesting, of them came to their affirmations by way of doubt

and fear; in this respect they were the very model of the modern existentialist. Snow was rather in the tradition of the Enlightenment, which took a benign view of nature and reason, and which conceived of progress in linear rather than dialectical terms, proceeding not by conflict and negation but by the steady, cumulative advance of knowledge and the steady, cumulative application of knowledge. Huxley had fought his battle on two fronts: against those who denied the truths of science and against those who denied all other truths; against the "individualists" who brooked no interference in the free market of society and against the "administrators" who were all too eager to refashion society according to their own designs. Snow's crusade was single-minded, based on a monolithic view both of the social problem and of the solution to that problem.

The recent emergence of a new form of Social Darwinism has brought with it a renewal of the Two Cultures debate, the latest version being even more ill-natured than the earlier ones. Again one is reminded of the Victorians, who were no mean polemicists, the disputes between Freeman and Froude, Kingsley and Newman, presaging some of the more notorious academic feuds of our time. But considering the issues at stake, the original Darwinian debate was far less acrimonious than might have been expected, certainly less so than the current controversy over Sociobiology. The famous meeting of the British Association for the Advancement of Science in 1860, when Wilberforce and Huxley traded insults, was civil compared with a meeting in 1978 of the American Association for the Advancement of Science, when Edward Wilson, professor at Harvard and leading proponent of Sociobiology, was greeted with shouts of "Fascist," "Nazi," "Racist," "Sexist," and had a bucket of water thrown over his head.

By now even the most benighted of Snow's "literary intellectuals" must be familiar with the basic tenets of Sociobiology. According to that doctrine, human emotions and ethical ideas and practices have been programmed to a substantial degree by natural selection over thousands of generations. These emotions, ideas, and practices have evolved and been incorporated into our genetic constitution. And such traits as altruism, which seem to contradict the self-serving, self-preserving function of natural selection, can be understood as a kind of higher selfishness, a form of kin selection only once removed from the more familiar kind of natural selection.

Because Sociobiology is so firmly rooted both in natural selection and in genetics—because, as the very term suggests, it purports to describe "the biological basis of all social behavior"[21] —it is obviously open to the charge of being materialistic and deterministic. Indeed, Wilson himself speaks of it as a form of "scientific materialism."[22] Yet it is ironic to find this charge so heatedly made by those who proudly subscribe to other forms of materialism and determinism: historical materialism and environmental determinism. It is also ironic that those who accuse the Sociobiologists of being politically inspired are themselves frankly political. A group of them, including some eminent professors at Harvard and their graduate students, have formed an organization called the Sociobiology Study Group of Science for the People, which issues the kind of manifestos and collective letters appropriate to a political sect. One of these public letters accuses the Sociobiologists of providing a "genetic justification of the status quo," and of reviving the doctrine that had led to sterilization laws in the United States and to the gas chambers of Nazi Germany.[23]

Protesting against this "vigilantism," Wilson insists that it is not he but his critics who are reductivist.[24] His theory, he argues, does not equate the genetic *is* with the ethical *ought,* if only because the two are presumed to be constantly evolving in response to changing conditions. So far from licensing the old kind of Social Darwinism, he points out that he has taken pains to establish a biological basis for altruism and morality. At times he seems to suggest that Sociobiology is not meant to provide a biological *basis* for behavior but only to establish its biological *limits*—limits within which individuals, groups, and societies have a large range of freedom for ethical choices, but beyond which they cannot go without violating their basic natures and ultimately destroying themselves.[25] If this modest interpretation is accepted, Sociobiology does not imply any kind of biological or genetic determinism. Instead, it becomes a refutation of social and environmental determinism, a denial that human beings are infinitely malleable and can be radically refashioned by changes in society, education, or the environment.

This modest reading of Sociobiology may be taken as a defense of the individual against the insidious pressures of society and culture, as well as against the more blatant actions of government and the state. Wilson quotes Lionel Trilling's rebuttal of the familiar charge that Freudianism is "reactionary" in presuming to define human nature in biological terms. For Trilling it is precisely the idea of a biological "given" that is liberating, because it prevents man from being overwhelmed by an otherwise pervasive and omnipotent culture. "Somewhere in the child," Trilling wrote, "somewhere in the adult, there is a hard, irreducible, stubborn core of biological urgency, and biological necessity, and biological *reason,* that culture cannot reach and that reserves the right, which sooner or later it will exercise, to judge the culture and resist and revise it."[26]

But just as Freud, it may be argued, pushed his biological given beyond that limited and limiting role, so that it was not simply a deterrent to the usurpations of society and culture but was a usurper in its own right, a determinism as powerful as any other, so Wilson has larger designs than he sometimes suggests. When he says that Sociobiology has finally reconciled the Two Cultures in the "blending of biology and the social sciences," he misstates the issue.[27] It is not science and social science that are the antagonists in the Two Cultures debate, but science and the humanities. The social sciences are all too easily "scientized." The great source of resistance to science, as Snow recognized, is the humanistic culture, which will hardly be reassured by some of Wilson's assertions, such as that "ethical philosophy must not be left in the hands of the merely wise," or that "the time has come for ethics to be removed temporarily from the hands of the philosophers and biologicized."[28] It would seem that Wilson, like Snow before him, does not want to reconcile science and ethics; he wants to subordinate ethics to science, to put ethics into the "hands" of the biologists.

Wilson and Snow are on the same side of the great divide, both champions of science against what they take to be the illusions, obfuscations, or plain ignorance of nonscientists. But politically, programmatically, they are on opposite sides. Snow assumed that if only scientists were given their head, if only they occupied their rightful place in the culture, the urgent social problems of the world could be solved. When he later said that he should have used, as an example of the egregious ignorance of humanists, molecular biology rather than the second law of thermodynamics, he could not have known that within a dozen years it would be molecular biology that would inspire Sociobiology, and that the Sociobiologist would prove to be a far more formidable opponent to his program of reform than the old-fashioned humanist.

Snow believed that science, by virtue of its sheer intellectual energy and creativity, would unleash an enormous force for good in the world. What Wilson did was to make of science itself a decisive check upon that force. Like the Malthusian checks on population, or the "iron laws" of Ricardian economics, so Wilson's genetics sets limits to social change. "The genes," he writes, "hold culture on a leash."[29] Where Snow's image of the scientist recalls the classical *conquistador*—audacious, fearless, seeking new worlds to conquer—Wilson's is reminiscent of the *bourgeois gentilhomme*—grateful to civilization (and evolution) for the goods it has bestowed on him, cautiously adding to his estate but never jeopardizing it by any rash speculation. This is hardly the fascist the "People's" scientists have made him out to be, but far from the brave adventurer Snow would have liked him to be.

Wilson's is only one of many signals sent out recently by scientists suggesting a retreat from the brave new world Snow had envisaged. Almost every literary season produces another book and another thesis citing new scientific (or pseudoscientific) reasons for retrenchment and constraint: zero population growth, zero economic growth, zero energy growth—the last, ironically, a presumed consequence of that law of thermodynamics which Snow had made a symbol of the scientific imagination. But the most ominous of the new scientific pessimisms is the retreat from science itself—what might be called "zero scientific growth."

One scientist commented on the Sociobiology controversy: "The real question, the question that gives the debate its emotional power, is: *do we really want to know?*"[30] The "we" in that quotation refers not to humanists but to scientists themselves. And that question has been raised not only in connection with Sociobiology but with other subjects of scientific inquiry touching upon race, sex, intelligence, even class. One recalls earlier qualms about atomic research. But then it was nothing less than the destruction of the world that was feared. Now it is knowledge about the world we have long inhabited and have long sought to understand.

If some scientists are fearful of what they might learn from science, if they are no longer certain they *want* to know what they can know, the reason may be that they are burdened with too heavy a responsibility. They no longer think it their duty to know all they can know. They now feel called upon to anticipate and judge the social and ethical consequences of their knowledge. It is as if they alone were the repositors of practical knowledge; as if there were no philosophers to speak to questions of ethics, or political philosophers (or, indeed, politicians) to politics; as if there were no historians, economists, theologians, poets, and artists to address other human and social concerns.

"Do we really want to know?" Snow—and Huxley, and Arnold too—would have regarded that question as the ultimate *trahison des clercs,* an unforgivable failure of nerve, a know-nothingness far worse than anything with which the humanist could ever be charged. This failure of nerve comes not from the hubris of humanists or their refusal to accredit the culture of science, but from the unwitting hubris of scientists, from their assumption that the salvation of the world—or its damnation—rests upon themselves alone, that, as Snow remarked not once but twice in the course of his lecture, "the scientists have the future in their bones."[31] That remark must have sent a chill down the spines of those of his own generation who recalled other occasions when intrepid voyagers into the new worlds of fascism and communism discovered there the "wave of the future," the "future that works."

The final irony is that just at this time, when the scientific culture seems to be torn by dissension and self-doubt, when the humanists might be forgiven some small expression of *Schadenfreude,* they themselves—or at least the most "advanced" among them, who pride themselves on being at the "cutting edge" of their disciplines—have chosen to capitulate. That capitulation started a long time ago, when modernism captured the arts, and when philosophy, the "mother of all the arts," modernized and "scientized" itself. Since then we have witnessed the attempt of political philosophy to transform itself into political science, history into social science, literary criticism into semiotics, and, most recently, theology into semantics. In each case the effect has been to "deconstruct" those disciplines, to desocialize, dehumanize, demoralize them by stripping them of any recognizable social and human reality. It is as if some humanists have decided that they too do not "really want to know" those truths about reality which they once thought it their most important mission to know.

This is the latest, most aggressive—and, one might argue, regressive—phase in this century-old debate between the Two Cultures. It is an effort to unite the Two Cultures analytically and linguistically, to create a language of discourse so recondite and internal, so concerned with the mode of discourse itself, that other modes of experience—history and politics, conduct and sensibility—are but dimly perceived as through a glass darkly. If the history of this controversy teaches us anything at all, it is that this strategy, too, will fail, that reality will reassert itself, and that the culture—or two cultures—will once again assume the task, however imperfectly and inconclusively, of interpreting reality.

Reviewing this checkered history, even the most unregenerate modernist might find himself looking back, with something more than nostalgia, to those Victorians who addressed themselves so forthrightly to their condition, who tried to salvage a sense of duty—a "peremptory and absolute" duty, at that[32]—from a world deprived of the traditional supports for duty, who tried to create an ethic that trod a fine line between defying nature and acquiescing in the imperatives of nature. They were as sensible as we are of the difficulties and deficiencies of a dualism that posits radically different modes of experience and knowledge. But they accommodated themselves to that dualism, suspecting that the alternative was worse, that any attempt to assimilate man more completely with nature would result in something like the "abolition of man," in C. S. Lewis's memorable phrase.[33]

The Victorian ethos that managed to sustain this precarious balance is, to be sure, beyond recall, largely because the Evangelical impulse from which it derived is irrevocably lost. But the memory of it, the history of it, is not lost. And that memory, of a culture living on sheer nerve and will, the nerve to know the worst and to will the best, may fortify us as we persist in our quest for some new synthesis that will herald some brave—or not so brave—new world.

❦ 5 ❦

Bentham versus Blackstone

❦❦❦❦❦❦❦❦❦❦❦

Jeremy Bentham's first published work, *A Fragment on Government,* appeared in 1776, a date memorable for other reasons. Even as a literary event it was eclipsed by such more notable works as *The Wealth of Nations* and *The Decline and Fall of the Roman Empire.* Yet there is a peculiar appropriateness in Bentham's maiden appearance at that time. For his philosophy was one of several versions of the "new science of politics" that competed for dominion in the New World.

Bentham himself was properly impressed by the historical importance of his work. His copy of the *Fragment* bore the handwritten note: "This was the very first publication by which men at large were invited to break loose from the trammels of authority and ancestor-worship on the field of law."[1] When the book was reissued in 1838 as part of Bentham's collected works, an admiring editor included that comment. It is an eminently quotable statement, and few of his biographers and commentators have been able to resist quoting it—or, more important, to resist accepting it at face value.

"The trammels of authority and ancestor-worship" refers to William Blackstone, whose *Commentaries on the Laws of England* was the authoritative exposition of English law. Bentham himself, as a young student of the law, had attended Blackstone's lectures at Oxford in the 1760s. More than half a century later, he recalled that even as a sixteen-year-old he had listened to those lectures with "rebel ears," although he had not had the audacity to think of "publishing my rebellion."[2] When he did get around to publishing it, in the *Fragment,* it created—again, as he later remembered it—a "sensation." He published it anonymously, not out of any lack of "audacity" but because he thought that secrecy would stimulate curiosity and thus sales. The strategy, he claimed, succeeded. The book was attributed to various authors, all of them "of the very first class": Lord Mansfield (Chief Justice of the King's Bench), Lord Camden (formerly Lord Chancellor), and John Dunning (formerly Solicitor-General, better known by his later title, Lord Ashburton).[3] The sensation, unfortunately, dissipated when the true authorship was revealed by a doting parent.

Such was Bentham's account, written in 1822 and first published as a "Historical Preface" to the 1838 edition of the *Fragment.* About fifty pages in length (half as long as the *Fragment* itself), rambling, anecdotal, often abusive, at times almost incoherent, the essay would surely have been dismissed as the meanderings of a man in his dotage, had it come from any less a personage than Bentham. At the very least, its allegations would have been subjected to scrutiny. Is there any independent evidence that the book was attributed to those notables, that it produced a "sensation," that Mansfield was "delighted" with it, while others greeted it with "alarm and displeasure"?[4] Almost all of Bentham's biographers, commentators, and editors have echoed his assertions, often without making it clear that they were his. Indeed, such facts as Bentham himself offers belie his claims. In the "Historical Preface" he reprinted the whole of one of the reviews (there were two in all), and explained that it would have stimulated controversy had a friend not chosen to reply to it, thus putting an end to the welcome publicity. But the review said almost nothing about the substance of the book, objecting rather to Bentham's "peculiar" and "tedious" mode of argument and his "conceit" in presuming to argue with Blackstone—hardly a sell-ing review. Nor was the complaint about the lack of advertise-ments and the difficulty of obtaining the book from the book-sellers—as if "the author may have had reasons for introducing it as privately as possible"—evidence of its having created a sensation.[5]*

There is a more interesting sense in which Bentham's account is self-contradictory. If the *Fragment* could have been attributed to such eminences of the legal establishment as Mansfield, Dun-ning, and Camden, if it could have been received warmly by Mansfield himself and (again according to Bentham) by such other Tories as Lord North and Samuel Johnson, and if these claims could have been accepted and perpetuated by generations of commentators—surely we ought to reconsider the conven-tional roles in which Bentham and Blackstone have been cast. Perhaps Blackstone was not quite the sacred cow of the establish-ment and Bentham the lone iconoclast bravely defying the "tram-mels of authority and ancestor-worship." Not the least of the curiosities of this affair is the fact that no one has thought to ask how so subversive a work could have been attributed to the very people whose views were being subverted.

One final oddity: Toward the end of the preface Bentham casually mentioned one other person to whom the book had been attributed, John Lind. Today that name is virtually unknown, but at the time it was far better known than Bentham's. Lind was the unofficial minister in London of the King of Poland, a friend of North and Mansfield and an occasional writer and journalist. In 1774 he wrote a critique of Blackstone which he gave Bentham for his comments. Bentham was so taken with the idea that after editing Lind's essay he decided to write his own, whereupon Lind good-naturedly turned over the subject to him. Although Ben-

*According to his friend and editor, John Bowring, the first edition consisted of five hundred copies. A year after publication, Bentham reported to his brother that the stock of one bookseller had been sold out, but he later discovered that a parcel of the books had been mislaid in the warehouse.[6]

tham privately acknowledged that Lind's was the "parent" work to which his own was "much indebted," he failed to make such an acknowledgment in public. Instead, he accused Lind of plagiarizing from him—the charge involving several sentences in a letter by Lind on another subject published in a newspaper.[7] Whatever else the story suggests about Bentham's character, it confirms the fact that Bentham was not alone in challenging the authority of Blackstone and that the intellectual atmosphere of the time was hardly as repressive and conformist as Bentham might lead one to think.

A Fragment on Government is sometimes described as a commentary on Blackstone's *Commentaries.*[8] It is in fact a commentary on seven pages of the introduction to that four-volume work. And those seven pages, as Bentham noted, were a "digression," casual reflections on the nature of sovereignty and the origins of society and government. Reading the few pages that inspired this impassioned critique, one is struck by how unprovocative they were even from Bentham's point of view. If one did not know otherwise, one might attribute some of Blackstone's sentences to Bentham himself: the pronouncement, for example, on the sovereignty of the legislature ("sovereignty and legislature are indeed convertible terms; one cannot subsist without the other"); or the absolute nature of sovereignty ("supreme, irresistible, absolute, uncontrolled"); or the requisites of sovereignty ("wisdom to discern the real interest of the community; goodness, to endeavour always to pursue that real interest; and strength, or power, to carry this knowledge and intention into action").[9] Even the account of the origins of society was less controversial than might be thought, since the "social contract" was described as a figurative expression which did not imply any actual historical contract or state of nature.[10] The only part of this section that was obviously objectionable to Bentham was the eulogy of "mixed government": a form of government "so admirably tempered and compounded" that it preserved all the virtues of the three classical forms and combined them in a harmonious whole.[11]

If Bentham made so much of this digression, it was because he was convinced that Blackstone was a "determined and persevering" enemy of reform and that "the interests of reformation, and through them the welfare of mankind, were inseparably connected with the downfall of his works."[12] And if he spent less time on the substantive issues and more on logical flaws—inconsistency, imprecision, faulty reasoning—it was because he believed that moral deficiencies revealed themselves in rational deficiences, that Blackstone's "antipathy to reformation" expressed itself in "obscure and crooked reasoning."[13]

The irony is that Blackstone, whatever might be said of his antipathy to reformation, did accomplish a considerable reform, and precisely of the kind that Bentham himself was later to undertake (with far less success). The *Commentaries,* after all, was the first serious attempt to systematize and clarify the entire body of English law. Elsewhere Bentham paid grudging tribute to it on this account, admitting that, for all its faults, it was a "work of light, in comparison with the darkness which previously covered the whole face of the law."[14] But in the *Fragment* the most he would concede was a certain felicity of style; and even this was cause for criticism since it served to make attractive "a work still more vicious in point of *matter* to the multitude of readers."[15]

Bentham's most devoted admirers would be hard put to absolve him of "crooked reasoning" (still more to attribute to him any stylistic felicity). A crucial part of his argument centered on a phrase that appeared not in this section but in the final volume of the *Commentaries*: "everything is now as it should be."[16] Bentham cited this as if it had been applied to the entire judicial and constitutional system of England. But in fact (as Bentham admitted at one point), it referred only to the Church's laws regarding heresy. On another occasion he deliberately omitted Blackstone's qualification of a statement, and then justified that omission in a typically obtuse fashion: "When a sentiment is expressed, and whether from caution, or from confusion of ideas, a clause is put in by way of qualifying it that turns it into nothing, in this case if we would form a fair estimate of the tendency and probable effect of the whole passage, the way is, I take it, to consider it as if no such clause were there."[17] Elsewhere he chose to disregard not only the qualification but the sentiment itself, the substance of Blackstone's opinion, when it belied the view that Bentham ascribed to him. Thus when Blackstone was perverse enough to criticize a particular law and propose a reform, Bentham found these so out of keeping with his "general disposition" that "I can scarce bring myself to attribute them to our Author"; at best they were evidence of "an occasional, and as it were forced contribution, to the cause of reformation," and therefore not to be taken seriously.[18]

If Bentham sometimes refused to attribute to Blackstone what Blackstone actually said, at other times he attributed to him opinions and words he never uttered. He made great play, for example, with the "perfection" claimed for the social contract: the *"perfect* habit of obedience" presumed to exist in political society and "perfectly" absent in natural society; the *"perfect state of nature"* or "state of society perfectly natural" as against a *"government* in this sense perfect."[19] From the repeated and italicized appearance of "perfect," and the large objection Bentham took to it, one might suppose that the word was Blackstone's. In fact, he never used it in this context. On the contrary, he went to some pains to make it clear that there never was any state of nature, that the very notion was "too wild to be seriously admitted."[20] His discussion of the subject was deliberately tentative and qualified, quite the opposite of anything like the "perfect state of nature" Bentham ascribed to him.

Nor did Blackstone credit the British constitution or government with "perfection," as Bentham claimed. Certainly in the seven pages under review, the government did not appear as "all-powerful + all-wise + all-honest = all-perfect."[21] The only time Blackstone used the word "perfection" in this context was when he spoke of those qualities of government—wisdom, goodness, and power—"the perfection of which are among the attributes of Him who is emphatically styled the Supreme Being."[22]* The point of this statement was exactly the opposite of that imputed to him by Bentham. It was God alone who had those virtues in "perfection"; human beings and institutions had them only to an imperfect degree. Even Blackstone's praise of mixed government was expressed in utilitarian and relative terms. He may have been mistaken or excessive in his praise, but not absurd or nonsensical.

In his preface Bentham announced that his task was essentially negative—to "overthrow" a work that was all the more "vicious" because it was so influential.[24] Toward the end he confronted the obvious question: If Blackstone's idea of the constitution was so thoroughly unsatisfactory, what was Bentham's own idea of it? His answer was disdainful and dismissive. "I may have settled it with myself and not think it worth giving; but if ever I do think it worth giving, it will hardly be in the form of a comment on a digression stuffed into the belly of a definition."[25]

---

*Elsewhere in the *Commentaries,* although not in the section analyzed in the *Fragment,* Blackstone did use language suggestive of "perfection." But when he did so, he qualified it by saying that while the principles of the constitution approached perfection, the practice fell short of it, which was why it was so important to understand and respect the principles. The last paragraph of the work, which he himself referred to as a "panegyric," concluded by speaking of the faults of the constitution:

> Nor have its faults been concealed from view; for faults it hath, lest we should be tempted to think it of more than human structure: defects, chiefly arising from the decays of time, or the rage of unskilful improvements in later ages. To sustain, to repair, to beautify this noble pile, is a charge entrusted principally to the nobility, and such gentlemen of the kingdom, as are delegated by their country to parliament. The protection of THE LIBERTY OF BRITAIN is a duty which they owe to themselves, who enjoy it; to their ancestors, who transmitted it down; and to their posterity, who will claim at their hands this, the best birthright, and noblest inheritance of mankind.[23]

One can imagine the ridicule with which he would have greeted such an evasion on Blackstone's part.

The *Fragment* itself yields only a few clues by way of an answer. The most positive idea in the book, and its most obvious claim to distinction, was the principle of utility. The opening page of the preface enunciated the "fundamental axiom": "It is the greatest happiness of the greatest number that is the measure of right and wrong."[26] But that idea was only occasionally invoked and not at all developed, and the axiom itself, as Bentham acknowledged, originated not with him but with Beccaria, Helvétius, and Priestley. More distinctive was Bentham's assertion that utility was "the sole and all-sufficient reason for every point of practice whatsoever."[27] While the principle of utility was common enough, in that exclusive and absolute form it may well have been unique to him. Thus he praised Hume for demonstrating that "the foundations of all *virtue* are laid in *utility,*" but went on to rebuke him for making "exceptions" to that principle.[28] Bentham's own principle, however, while absolute and unqualified, had little positive substance; it was not even related to the "greatest happiness" axiom he had enunciated earlier. Instead, it served an essentially negative, critical function. There is surely some truth in Bentham's criticism of Blackstone: that by being an "expositor" of the law rather than a "censor" (critic), by giving reasons for the law as it is rather than as it ought to be, Blackstone was bestowing upon the law an implicit "approbation."[29] The converse could be said of Bentham, who assumed the exclusive role of "censor"; by making utility the sole basis of the law as it ought to be and ignoring the reasons for the law as it is, Bentham implicitly illegitimized the existing body of law.

On one subject Bentham and Blackstone were in agreement: their opposition to American independence. Although the subject as such was not mentioned either in the *Commentaries* or in the *Fragment* (even in the later editions of those works), their views may be deduced from their discussion of other issues—and from what was not discussed.* Blackstone's opposition to independence, for example, could have been used by Bentham as an example of his incorrigible "antipathy to reformation"—had Bentham himself not been equally opposed to it. Blackstone's attitude is not surprising; as a staunch defender of the British Constitution and a supporter of the Tory government, he was bound to resist the Revolution. Bentham, on the other hand, professedly independent, untrammeled by authority and unawed by the constitution, might have been expected to sympathize with the American cause. How could he do less than Edmund Burke?

Bentham did, in fact, do far less. At one point in the *Fragment* he seemed to suggest that his philosophy allowed for a greater tolerance of revolution, in principle at least, than Blackstone's. Blackstone's idea of a social contract, Bentham argued, made "a *necessity* of submission"; having contracted to enter society and form a government, to exchange their wills for the will of the sovereign, the people could not reverse that decision.[31] This might have been a telling argument against a Hobbesian contract, but not against the Lockean variety which Blackstone held to and which posited, in effect, two contracts, one establishing society and the other government, so that the latter could be overthrown without reverting to a state of nature. This was a small difficulty, however, compared with what was to follow. For having accused Blackstone of making a necessity of submission, Bentham then

---

*Again and again one awaits some reference in the *Fragment* to America: in the chapter on the "Formation of Government," when Bentham alluded to the American Indians but not to the colonists; or when he wondered at what point the Dutch colonies, claiming independence from Spain, could be said to be in a state of rebellion and therefore in a state of nature; or in the following chapter, when he cited numerous cases of political conflict (between the Spaniards and Mexicans, Charlemagne and the Saxons, and other more obscure examples) without ever mentioning the obvious case of George III and the Americans. He even derided Blackstone's use of the word "founders," again without any reference to America.[30]

proceeded to accuse him of being "eager to excite men to disobedience," and to do so upon "the most frivolous pretences," indeed, upon "any pretence whatsoever." This incitement to sedition Bentham found in the doctrines of natural and divine law. Blackstone had written that no human laws should be "suffered to contradict" the laws of nature and of revelation, and if any did so, "we are BOUND TO TRANSGRESS that human law." The practical effect of this injunction, Bentham said, was to force resistance "as a point of *duty,*" to "impel a man, by the force of conscience, to rise up in arms against any law whatever that he happens not to like."[32]*

In place of this "dangerous maxim" Bentham proposed the doctrine of utility, which permitted each man to calculate his own "juncture for resistance" against the "probable mischiefs of submission." While this calculus might justify the resistance of any particular individual, it did not provide any "common sign" or "common signal" that could serve as a collective call to resistance. In the absence of such a common sign, there were no grounds for revolution, and the sovereign remained inviolate. Moreover, sovereignty itself was unlimited. "Unless such a sign then, which I think impossible, can be shown, the field, if anyone may say so, of the supreme governor's authority, though not infinite, must unavoidably, I think, unless where limited by express convention, be allowed to be indefinite."[34] Lest it be thought that "express convention" referred to a written constitution limiting the sovereign authority, Bentham explained in a footnote that what he had in mind was the case of a state which had submitted itself to the government of another. Whatever

---

*This is, in fact, the way some radicals read Blackstone. William Cobbett, for example, much preferred him to Bentham (even the later Bentham, who professed to be a radical). In 1818, at a time of social unrest and political agitation, Cobbett cited Blackstone (perhaps not quite accurately) on the right of resistance. "I say, therefore, upon this point, what JUDGE BLACKSTONE says: and that is, that the right to resist oppression always exists, but that those who compose the nation at any given time must be left to judge for themselves when oppression has arrived at a pitch to justify the exercise of such right."[33]

infelicities or ambiguities might be found in this passage (it was typical of Bentham's mode of expression and reasoning), the burden of his argument was clear. Revolution was "impossible" and sovereignty was "indefinite." The supreme body, the legislature, had no "assignable" or "certain" bounds; there was nothing "they *cannot* do," nothing that was "illegal" or "void" or "exceeding their authority."[35]

Since sovereignty was absolute, the question of whether a government was free or despotic depended not upon any "limitation of power" but upon "circumstances of a very different complexion":

> On the manner in which that whole mass of power, which, taken together, is supreme, is, in a free state, distributed among the several ranks of persons that are sharers in it:——on the source from whence their titles to it are successively derived:——on the frequent and easy changes of condition between the governors and governed; whereby the interests of the one class are more or less indistinguishably blended with those of the other:——on the responsibility of the governors; or the right which a subject has of having the reasons publicly assigned and canvassed of every act of power that is exerted over him:——on the liberty of the press; or the security with which every man, be he of the one class or the other, may make known his complaints and remonstrances to the whole community:——on the liberty of public association; or the security with which malcontents may communicate their sentiments, concert their plans, and practise every mode of opposition short of actual revolt, before the executive power can be legally justified in disturbing them.[36]

This passage may seem to support the claim that Bentham was a liberal in the American tradition established by the Founding Fathers. But in the context of the book as a whole, that claim is dubious. Here, as in his later writings, Bentham insisted that it was important to provide for good government without in any way limiting the power of government; indeed, the legislature was required to have unlimited power in order to satisfy the principle of utility and achieve the greatest happiness of the greatest number. It is questionable whether this doctrine of an "omnicompetent legislature,"[37] subject only to the kinds of conditions Bentham specified—frequent elections, publicity, a free press, and freedom of association—is "liberal" in the usual meaning of that word, and even more questionable whether it resembles anything remotely like the American mode of liberalism, which depends precisely upon the limitation of power.

The denial of any limitation on power is hardly consistent with the kind of government established in the wake of the American Revolution. Indeed, the denial of the possibility of revolution would seem to preclude any kind of American revolution. Yet Bentham later gave quite a different account of his early views. In the preface to the *Fragment* written half a century later, he contrasted the English government, "the least bad of all bad governments," with that of the United States, "the first of all governments to which the epithet of good, in the positive sense of the word, could with propriety be attached."[38] He did not specify what was good about the American government, but since he never wavered in his belief that checks and balances, the separation of powers, judicial review, a bicameral legislature, and a bill of rights were unequivocally bad, the "epithet of good" must have been considerably qualified.

Bentham also later claimed that he had not opposed the American Revolution as such but had only objected to the ground on which the Americans had justified their revolution —the principle of natural right instead of utility.[39] This is a plausible view of the matter, but not, as it happens, a true one. In 1776, when Lind was writing a pamphlet attacking the colonists, Bentham prepared an outline of the arguments that should be used against them. Making no mention of either utility or rights, he based his case entirely on the principle of sovereignty: the "power vested in the crown" which invalidated the American claim to independence.[40] Nor did he alter his position after independence had been achieved. Five years after the end of the

American war, having almost completed his *Principles of Morals and Legislation,* he prepared to send a copy to Benjamin Franklin, with a letter candidly expressing his disapproval of the revolution. "If any . . . of the ideas contained in it [the book] should be the means of adding to the prosperity of *your* country (since the unhappy distinction is now made) it will be some consolation for the misfortunes you have been a means of bringing upon *mine.*"[41]

Even the reference in the *Fragment* to the liberty of the press —one of the very few times the word "liberty" appears in that book—turns out to be problematic in the light of Bentham's other writings at the time. Among his manuscripts is a thirty-page document entitled "Plan for a Government Newspaper," written soon after the publication of the *Fragment.* Provoked by the "malignant," "virulent," "incendiary" attacks on the government in the opposition press (attacks directed especially against Lord North's policy on America), he recommended that the government establish its own newspaper to present its own point of view. The bulk of his proposal consisted of a series of "maneuvers" and "screens" designed to conceal the government's ownership and control of the paper: a title containing some such word as "candid" or "impartial"; a price low enough to attract circulation but not so low as to arouse suspicion about the subsidy; a printer known to have been prosecuted under the libel laws; and occasional articles mildly critical of the government.

A government-owned newspaper was justified, Bentham argued, because "the business of conducting newspapers may be considered a very important branch of national education." While a minister was not authorized to take that business *"out* of improper hands," he did have the power to "put it *into* hands that he thinks proper."[42] Bentham did not address himself to the propriety of secrecy and deception, the "maneuvers" and "screens" to prevent the public from knowing that the paper was owned and controlled by the government. Nor did he try to reconcile these stratagems with the principle of publicity he made so much of on other occasions, and which was one of his main securities against the abuse of power. Although nothing came of this proposal, it hardly inspires confidence in Bentham's solicitude for the liberty of the press. And it reminds us once more how equivocal his liberalism was.

If Bentham was not as liberal and progressive as he is often made out to be, neither was Blackstone as benighted and reactionary. It is curious to find that only two years after his impassioned attack on Blackstone, Bentham endorsed a penal bill drafted by Blackstone and William Eden; the only changes he recommended were designed to make the regimen of the prisoners more arduous and to "augment the terror" of punishment. It was this bill, providing for prisons in the form of "Houses of Hard Labour," that later inspired Bentham's first reform proposal, the Panopticon; and his proposal was considerably harsher than Blackstone's.[43] Blackstone also anticipated Bentham in advocating reforms of the criminal law, the game laws, and the laws governing property and inheritance. Even on the subject of parliamentary reform, Blackstone was amenable to change: in the *Commentaries* he criticized the rotten boroughs and suggested that there might be reason to favor a "more complete representation of the people."[44]

But it was not for these reasons that the Americans, both before and after the Revolution, read Blackstone so diligently and, for the most part (with the notable exception of Jefferson), so respectfully. Long before Bentham proposed to create a "science" of the law by codifying and systematizing it, Blackstone had done just that. He had, in fact, used that very word, referring to the *Commentaries* as an attempt to create a "science of the law."[45] Mill is often quoted as saying of Bentham: "He found the philosophy of law a chaos, he left it a science."[46] But the same can be said

—indeed, has been said—about Blackstone. The nineteenth-century jurist James Fitzjames Stephen was not alone in claiming that it was Blackstone who "first rescued the law of England from chaos."[47]

Daniel Boorstin has argued that in making law accessible not only to lawyers but to all educated laymen, Blackstone "did more than any other writer in the English-speaking world to break down the lawyer's monopoly of legal knowledge."[48] This itself, as Bentham pointed out on other occasions, had a democratic effect, democratizing the law by demystifying it, as we would now say. It also had the effect of instilling among Americans a respect for English common law and principles of government. This is what Burke had in mind when he pointed out, on the eve of the Revolution, that nearly as many copies of the *Commentaries* had been sold in America as in England. That legal training, he said, gave the Americans the habit of thinking in terms of principles rather than mere grievances. The principles, moreover, were those of the mother country. "They are therefore not only devoted to liberty, but to liberty according to English ideas, and on English principles."[49]

However much Blackstone himself opposed the American Revolution, he gave the revolutionists the heritage of parliamentary and legal institutions that has come down to us today as the "Anglo-American" tradition. That tradition has been much modified over the years, and in some respects (the principle of "one man one vote," for example) in ways that might have displeased Blackstone and would certainly have pleased Bentham. But in other respects we are even further from Bentham today than we ever were, further not only from his idea of an "omni-competent legislature" but also from his proposals for legal reforms: the abolition of the jury system, the elimination of legal procedures that impede the swift execution of justice, and changes in the rules of evidence to admit whatever evidence, however obtained and from whatever source, a judge might deem relevant (including the testimony of a wife against her husband or a lawyer against his client).

The conflict between Bentham and Blackstone reflected a profound difference of philosophy and disposition. What Blackstone and the Founding Fathers had in common, and what Bentham notably lacked, was a large tolerance for complexity. When Bentham quarreled with the idea of mixed government, he was not only opposing the particular "mix" favored by Blackstone; he was rejecting any kind of mix, any multiplicity of principles and institutions. His own "political and moral science" derived from a single principle: the "sole and all-sufficient" principle of utility.[50] It was the singleness of that principle, as much as the principle itself, that he took to be an essential part of his science, just as it was the singleness of the legislature ("omnicompetent" and unicameral) that he took to be an essential feature of a rational polity.

The Founding Fathers, on the other hand, like Montesquieu, believed simplicity to be a feature of despotism and complexity a condition of liberty. So far from relying on a single principle, their "science of politics" was deliberately based upon the "efficacy of various principles." Even while establishing a new nation and a new regime—and a republic at that—they deliberately retained as many features of the British system of law and government as were compatible with republicanism. Indeed, it was precisely a new government, and a republican one, that they believed most in need of a plurality of principles and competing institutions, of all the means that resourceful men could devise so that "the excellencies of republican government may be retained and its imperfections lessened or avoided."[51] Thus in addition to the separation of powers, checks and balances, judicial review, and bicameral legislature, they introduced one additional principle: federalism.

It is little wonder, then, that Blackstone, not Bentham, was a guiding spirit in the early years of the Republic. "In the history of American institutions," Boorstin has written, "no other book —except the Bible—has played so great a role as Blackstone's *Commentaries on the Law of England.*"[52] Bentham's works, by contrast, were almost unknown in America during the formative years of the Republic and well into the nineteenth century. If today it is Bentham who more often engages our attention, who appears as the more "modern" and "relevant" thinker, that can only testify to a profound misunderstanding cither of Bentham or of America.

❦ 6 ❦

Bentham's Utopia

〰〰〰〰〰〰〰〰〰

R. H. Tawney once wrote: "There is no touchstone, except the treatment of childhood, which reveals the true character of a social philosophy more clearly than the spirit in which it regards the misfortunes of those of its members who fall by the way."[1] Bentham's "Pauper Management" plan may serve as such a touchstone.

The plan has generally been taken to exemplify what one admirer has described as "the humble, rational, humanitarian spirit of this great man."[2] To some commentators it has seemed so progressive as to be in advance not only of Bentham's own time but of theirs—indeed, of ours. In 1841 the editor of his *Collected Works* remarked upon the "practical sagacity" which permitted Bentham to anticipate the "civilizing benefits" of reforms that found their way, decades later, into the New Poor Law of 1834—"benefits which may then have appeared as the wildest Utopianism, but which have of late been on so large a scale practically and speedily realized."[3] A century later the same judgment, often couched in the very same words, was echoed in scholarly volumes commemorating the bicentenary of his birth. One writer praised him for "anticipating specific nineteenth century reforms"; his proposal, "much ahead of its time and utopian in many ways," clearly foresaw its "civilizing benefits."[4] Another described it as a plan for "garden communities" in which paupers would enjoy advantages not available even to the rich—healthful labor, steam heat, running water, and schools; "I do not know," he added, "whether such a community is practicable, but at least I have seen one in operation, an ancient abandoned estate in South Carolina, converted by the Farm Security Administration into a beautiful community, for people who had been destitute."[5] Still another, a distinguished economist, was pleased to note that the plan was not utopian, but rather "comprehensive, radical and progressive without being visionary."[6]

Later commentators sounded the same note. In 1963 Bentham's biographer offered it as evidence of his "secular, scientific, practical, democratic bias," the "principle of utility in practice"; Bentham, she reported, "rejoiced to imagine thriving houses of industry filled with happy busy people."[7] Two years later, at the height of the "war against poverty," a faculty seminar at the University of California was introduced to this model plan of reform and rehabilitation, in which relief was combined with such positive measures as "education and health care, assistance and insurance, and cooperative actions on the part of the self-maintaining poor"; none of the latest ideas about poverty, the group was assured, would have been novel to Bentham.[8] As recently as 1981 an entire book devoted to this plan concluded that, whatever might be said in criticism of this or that detail, the proposal as a whole resembled nothing so much as a "welfare state," a state that "assumes the responsibility of providing the means which assure the general well-being of its subjects."[9]

The project that has been so generously commended is *Outline of a Work entitled Pauper Management Improved.* Published serially in 1798 in the *Annals of Agriculture* edited by Arthur Young, it was reprinted twice during Bentham's lifetime (in 1802 and 1812), and toward the end of his life he made plans to reissue it.[10] The several manuscript versions clarify and elaborate upon the published work but do not alter it in any essential respect. Thus it cannot be said to represent a juvenile enthusiasm or passing

aberration on his part. Nor was there anything private or recondite about it, anything not publicly available to contemporaries
and historians alike.

Pauper Management was a companion piece to the *Panopticon,*
Bentham's plan for a model prison, published seven years earlier.[11]
The architectural design was basically the same: "circularly polygonal," with the inspector's lodge in the center permitting total
visibility of the inmates. It reproduced the earlier plan even in
small details, such as the chapel in the form of a stage lowered from
the ceiling, so that the inhabitants could watch and hear the
religious services without having to leave their quarters. More
interesting were the economic and organizational similarities. Like
the model prison, the poorhouses—"industry-houses," Bentham
called them—were to be privately owned and managed. What
differences there were in the two plans came from the difference of
magnitude. The Panopticon-prison, a single unit containing two
thousand prisoners, could be conveniently owned and managed by
a single person (Bentham himself, as it happened). The industry-
houses were a quite different matter, for they were to have
"undivided authority" over the "whole body of the burdensome
poor" throughout all of "South Britain" (i.e., England). Initially
there were were to be 250 houses accommodating 500,000 people;
by the end of twenty-one years, the system would comprise 500
houses and a million people. Since a single proprietor was obviously inappropriate for an institution on this scale, Bentham
proposed the next best thing: a joint-stock company. The National
Charity Company, as he named it, was to be established on
"mercantile principles" on the model of the East India Company,
and was to be managed by a board of directors elected by the
shareholders. It would have a capitalization of four to six million
pounds, to be raised by private subscription, preferably in shares of
small denomination. It would also receive an annual subsidy from
the government equal to the poor-rates.[12]

Here, as in the *Panopticon,* Bentham defended the idea of a
private company—and a private monopoly, at that—in place of

the existing system of poor relief administered by local authorities. Such a company, he argued, would be more economical and better managed than a public, pluralistic system. "The mind," he conceded, "has a natural leaning towards the system of divided management." And the English mind more than most. The English could conceive of three or four hundred individuals under one management, but boggled at the thought of half a million under the "undivided authority" of a single company. Other countries were less inhibited. In Hindustan, for example, "you see twenty or thirty millions under the management, and much more absolute government of one Board, and those spread over a surface of country several times as large as South Britain." What Hindustan could do, surely the English could do as well. A National Charity Company would be "but child's play to a Director of the East India Company." Only such a company, which was both private and monopolistic, could do the job, since government was notoriously inefficient. "The race between the individual and government exertion in the line of economical improvement is the race between the greyhound and the sloth."[13]

The individual industry-houses, as well as the company as a whole, would be privately owned and managed, the company selling the contract for each house by auction to the highest bidder. The purchaser would then become the governor of the house, and his authority would be "absolute over the whole establishment." Since the paramount motive of every man was his personal interest, the only way of ensuring the performance of duty was by means of the "Duty and Interest junction principle." Thus a contractor, liable to the "whole loss" or "whole profit" of the enterprise, was more apt to carry out his responsibilities than an official on a fixed salary.[14] In his manuscripts Bentham elaborated upon this, defending the contracting, or "farming," system against such prominent critics as Montesquieu, Adam Smith, and Richard Burn (author of the influential *History of the Poor Laws*). These men, Bentham protested, had made a "hob-goblin" of the farmer of the poor, encouraging the envy and suspicion that attached to all those through whose hands money passed. So far from being "abominable," as these critics thought, farming was "the best mode even under the existing system," and would be still better under the new one, since it was "the strongest stimulation to what is good in management and the strongest check to what is bad."[15]*

The principle of self-interest, or private profit, was carried out in such other details of the plan as the "life assurance principle," which gave the officials of the house a "pecuniary and never ceasing interest" in the lives of the inmates. Thus they would receive "headmoney" for every year of every child's life, forfeit a specified sum for every woman dying in childbirth, and get a "bounty" in especially profitable years. Only by such means could "genuine and *efficient* humanity" be promoted.

> Every system of management which has disinterestedness, pretended or real, for its foundation, is rotten at the root, susceptible

*The contracting, or farming, system had been prevalent earlier in the century, but by this time, as the result of the efforts of reformers, had fallen into disrepute, so that most poorhouses were parish-owned and run by salaried officials and public supervisors. Even these poorhouses were being bypassed by the elaborate system of outdoor relief, the boarding-out system for children, and such specialized institutions as the Magdalen Asylum for "penitent prostitutes," the Marine Society for indigent sailors, and a variety of other philanthropic establishments.

In one manuscript Bentham suggested that in the distant future government management might be feasible:

> The present seems to be precisely the period for the establishment of an institution such as that proposed: the state of society and the progress made by political knowledge is up to the requisite pitch, and is not yet beyond it. The economy of the Joint Stock Company management is up to it, and the economy of Government management is not yet up to it. . . .
>
> Were the institution to wait for its establishment another century or even half century, it is possible that by that time the discipline of Government might have made such a progress, and to such a degree outgrown its present habitual disease of relaxation as that the business might be carried on in Government account instead of Company account.[16]

of a momentary prosperity at the outset, but sure to perish at the long run. That principle of action is most to be depended upon, whose influence is most powerful, most constant, most uniform, most lasting, and most general among mankind. Personal interest is that principle: a system of economy built on any other foundation is built upon a quicksand.[17]

Whatever abuse might creep into this system would be checked by the "principle of publicity." In the *Panopticon* this took the form of a "visitor's gallery"; here Bentham spoke of a "concourse" of visitors, whose comments and scrutiny would be "a spur to improvement and a check to abuse."[18] A more important mode of "publicity" was an elaborate system of bookkeeping, which would expose every aspect of the economy, management, and organization of the industry-houses. The most obvious function of the bookkeeping system was economic. Because of the sheer size of the enterprise, the pettiest sum was greatly magnified, so that a comparative analysis of the expenditures and earnings in each house could suggest savings that would permit the company to achieve "the highest possible pitch of perfection."[19] The bookkeeping system would also ensure the proper discharge of the company's obligations to its stockholders, to the ratepayers, and to the financial and industrial community. If it revealed, for example, any undue competition with other businesses, the Privy Council might intervene to prevent such competition.

A more novel use of accounts was for purposes of discipline and justice. Ideal justice was a "domestic tribunal" presided over by a "wise and good man." But the industry-house would surpass even that in "simplicity and perfection," its architecture enabling every act of misconduct to be known "the instance of its being committed," and its bookkeeping system (Complaint, Misbehavior, Punishment, and Merit books) ensuring, in effect, instant justice, since "delinquency, complaint, trial, sentence, execution" would all be telescoped in time and place. (Execution of the sentence, because the house would double as a jail.) This "unexampled perfection" of justice would provide the pauper with an "unexampled degree of protection."* And all of this without detracting from the "absolute power" of the governor. Since everything was recorded, everything was known; hence absolute power was accompanied by absolute responsibility.[20]

In this plan of "Pauper Management," "management" took precedence over "pauper." Thus the book opened with an account of the "managing authority," and only in the course of defining that authority did there emerge a definition of the paupers, or "burdensome poor," over whom authority was to be exercised. The opening sentence was unambiguous: "The management of the concerns of the poor, throughout South Britain, to be vested in *one* authority, and the expense charged upon *one* fund."[21] Commentators have focused upon what was a sufficiently radical idea at the time: the replacement of the existing system of local authorities by a single authority for all of England. But an even more radical principle was implied here, which became explicit later in the stipulation that there would be "no relief but upon the terms of coming into the *house*."[22] At a time when the bulk of relief was given in the form of "outdoor relief"—doles, wage supplements, family allowances, rent allowances, grants in kind, work projects—Bentham was proposing to create a single system of *indoor* relief. The National Charity Company was to be the exclusive agent

*This "unexampled degree of protection" did not mean an exactly reciprocal relationship between the pauper and the official. A pauper could bring charges against an official, as an official could against a pauper; but whereas the pauper could be punished for "groundless" complaints, the official could not. Similarly, in the Common (i.e., Pauper) Misbehavior Book, the name of the offender would be cited, whereas in the Officer's Misbehavior Book ("if there be one"), it would not. It is also noteworthy that visitors might examine the Behavior books and even interview officials and paupers, but their power was limited to adding to the minutes of the book, which then became the exclusive responsibility of the board of directors.

of relief, and all relief was to be given within the confines of the industry-houses.*

It was the total abolition of all alternative forms of relief that was the truly radical innovation of this plan. For this would transform not only the mode of relief but the status of the recipient of relief. In the existing amorphous and polymorphous system, where the laborer might derive part of his income from his own labor and part from the parish, or where an elderly person might have his rent paid by the parish but be otherwise self-supporting, there was no sharp line separating the "independent" poor from the "pauper." In Bentham's plan the line between the two would be sharp and unmistakable. Indeed, the two groups would be literally, physically separated. In his manuscripts Bentham suggested that his proposal be looked on as a kind of "domestic colony." "Colonize at home," he argued, and you could have all the advantages of colonies without the disadvantages of foreign colonies.[24]

The inhabitants of that "domestic colony," segregated from the rest of the poor, would have the unambiguous status of pauper. Moreover, it was not only the pauper, as that word was conventionally used, who would have that status. So too would all the other inhabitants of the colony. For the National Charity Company was charged with seeking out and bringing into the industry-house groups of the poor who were not "burdensome," not paupers in the usual sense. To facilitate that task, it was to have special "coercive powers":

> Powers for *apprehending* all persons, able-bodied or otherwise, having neither visible or assignable property, nor honest and sufficient means of livelihood, and detaining and employing them. . . . Powers for apprehending non-adults of divers descrip-

---

*Two years earlier Bentham had written a long critique of Pitt's Poor Law Bill of 1796, which proposed an even more elaborate and generous system of outdoor relief. He later claimed that this manuscript was responsible for the withdrawal of Pitt's bill.[23]

tions, being without prospect of honest education, and causing them to be bound to the company in quality of apprentices. . . . Powers for apprehending insolvent fathers of chargeable bastards and detaining them until they have worked out their composition money . . . also mothers of ditto for a certain time.[25]

Unlike the conventional system in which the pauper defined himself, so to speak, by his own action in applying for relief, here he was to be defined by the company, which alone had the power to determine whether he had visible property, honest means of livelihood, or the prospect of education, and was therefore a proper candidate for the industry-house.

A policy of "coercion" or "compulsion," Bentham explained, was "indispensable" to his proposal. Even under the system of outdoor relief, there were those who preferred begging to parish relief. With the substitution of the industry-house for outdoor relief, the incentive to begging was even greater. In this situation, the "extirpation of mendicity" could only be effected by a policy of coercion—the beggar had to be forced into the house.[26] The logic of this argument also accounts for the principle of exclusiveness: *"one* authority" and *"one* fund."[27] So long as either alternative, outdoor relief or begging, was available, no one would apply for workhouse relief. To make the industry-house effective, it had to be the sole agency of relief, and not only for those actually seeking relief but for all those who had no visible, honest means of support; if the former entered the house voluntarily, the latter had to be brought in forcibly. To carry out this policy, the company would delegate its "coercive powers" to the governor or chaplain of the industry-house, who would have the authority to apprehend and confine beggars without the usual legal order issued by a magistrate. "Intervention of a magistrate (unless the chaplain should be nominated to the magistracy) would produce complication and delay, and might render the execution of the law less steady."[28]

If beggars had to be coerced into the house, so did "habitual depredators":

The habit of depredation may be inferred with the most perfect certainty, and without the possibility of injury, from the want of honest means of livelihood (sufficient property as well as honest occupation included), coupled with the non-exercise of mendicity: for existence has no other means of support. What is *not* known is whether a man is a smuggler, a sharper, a coiner, a thief, a highwayman, or an incendiary:—what *is* known is that he is one or other of these, or several in one.[29]

If any of these crimes could be "proved in a legal way," the man would be dealt with as a criminal. It was when the case against him was "indirect," "negative," or not legally provable that he fell within the category of "depredator." "It would be a sad inconsistency," Bentham commented, "to extirpate the undangerous habit [begging], and leave the dangerous habit [depredation] untouched."[30]

And if the habitual depredator, so too the "stigmatized" depredator, who had been tried for a crime, had been convicted, and had already served his sentence. And if the stigmatized, then also the "suspected" depredator, who had been tried and been acquitted. And so too the wives and children of habitual, stigmatized, and suspected depredators, who were themselves "presumed" to be depredators by the fact of kinship (common-law wives by the fact of cohabitation). To be sure, it would be unjust to punish these "disreputable classes," since the stigmatized had already completed their punishment and the suspected had been acquitted. But confinement in an industry-house, Bentham insisted, was not a "punishment." It was a "remedy," and one not likely to be abused since the genuinely reformed man or the genuinely innocent one would not be wanting for legitimate employment.[31]

Because positive evidence of depredation was, in the nature of the case, unavailable (if there were such evidence, the person would be a criminal rather than a depredator), "suspicions" would be considered grounds for interrogation, and suspicious replies for confinement in the house. An oath by a "person of character" testifying to his suspicions, an accusation unacceptable in a court of law, "strangeship to the place" (a newcomer to the area) without evident means of support—these were sufficient warrant for confinement. To facilitate this process, a *"universal register* of names, abodes and occupations" would be established. Anticipating the objection that such a register was inimical to liberty, Bentham argued that the information was already exacted for purposes of taxation from the "affluent and undangerous classes." Why not, then, from the "disreputable classes"?[32]* Nor was he disturbed by the thought that this procedure violated the laws against self-incrimination. Whatever the wisdom of these laws (and he himself had little use for them), the issue was irrelevant, for here there was "no crime, no punishment, no crimination, no self-crimination."[35]

The same logic that dictated the commitment to the industry-house of one after another variety of depredator—if one, why not another?—made for the inclusion of still other groups: transported prisoners confined overnight in the "strong-ward" of the house; other prisoners more conveniently kept there than in the ordinary jail; "unchaste hands," such as "prostitutes, mothers of bastards, loose women, procuresses"; unruly apprentices, children, or wives committed at the instance of masters, fathers, or husbands; and "conversely," victimized apprentices, children, or wives fleeing from tyrannical masters, fathers, or husbands. (This was not quite the converse, since in each case it was the subordi-

---

*Bentham expected a great deal of resistance to such a register. The English, he complained, preferred "the most inveterate mischiefs to the most simple and efficient, if unaccustomed, remedies." He himself favored another mode of identification but confessed that he was loath to mention it, even in his manuscripts, for it would be "shrunk from as horrible or laughed at as ridiculous"; yet it was a "moral preservative and political security of the very first order." A penciled note in the margin identified it as an "identity wash."[33] Bentham's reluctance to mention it may be explained by the fact that twenty years earlier he had been severely criticized for proposing, in his pamphlet *View of the Hard Labour Bill,* that a chemical wash be applied to the face of every prisoner, spelling out his name and jail.[34]

nate who ended up in the house, regardless of guilt.) Eventually, Bentham suggested, "the whole system of imprisonment might be undertaken by the company," the only prisoners not easily accommodated, without additional facilities, being "debtors and delinquents from the higher lines of life."[36]

The expansiveness of the scheme depended on the proposition "No crime, no punishment," which recurred at crucial points of the argument. The double-barreled formula performed a double function: to admit those who had not committed a crime, and to do so without the usual legal procedures attaching to punishment. Thus Bentham criticized the Vagrancy Act then in force, which consigned vagrants to houses of correction upon the order of a justice of the peace, as a violation of justice "by punishing, as for delinquency, without proof"; if there had been proof, the culprit would have been committed to a jail rather than a house of correction. Commitment to an industry-house, on the other hand, involved neither a charge of delinquency nor the exaction of punishment; therefore there was no need for legal proceedings and no possibility of "injustice."[37] He also thought his plan preferable to the older law, which bound the vagrant over to the service of the master. That law was naturally odious in a country that "piques itself so much in its regard for liberty." The industry-house was less objectionable since the master was a large, responsible establishment rather than a single, possibly tyrannical individual.[38]

Although Bentham was willing to use his countrymen's "regard for liberty" as an argument against other policies, he was frank to admit that he himself did not share that regard and that his own plan could be objected to on the same ground. What was important was not liberty but security.

Objection—liberty infringed. Answer—liberty of doing mischief. As security is increased, liberty is diminished.[39]

Public security commands it [compulsion in the case of "stigmatized hands"]. Justice does not forbid it.[40]

That it [the "Universal Register"] would be an infringement upon liberty is not to be denied: for in proportion as security is established, liberty is restricted. To one branch of liberty—the liberty of doing mischief—it would be not prejudicial only, but destructive.[41]

But was not the denial of liberty, the fact of compulsion, a form of punishment? Here the argument turned not only upon the security of society but upon the nature of those who were properly subject to the coercion of society—who were incapacitated for liberty and benefited from coercion.

It is not for punishment that the whole race of mankind is placed in a state of wardship—that is in a state of coercion—till its arrival at the prescribed period of intellectual maturity. It is not for punishment that the insane of all ages are committed to the custody of sounder minds. The persons in question are a sort of forward children—a set of persons not altogether sound in mind —not altogether possessed of that moral sanity without which a man can not in justice to himself any more than to the community be intrusted with the uncontrolled management of his own conduct and affairs.[42]

Once committed to the house, for whatever reason—as pauper, beggar, or depredator, as wife, apprentice, or child—each person was subject to the "self-liberation principle": "No relief but upon the terms of coming into the house . . . and working out the expense."[43] Release would come when that "self-liberation account" was fulfilled, when "the value of labour has balanced the expense of relief." As in the marketplace, so in the industry-house, everyone had to earn his keep. Here, too, the bookkeeping system was crucial. The debit side of the inmate's account included not only the expense of maintaining him but also the cost of apprehending and conveying him to the house, the reward paid for him, a charge for insurance (to reimburse the company in case he should die before his account was balanced), and a sum equivalent to the "ordinary profit" on invested capital.[44]

Within the house the principle of economy was to be reinforced by the principle of "suitability," to ensure that the condition of the pauper be no "more desirable" than that of the poorest man outside.[45] The application of these principles was worked out in the greatest detail. Meat, for example, "the greatest article of excess in the existing poorhouses," would be greatly reduced or eliminated (if Hindus could get on without it, so could the English); bread would be replaced by cheaper substitutes; and experiments would be conducted to determine the minimum quantity and quality of food consistent with good health (possibly two meals a day instead of three).[46] Clogs would be worn in place of shoes, and uniforms of the most economical sort. ("Soldiers wear uniforms, why not paupers?—those who save the country, why not those who are saved by it?")[47] Beds would consist of large wooden frames drawn up by pulleys during the day or reversed to form tables and benches; at night each frame would sleep several persons, children of "an innocent and unobserving age" alternating with adults. By these means each room could be made to accommodate twenty-four single adults or sixteen married people and thirty-two children. An infirmary would provide for the sick, with special huts for those with noxious or contagious diseases. (At first Bentham spoke of them as individual huts, but after working out the cost of construction, he decided upon four-person huts for venereal cases and two-person huts for other infectious diseases.)[48] In his manuscripts (although not in the book) Bentham admitted that some of these proposals might strike other reformers as inhumane. "I am fighting some of my best and most respected friends. . . . I am fighting myself likewise." But he would not succumb to "false humanity." "The stronger my propensity to give way to it, the more strenuous my efforts to subdue it."[49]

On the credit side of the self-liberation account was the profit to be derived from the pauper's labor. (The annual government subsidy equivalent to the poor rates did not enter these calculations, even to the extent of reducing interest charges or overhead costs.) Here the governing principle was the "all-employing principle": "Not one in a hundred is absolutely incapable of all employment. Not the motion of a finger, not a step, not a wink, not a whisper, but might be turned to account in the way of profit in a system of such magnitude." The bedridden might be inspectors, the blind could knit or spin—even the insane could work, under careful direction. Thus "employment might be afforded to every *fragment* of ability, however minute." Productivity would be further enhanced by the division of labor, job rotation, employment at maximal capacity (a man not being used where a woman would do, or an adult in place of a child), payment by piece-work, special prizes ("by paying one or a few victors, you get the result of the extra exertions of the whole multitude of competitors"), and honoraria which produced the same effect without cost. Laziness would be discouraged by the "earn first" principle: the withholding of food until the task was completed. And waste would be eliminated by consuming within the house whatever products were unfit for sale.[50]

The self-liberation account was meant to do for the inmate what the contract did for the governor: effect the "junction" of duty and interest. It was to the pauper's interest to work hard since the more he earned the sooner he would be released. But there is an inconsistency here that Bentham did not confront. While the principle of self-liberation implied that the pauper would be discharged as soon as his account was balanced, the principle of contract held out the promise of substantial profits over and above the "ordinary profit" on capital investment. On Bentham's calculations, the cost of maintaining a pauper would be no more than 4d a day for a man and 3d for a woman, while the yield from their labor would be no less than 1s and 6d respectively, with a "still more advantageous" profit in the case of children.[51] Thus the company's earnings would be far greater than that required for the balancing of the pauper's account. "The

Company," Bentham noted, "need never be a loser, but may be a gainer if it pleases."[52] But to the extent to which the company was a "gainer," the pauper had to be a "loser," since he was working beyond the balance of his account.

If Bentham was unaware of this difficulty, he was very much aware of another. While the rationale of the enterprise depended upon its profitability, that profitability represented a threat to competing enterprises. To minimize that threat without jeopardizing profits, Bentham pledged the company to refrain from occupations that would bring it into competition with private industry and to pay lower wages so as to encourage the poor to seek private employment. (To be sure, the latter provision would retard the fulfillment of the self-liberation account, thus delaying the pauper's return to the free market.) The desire to placate commercial interests may well have contributed to the unique character of the plan. For the curious thing is that while it provided most ingeniously for beggars, depredators, and especially children, it paid little attention to the honest, "able-bodied" paupers. That neglect is all the more conspicuous because these paupers were the most obvious responsibility of a National Charity Company as well as the most obvious source of profit. Yet Bentham repeatedly disclaimed any designs upon them and belittled their importance to his plan.

For able-bodied, honest paupers, the industry-house was to be "a makeshift, a dernier resort." And for the industry-house, they were to be only a small part of the labor force, since they constituted the "coming-and-going stock" rather than the "longer-staying" or "permanent" stock. The latter contributed most substantially to the economy of the enterprise, and they were precisely the unable and the dishonest. "The refuse of the population, able as well as unable, is the lot best adapted to the situation of the Company"; "what the Company gets of the national stock of industry and ability is all along but the refuse." But the company knew how to make the best of that refuse. "So many Industry-houses, so many crucibles, in which dross of this kind is converted into sterling."[53]

One can now appreciate the importance of the "all-employing principle," by which the sick, blind, lame, aged, and young, who could not earn their keep elsewhere, were found capable of earning "more than a maintenance" in this establishment. By practicing every economy and exploiting every "fragment of ability," the industry-house, and only the industry-house, could make them a source of profitable labor. And a source, moreover, of permanently profitable labor: since they were incapable of maintaining themselves outside the house, they were necessarily part of the "permanent stock" of the house. One can also understand why the appendages to the plan—beggars and all the varieties of depredators—proliferated so rapidly as almost to obscure what might have been thought to be its primary purpose. For these were indeed "best adapted to the situation of the company," being more capable of profitable labor than the physically disabled and, unlike the honest pauper, neither seeking employment nor being sought after by private employers. To be sure, beggars and depredators were not bound to the house as inexorably as the disabled, since they could more easily work off their accounts. But Bentham compensated for this by stipulating that, unlike the others, they were not to be automatically released when their accounts were balanced. Instead, they were to be retained until a "responsible person" undertook to employ them for a specified period, after which they would return to the house—"and so *toties quoties.*"[54] In effect, this provision transformed them from "coming-and-going" stock into "longer-staying" stock. Thus the more permanent part of the labor force of the house would be augmented by those who, by *"positive* institution" rather than *"natural* state and condition," were to be "fixed within the pale of the establishment for a long and determinate time."[55]

There was still another class, more numerous and important than the others, which was in the house as much by virtue of "positive institution" as by "natural state." This was the "indigenous" class: those born in the house or entering it as minors, all of whom would remain in it until adulthood. His plan, Bentham observed, "would be incomplete if the rising generation were left out of it."[56] He provided for that rising generation so well that at the end of twenty-one years, the indigenous class was to equal in number all the other groups combined, doubling the size of the enterprise from 250 to 500 houses and the number of inmates from half a million to a million. (His notes gave the total population of England at the time as nine million.)[57]

As beggars and depredators were more important to the scheme than honest, able-bodied paupers, so the rising generation was more important still, and was conceived as such from the outset. One of the two questionnaires prefacing the book was a "Non-Adult Value Table," and the very first page of the book spoke of the "growing produce of the labour of all non-adult paupers." These "non-adult paupers" included orphans, abandoned children, and the children of the inmates, all of whom were to be "bound to the company in quality of *apprentices*—males, till twenty-one or twenty-three; females, till twenty-one or nineteen: without prejudice to marriage."[58] The last clause meant that they would be free to marry but that marriage would not release them from the bonds of apprenticeship. Nor could they leave the house with their parents, for their apprenticeship would continue until they themselves reached adulthood. The children of beggars and depredators would remain even longer, since they would start working out their accounts only after they had completed their apprenticeship.[59]*

Even more than the "refuse of the population," the apprentices were the "very essence of the plan," the "chief basis of the company's profit-seeking arrangements."[61] The profit from apprentice labor, Bentham calculated, would be even greater than

---

*In the manuscripts Bentham proposed "augmenting the stock of apprentices" by admitting pregnant women who were not indigent, on condition that their infants be turned over to the company.[60]

the 300 percent profit anticipated from adult male labor, and would more than equal the amount of the poor rates. He was especially pleased to compare the "negative pecuniary value" of the ordinary child with the "positive value" of the company's child, "an inexhaustible source of wealth, population, and happiness to the state"—and, by the same token, to the company.[62] In his book Bentham presented this aspect of his plan without apology or excuse, indeed as cause for pride. In his manuscripts, however, he felt the need to justify it. Just as the children of laborers were "a part of the property of their parents," who could extract from them whatever "profit or pleasure" they thought fit, so pauper children were "as naturally a portion of the property of the public"—and of the company acting on its behalf.

> To them belongs the profit derivable from whatever services it can contrive to extract from them during their non-age, saving in this case as in the case of the real parent the regard due to their own instincts and sensibilities. It has it in its power to reap the profit, and there is no reason why it should abstain from exercising that power. The greater this profit, the greater the extent that may be given to the service.[63]

The company, moreover, was in a better position to "reap the profit" than parents who, "for want of time, opportunity, intelligence and capital," did not properly utilize the labor of their children.[64] And unlike the ordinary poorhouse, which discharged the young as soon as they entered their most productive years, the company would retain its apprentice stock for a long period, including a year or two "during which their ability in every point of view will be at the highest pitch."[65] The book did not specify the age at which these apprentices would start to work, but the manuscripts put it at four—this in contrast to the customary apprenticeship age of fourteen. At four, Bentham insisted, children became capable of work, and at that age their work began to show a profit. To start later was a deplorable waste of time.

Ten years, ten precious years, may be looked upon in the existing state of things as the waste period of human life, the period lost to industry. . . . Ten precious years in which nothing is done! nothing for industry! nothing for improvement, moral or intellectual![66]

Again, in the manuscripts although not in the book, Bentham took cognizance of the conventional argument against child labor. "There is a degree of cruelty, I have heard it said, in shutting up children in a manufactory, especially at a tender age." But that argument was groundless, for unless "shutting up" meant "unnecessary confinement," there was no cruelty. On the contrary, "the cruelty would be in not doing it."[67] Nor was there any cruelty in the austere and rigorous regimen of the industry-house. Compounding the wastefulness of those "ten precious years" was the wastefulness of the ordinary family and of the conventional poorhouse. Indeed, the latter was even more profligate, serving meat more often than was the custom in private homes, allowing the boys as much as 4d a week pocket-money (which was more, Bentham noted, than he had had as a schoolboy at Westminster), and otherwise indulging the children in "luxurious and expensive" habits that were as detrimental to them as to society.[68]

The truth is, under the existing system of laws and under the prevailing system of sentiments and affections, not only these poor children, but the dependent Poor in general may be termed the spoiled children of the rich: benevolence the seed: mischief and misery the fruit.[69]

The industry-house would prevent that "mischief and misery" by sheltering its children from the very knowledge of such luxuries. Within the house they would be separated from their fathers (who would be permitted to "view" them but not speak with them except in the presence of specified authorities), as well as from older paupers who might excite in them "hankerings after emancipation" by painting "flattering pictures of the world at large."[70]* In the "sequestered though public sanctuary" of the industry-house, "habit is formed, fashion is unknown"—the habit of "systematical frugality" as against the "unsatisfiable desires" of false fashion.[72]

In this as in other respects the industry-house was superior even to the rich family, let alone the poor. Unlike parental care, which was apt "to be relaxed by casual want of affection, or to be misguided by ignorance, prejudice or caprice," the industry-house would function in a manner that was "uniform, systematical, governed by principle." Professional attendants, machinery, experiments, and a rational ordering of the necessities of life would assure the children the "most advantageous" amount and form of exercise, fresh air, and food. What was most advantageous to the inmates was also what was most economical for the company. Thus a large number of infants would be rocked in a single crib by the "slight exertion of a feeble hand," or aired together in a single carriage drawn by an ass or an older child; 140 infants and four nurses would be lodged in a single room; each woman delivered of a child would be given two to suckle (and mothers of bastards would be detained for that purpose alone); clothing would be made out of the discarded garments of the poor ("old materials being preferable for this purpose to new on account of their softness"); and food would be the minimum consistent with health (a one-year-old could be fed for no more than 2d a day, a two-year-old for 2½d, and so on).[73]

Still more advantageous was the education of the children in the industry-house. This was of the greatest importance, Bentham explained, because it affected not only the half-million apprentices over whom the company would have a "direct and all-

---

*In practice, there would be large exceptions to this principle of "separation." The piece-work system, for example, requiring people to work together, would be governed instead by the principle of "aggregation."[71] And the proposed sleeping arrangements would have very young children sharing beds with adults.

commanding authority," but the rest of society, over whom it would have an "all-prevailing, though less certain and immediate influence." Whereas traditionally the education of the poor was shaped by the "remote and casual example of the rich," now it would be shaped by the "direct and constant exercise of plastic power." And a "plastic power" far more effective than anything previously known. "The influence of the schoolmaster on the conduct of the pupil in ordinary life is as nothing compared with the influence exercised by the company over these its wards."[74]

That power derived in part from the fact that the company combined in itself the authority of schoolmaster, parent, and employer, and in part from a concept of education that equated it with all of life and thus with "the whole of the individual's time." "The proper end of education," Bentham declared, "is no other than the proper end of life—well being."[75]* And the well-being not only of the "individual to be educated" but also of "the parties at whose expense and by whose care he is to be educated—viz. the proposed company."[76] The well-being of both parties was best served by combining education—that is to say, every aspect of life—with every other aspect, so that everything had a multiple utility. Thus "no portion of time ought to be directed exclusively to the single purpose of comfort"; exercise was best when "infused into the mass of occupation"; amusement was no less amusing when it had "the faculty of leading to profit"; the optimum amount of sleep was "the least that can be made sufficient for health and strength";† and health and strength were themselves "the natural, though but collateral results" of

*This definition of education might have been taken almost verbatim from Helvétius. It is probable that Bentham, a great admirer of Helvétius, did adopt it from him and did not attribute it to him because the substance of education, as Helvétius understood it, was so different from what Bentham was here proposing.

†"Sleep is not life but the cessation of life: lying a-bed without sleep is a habit productive of relaxation, and thus pernicious to bodily health: and in so far as it is idleness, pernicious to moral health."

productive labor. The common denominator of all these activities, and occupying far the greatest part of the child's life in the industry-house, was "productive labour," defined as occupations "having profit for their object."[77] Thus productive labor was the heart of this plan of "pauper education"—which, in turn, was to be the basis of the "great system of national education" that would "substitute garden culture to barrenness or weeds."[78]

About education in the more conventional sense, Bentham said relatively little. Of the fifteen items listed as the "ends" of pauper education, only two involved conventional learning: the tenth, "intellectual strength," and the fifteenth, "suitable instruction—instruction in all suitable points of art and knowledge." But the former excluded any learning that did not serve other ends; and the latter was made dependent upon the capacity of the particular child and the utility of a particular subject in his particular "situation." A footnote deferred to a later part of the book the question of "whether any instruction of the literary kind ought to be administered."[79] But the only later allusion to this subject was in the list of "comforts" enjoyed by the company's apprentices, one of which was "exemption from intellectual exercise of the most painful kind," notably from the study of languages.[80]* His manuscripts are only slightly more revealing. There he specified that reading, "the ground work of everything else," was to be taught "before the body is fit for profit-yielding occupations," and after that age only on the Sabbath when there was no labor.[82] Since elsewhere he had specified that work was to start at the age of four, presumably education was to be confined (except for the Sabbath) to the period before four.†

---

*It is ironic that for all of Bentham's contempt for "dead languages," here and in his *Chrestomathia,* his much prized "Nomenclature" should have been so largely derived from them. Thus in defending the name "Panopticon," he explained that it would be unintelligible to those "who have not some little intercourse with living science or with dead languages."[81]

†The education plan developed in Bentham's *Chrestomathia,* published in 1816, has the pupils starting at the earliest possible age and continuing to the age

It is extraordinary that a plan otherwise so detailed (specifying how sheets were to be fastened to the bed, whether hats should have brims, and at what points garments should be reinforced) should have been so vague about the time allotted to instruction, the method of instruction, and the subjects to be taught. What is clear, however, is Bentham's objection, on utilitarian grounds, to most of conventional education. "Exercises of the mind," he explained, "lie under a special disadvantage," since they involved "pain and pain only" in the present, and for a long time were "incapable of affording anything like pleasure." Indeed, most of "liberal education" was not only painful to acquire but useless or pernicious once acquired. Languages implied a preference for words over things; poetry was "misrepresentation in meter"; oratory was "misrepresentation for the purposes of inflammation"; philosophy was "nonsense and quibbles upon words"; history was "of use to none but politicians"; geography was only an appendage to history; law was too difficult; and the "Rights of Man," insofar as they were not part of the law, were against the law, and thus a sanction for "treason, murder, personal violence, robbery, etc."[84] Even "useful studies"—natural history, chemistry, mechanics, mathematics, agriculture, gardening, veterinary medicine, and morality—should be taught only in their most concrete forms: the "domestic" branch of chemistry, for example, which was "the art of making the most of everything"; and the practical aspects of mechanics, such as land-surveying and navigating (and the propositions only, not the theoretical demonstrations).[85]

The last of the "useful studies," morality, occupied Bentham

---

of fourteen—this on a daily basis. But that plan, as he specified on the title page, was intended for the "middling and higher ranks in life."

It might be thought odd that Bentham, who was notably irreligious (indeed, anti-religious), should have respected the prohibition against work on the Sabbath. In a tract written before the *Panopticon,* he had proposed that voluntary labor be permitted in prison on the Sabbath—a proposal rejected in the act subsequently passed by Parliament. He did not raise the issue in the *Panopticon,* nor did he do so here.[83]

at some length. The subject, he said, was essentially a sermon on the text, "Study to be quiet and mind your own business," and was intended to impress the children with two basic propositions:

1. That the condition they are doomed to is as good a one, i.e., as favourable to happiness as any other.
2. That if it were not, no efforts which they could use by the display of collective force would have any tendency to improve it.[86]

Perhaps the most unexpected subject to appear under the category of "useful studies" was music; indeed, one of the "collateral uses" of the industry-house was to serve as a "National Music Seminary."[87] A primary function of education, Bentham reasoned, was to fill up the "vacuum in the mind"—"if not stocked with good, it will be with evil." And music was one of the goods with which it could most usefully be stocked. "The more occupied a man's mind is with music, [he] is so much the less exposed to the temptations of engaging in any such pernicious enterprises." In the past half-century, Bentham observed, "God Save the King" had more than once served as a "preservator of peace" and an instrument of "loyalty and public tranquillity." And he quoted approvingly the "proposition": "The man who has not music in his soul/ Is fit for treasons, stratagems and spoils."[88]*

In the course of defending the teaching of "morality," Bentham was inspired to some general reflections on liberty and authority which throw light on the philosophical rationale not only of this idea of morality but of the plan as a whole.

Subjection, subjection not liberty, be it remembered, is the natural state of man.[90]

---

*This "proposition" was a foreshortened and slightly altered form of the quotation from *The Merchant of Venice*. Bentham also disputed the notion that singing was related to drunkenness; on the contrary, it discouraged drunkenness, as it did all "solicitations of promiscuous pleasure."[89]

Every child during his period of weakness, every man for the first 16 or 18 years of his life, is a slave. Every family is by nature an absolute monarchy. The little monarchy like a great one may be limited, but if it be, and in proportion as it is, it is by government that it is limited, not by nature.[91]

Tear up the most salutary as well as the deepest rooted habits, tear asunder every bond of society, democratize the whole face of the earth, dye it with the blood of the inhabitants, still your republic if it has parents and children in it, will after all be but a cluster of little monarchies: still your code of the rights of man will be the most foolish as well as the most mischievous of all dreams.[92]

Early in the book Bentham had insisted that the condition of paupers within the industry-house should be no more "desirable" than that of the independent poor outside.[93] But after describing the care and education of the children, he was so impressed by his arrangements that he saw the condition of the company's wards as "obviously more eligible" than that of the children of even the better classes of the independent poor. So much more eligible, indeed, that he expected parents not only of the poor but even of the "superior classes" to enroll their children voluntarily as apprentices in the houses.[94]

Earlier, too, Bentham had denied to the apprentices any "comfort" not conducive to productive labor, and had prided himself on devising a regimen of austerity compared with which the poorhouses were "luxurious."[95] Yet his last chapter, on "Pauper Comforts," was positively euphoric. He then found that the comforts he had designed for the inmates of his house were such as to evoke the gospel, "Blessed are the poor for theirs is the kingdom of heaven." These comforts were indeed remarkable:

1. Extraordinary security in respect to health . . . better security not only than is to be found in a poor-house under the existing

order of things, but than can be found within the circle of a private family, even in a high sphere, not to say the highest.

2. Consciousness of a superior probability of long life and health.

3. Security against want of every kind.

4. Consciousness of security against want.

5. Constant cleanliness and tidiness.

6. Employment favorable to health and recreation. . . .

And so it went, through fifteen items, alternately mundane ("nights comfortable") and sublime ("a clear conscience brightened by religious hopes").[96]

The comforts of the apprentices were even more impressive than those of the adult paupers. To the adult, "tranquillity" meant being spared the disturbing changes that went on in public institutions. To the child, it also meant being spared the discomfort of first being boarded out in the country and then having to return to town; for the company's child, "it is all country— no transition from rural liberty to town confinement." Similarly, the "security against oppression from officers" was especially meaningful to the child, who would not have to suffer the "temper and humour," "caprice and tyranny," of parents, schoolmasters, and other children. "*Here* no instance of any act of authority, or exercise of coercion, on the part of anybody towards anybody, but what will be immediately and universally known; therefore, humanly speaking, no possibility of abuse." By the same token, the apprentice would be secure from punishment: "No cessation of inspection, no transgression; no transgression, no punishment."[97]

To the objection that it was a disadvantage to the child to be deprived of the "natural affection" of a real father, Bentham replied that this was, in fact, a positive advantage, the "appointed Father" being so much superior to the natural one. The natural father had an interest distinct from and opposed to that of his child; the appointed one had no such interest. In the natural father, especially of a "rude and uneducated" nature, fondness was often the source of anger, caprice, and negligence; he might be "tender and affectionate" but also "rough and brutal"; the appointed father was "indifferent," and therefore not prone to such irrationalities and excesses. The "government" of the natural father was "hidden, and without account and without appeal"; that of the appointed father was subject to observation, therefore accountable and reformable. The government of the natural father, "essentially variable, essentially uncertain," could derive no improvement from experience; that of the appointed father had "the attribute of perfectibility" characteristic of the entire plan.[98]

Another inestimable comfort enjoyed by the apprentice was "matrimony allowed at the earliest period compatible with health." The desirability of early matrimony was deduced from a simple utilitarian calculus. Maximum happiness meant the maximum duration of any pleasure; maximum duration meant the earliest commencement of the pleasure; hence whatever time was "suffered" in celibacy which could have been spent in the matrimonial state was "so much lost to happiness." In ordinary life, so many "inconveniences" attached to early matrimony that they detracted from happiness. But the industry-house obviated the financial inconvenience by imposing a systematic regimen of economy, work, and child care; and the moral inconvenience— the difficulty of undertaking "family government" before attaining the maturity of "self-government"—by keeping the married apprentice in the same state of "subjection" as the unmarried one. There remained only the physical inconvenience: the possibility that a "too early sexual indulgence" might lead to a "premature termination" of the sexual faculty. Here the industry-house would perform a most valuable service in determining, by means of experiments, the optimum starting age and duration of sexual activity.

Nature shows the commencement of the ability. Nature shows the commencement of the desire. How long must the ability

continue useless? How long must the desire be a source of vexa-
tion, instead of enjoyment? . . .

Fiat lux were the words of the Almighty. *Fiat experimentum*
were the words of the brightest genius he ever made. O chemists!
Much have your crucibles shown us of dead matter: but the
Industry-house is a crucible for men![99]

Even before the "crucible for men" could carry out these
experiments, Bentham was convinced that the most "exquisite"
of pleasures was most intense and productive in the early years.
The Chinese, he quoted one authority, married earlier than Euro-
peans, were harder-working, less diseased and debauched, and
more prolific. He also cited the case of France in its golden age,
when royalty and the highest nobility were often married before
the age of fourteen. His own apprentices would be similarly
favored. "What under the French monarchy was the best privilege of the Prince, is in our Utopia the universal lot of the whole
community." They were, in fact, to enjoy a privilege forfeited
by modern royalty, who were in a sorry state. "Princes un-
matched, or late matched, or unprosperously matched, or incon-
gruously matched. Princesses—five remaining—all ripe, but all
too high, for happiness." The apprentices, by contrast, were in a
veritable "Utopia," thanks to the enlightened economy of the
industry-house.

> And to what would they be indebted for this gentlest of all
> revolutions? To what, but to economy? Which dreads no longer
> the multiplication of man, now that she has shown by what secure
> and unperishable means infant man, a drug at present so much
> worse than worthless, may be endowed with an indubitable and
> universal value.[100]

This paean to early marriage, and to the abundant progeny
resulting from that happy state, suggests once again the expansiveness of the plan. For the appendages were now acquiring
appendages of their own, the apprentices being encouraged to
produce still another generation of apprentices, which would

become part of the indigenous population of the houses. Bentham did not at this point elaborate upon the economy that "dreads no longer the multiplication of man," except to repeat the assurance that the only way of "promoting marriage without doing mischief" was by making the child a source of positive value. "In this way, so long as land lasts, you may go on increasing population without end and without expense. . . . Give them a value and you may have them without end."[101] The industry-house, at any rate, could have them "without end," for it alone could give the child the highest economic value.*

The revolutionary potential of this "Utopia," "this gentlest of all revolutions," has not yet been exhausted. Beyond the satisfaction of material needs, beyond sexual gratification to an uncommon degree and fecundity in uncommon measure, the apprentices were to enjoy one other comfort that was even more remarkable: "No sense of deprivation, none of the pains attendant on the emotions of regret, discontent and envy."[103] This is surely the ultimate in utopianism: the security against unrequited desire. And it was to be achieved not, as some utopians would have it, by requiting all desires but by eliminating desire itself.

This principle had been implicit early in the book, in the elaborate provisions, for example, for the separation of young and old, the indigenous and non-indigenous population. But whereas earlier the elimination of desire had been a means to assure maximum economy, now it became an end in itself. And that end was to be achieved by the simplest of "efficient causes":

---

*Malthus's *Essay on Population* was published just before the final installment of Bentham's work appeared. That essay was, of course, diametrically opposed to this paean to population. Godwin's utopianism, which had provoked Malthus, was as nothing compared with Bentham's, because Godwin at least envisaged a future in which sensuality would be diminished and propagation eventually ceased. Although Bentham never repudiated this section of the book, he was evidently sufficiently discomfited by it to delete it from the later editions that appeared during his lifetime. It was restored in the posthumous edition of his *Collected Works,* without mention of the earlier deletion.[102]

"inexperience and ignorance for any fare more palatable than what they possess," "desires not crossed but prevented." This, the ultimate in security and felicity, was to be the enviable lot of the company's apprentices, making their condition superior to that of "any other class of the same age, the very highest not excepted."[104] Bentham closed his book on this happy note:

In the article of diet, no unsatisfied longings, no repinings— nothing within knowledge that is not within reach. That he who has been habituated to poignancy and variety of diet suffers on being reduced to simple and insipid fare is not to be doubted; but that the enjoyment of him who has never known any sort but one, though it were the most insipid sort, does not yield in anything to that of the most luxurious feeder, seems equally out of doubt. In this way all the efforts of art are but a vain struggle to pass the limits set to enjoyment by the hand of nature.[105]*

This, finally, was what Bentham was pleased to call "our Utopia."[107] The term was not an idle conceit or casual afterthought. In his introductory letter in the *Annals* he had described his plan as "the Romance, the Utopia," hastening to add that this did not mean that it was unrealizable, only that it had not yet been realized. "In proportion as a thing is excellent when established, is it anything but romance, and theory, and speculation till the touch of the seal or the sceptre has converted it into practice?"[108] In his notes he countered the objection that his proposal would be judged "too good—it is so good as to be *Utopian.*" Unlike More's *Utopia,* he insisted, his plan provided for the "efficient causes" that would produce the desired effects.[109]

Whatever else might be said about this plan, one cannot deny its boldness and originality. To conceive of a scheme on this scale, encompassing over one-tenth of the population of England, was

---

*This argument was made more succinctly in the manuscripts: "It is by diminishing wants not by multiplying them that the capacity of population is increased. Of increasing wants there is no end. In withholding the means of gratification there can be no hardship where there is no desire."[106]

itself a notable feat of imagination. To propose a regimen as austere, rigorous, and repressive as this was even more remarkable. And then to praise it as the very "pitch of perfection"— providing such "comforts" as the "security against want of every kind," the "consciousness of security against want," and, the ultimate of comforts, the unconsciousness of want itself—was still more extraordinary. The vision of half-a-million young people, knowing of nothing and aspiring to nothing beyond the confines of such an institution, would boggle a more conventional mind. But then a more conventional mind would have balked at describing any pauper institution, still less this one, as a utopia.

It is almost anti-climactic to comment on Bentham's personal interest in the plan. In the case of the Panopticon-prison, his interest was unambiguous. He officially submitted a contract to the government naming himself as owner, manager, and chief jailer ("the spider in the web," Edmund Burke said when he was shown the plan).[110] He spent years soliciting that contract and then, when it was finally rejected, petitioning the government for restitution. If he pursued the pauper plan less vigorously, it was probably because of the difficulties he encountered with the earlier one. He did, however, draw up and circulate an appeal for funds for a National Charity Company, the money to be used to acquire more information and to promote support for it in Parliament.[111] And he never ceased to recommend it as a model plan and to deplore the fact that it was not adopted.

In his memoirs Bentham spoke of the prison and pauper plans as part of a single master-plan: "the Panopticon in both its branches—the prison branch and the pauper branch."[112] And he associated himself personally with both, so that when he failed to achieve the position of prison-keeper, he also felt deprived of the position of "Sub-Regulus of the Poor," as he entitled it.[113] Because he identified the two so closely, he extended the prison scheme to include all the prisoners in the country, just as the pauper scheme included all the paupers. The failure of both rankled so deeply and so long that decades later he was still bitterly complaining: "But for George the Third, all the prisoners in England would, years ago, have been under my management. But for George the Third, all the paupers in the country would, long ago, have been under my management."[114]

It is not surprising to find the author of this utopia composing his own epigraph:

J.B. the most ambitious of the ambitious. His empire—the empire he aspires to, extending to and comprehending the whole human race, in all places, in all habitable places of the earth, at all future time. J.B. the most philanthropic of the philanthropic; philanthropy the end and instrument of his ambition. Limits it has no other than those of the earth.[115]

What is surprising is to find so many reputable scholars taking so benign a view of him—praising him, for example, as "A Modest Utopian" (the chapter title of one book), who never indulged in the kind of "glorious visions" that marred the work of his heirs (the Fabians) and who wanted only to "make it easier for men to live as they liked."[116]

An explanation for this remarkable phenomenon would require nothing less than an analysis of utilitarianism in the largest sense: as a philosophy that professes to be eminently rational and pragmatic, untainted by any metaphysical or religious assumptions; and as a practical program based upon the simple principle of "the greatest happiness of the greatest number." How can one quarrel with such a sensible philosophy and such a commendable program? One may perhaps start by taking seriously Bentham's own proposals for reform, proposals which he himself took seriously, which he was prepared to stake his reputation on, and which he regarded as the very embodiment of that philosophy and that program.

7

Godwin's
Utopia

"Utopian" is one of the more ambiguous words in our vocabulary. To some it signifies an ideal that is commendable if not entirely realistic, a goal to aspire to, a vision of excellence that leads us, if not to the best, then at least to the better—a benign and altogether innocent image. To others it suggests exactly the opposite, a dangerous illusion which tempts us, in the name of the best, to reject the better and end up with the worse. The yearning for perfection that makes reality seem irredeemably flawed creates so large a discrepancy between the ideal and the reality that nothing less will suffice than a total transformation of reality—of society, the polity, the economy, above all, of human nature.

There are utopians and utopians, to be sure. The word "utopia" was first coined by Thomas More, who was perhaps the least utopian of them all. The title of his book gave notice that the *Utopia* he was describing was "nowhere," that his visionary society was just that, an imaginary construct meant to dramatize ideas, not a blueprint for an ideal or potentially real society. And the other conspicuously Greek neologisms in this Latin book also testified to its fancifulness: the river Anydrus meaning "not water," the philosopher Hythlodaeus, "purveyor of nonsense," the magistrate Ademus, "not people." Later utopians, products of the Enlightenment, were less modest than More. Believing in the infinite power of human reason, they were confident that everything rational was realizable; all that was needed was to conceive the good and will it into existence or await its realization in the course of the necessary progress of history. Their utopias, so far from being located in a never-never world, were designed for a real place (as in the communities of Fourier and Owen), a real time (as in the historical schemas of Condorcet, Saint-Simon, and Comte), and real people (as in the totally rational human beings of Godwin).

William Godwin was perhaps the most ambitious utopian of all, so ambitious that he would have spurned that label. He also spurned the familiar forms of the genre: the blueprint of a new society and the prospectus of the stages of history. His work was intended as nothing less than a "science" of politics and morals, a systematic elucidation of principles that were absolutely valid and universally applicable, an irrefutable demonstration of "the one best mode of social existence" for all of mankind.[1] Published in two volumes in 1793, it had the appropriately imposing title, *An Enquiry Concerning Political Justice, and its Influence on General Virtue and Happiness.* Its basic premise was the perfectibility of mankind, the development of human beings who would be perfectly rational and moral and, therefore, perfectly free and equal.

If perfectibility had so far eluded mankind, Godwin argued, it was only because of the corrupting and coercive effect of government. While monarchy was the worst form of government, it was not this or that form of government that was evil but government as such. Even the most democratic government was unjust because its characteristic and commonly admired features—the separation and balance of powers, representation, elections, voting, the ballot—violated either reason or liberty or both. On the same grounds, all the institutions created and sanctioned by government were deemed to be unjust: constitutions, laws, courts, contracts, juries, punishments, prisons, private property, marriage, the family, religion, schools. And so too all collective or cooperative enterprises, whether voluntary or compulsory: work that required any form of organization, social clubs, musical concerts, theatrical performances. (Concerts and plays were objectionable, Godwin explained, because rational men had no desire to "repeat words and ideas not their own," to "execute the compositions of others," or to engage in other activities requiring an "absurd and vicious cooperation.")[2]

Liberated from these oppressive and corrupting institutions, mankind would be rational and virtuous, free and equal. There would be no passion or prejudice to inhibit the intellect, no error or falsehood to stand in the way of truth, no self-love or self-interest to interfere with benevolence, no acquisitiveness or competitiveness to undermine equality, no coercion or cooperation to restrict individuality. Without marriage or any other contracts or promises to bind them to a future course of action ("to disarm my future wisdom by my past folly"), individuals would be free and rational at every moment of their lives.[3] And without families to divert them from their higher obligations, they would be at liberty to devote themselves to humanity at large.

In a much quoted passage, Godwin illustrated the "science of morals" that was at the heart of his political science.[4] If the philosopher Fénelon and his chambermaid were trapped in a fire and only one of them could be rescued, that person should be Fénelon, who was of "more worth and importance" than the maid, just as a man was more worthy and important than a beast. This choice was so self-evidently just by every principle of reason and utility that the maid herself would acquiesce in it. Moreover, it was equally just and compelling if the chambermaid should happen to be the rescuer's wife or mother. "What magic is there in the pronoun 'my,' to overturn the decisions of everlasting truth? My wife or my mother may be a fool or a prostitute, malicious, lying or dishonest. If they be, of what consequence is it that they are mine?"[5] (In the second edition, hoping to mitigate the harshness of this passage, Godwin changed the chambermaid to a valet, and the wife or mother who might be a prostitute to a brother or father who might be profligate.)

Toward the end of the book, contemplating the inventions that would enable one man to do alone what now required the cooperative effort of many, thus doing away with the evil of "common labour" (and doing away with most individual labor as well, since half an hour a day would suffice to provide all of a person's needs), Godwin cited the "conjecture" of Benjamin Franklin that "mind would one day become omnipotent over matter."[6] That conjecture suggested to Godwin the bolder one that mind would become omnipotent over bodily matter as well. Just as in political and social affairs men would achieve a perfectly voluntary state, so too in the functioning of their bodies. "If volition can now do something, why should it not go on to do still more and more?" If it could cure all our social ills, why not our physical and mental ills? And why should it not, finally, result in the "total extirpation of the infirmities of our nature" —disease, sleep, languor, anguish, melancholy, resentment?[7]

There was yet another infirmity that would be extirpated once the omnipotence of mind established itself, and that was sexuality. In the opening paragraph of the book, Godwin had asserted, as a self-evident principle, "that the happiness of the human species is the most desirable object for human science to promote; and that intellectual and moral happiness or pleasure is extremely to be preferred to those which are precarious and transitory."[8] By the end of the book it appeared that among the most precarious and transitory, and hence least desirable, pleasures were those of sex. "The tendency of a cultivated and virtuous mind is to render us indifferent to the gratification of sense," and especially to sensory gratification of a "mere animal function."[9] Thus an enlightened mankind could look forward to the diminution and eventual elimination of sexuality. Lest this happy state of affairs result, as it inevitably would, in the depopulation of the earth, Godwin introduced an even bolder suggestion: that men might become immortal. He did not commit himself to immortality as a certainty, only as a real possibility; what was certain was the infinite prolongation of life. It was this combination of celibacy and immortality, or near-immortality, that inspired the most memorable passage in the book, the image of a world in a permanent condition of perfection because it was in a permanent state of maturity.

> The men therefore who exist when the earth shall refuse itself to a more extended population, will cease to propagate, for they will no longer have any motive, either of error or duty, to induce them. In addition to this they will perhaps be immortal. The whole will be a people of men, and not of children. Generation will not succeed generation, nor truth have in a certain degree to recommence her career at the end of every thirty years.[10]

After this edenic vision of mankind purged of all the imperfections of human nature, to say nothing of all political and social evils—"there will be no war, no crimes, no administration of justice, as it is called, and no government," all this possibly within the lifetime of "the present race of men"—it was anticlimactic to be told that these were matters of "probable conjecture," which did not affect the truth of the "grand argument" of the rest of the book.[11] This disclaimer, coming in the final sentence of the chapter, was too belated and too feeble to diminish the effect of the dramatic image of mankind in a perfect state of reason, virtue, and freedom. Even if it were perfectibility rather than perfection that Godwin held out as the promise of the future, this too was intoxicating enough, for perfectibility had no limits, no foreseeable end. Nor was it only in the grande finale of the book that perfectibility made its appearance. From the beginning it had been at the heart of his "grand argument": "There is no characteristic of man, which seems at present at least so eminently to distinguish him, or to be of so much importance in every branch of moral science, as his perfectibility."[12]

Any resemblance between this Godwin and the subject of the biography by Peter H. Marshall is purely coincidental. The details and even many of the quotations are the same, but the totality is quite different. Marshall's Godwin is no utopian but a philosopher and humanist on a par with "Hobbes, Locke, Rousseau and Mill." And *Political Justice,* so far from being the work of an "idle visionary," offers nothing more visionary than the idea that everyone is capable of improvement and that "education and enlightenment could bring about a better order of things on earth."[13]

The admiring biographer is not troubled by difficulties that might occur to other readers of Godwin: the contradiction, for example, between the claims of individuality and morality (the person who is so solicitous of his own freedom that he cannot commit himself to another in marriage, but who is prepared to submerge his own self for the "love of my species");[14] or between the principles of equality and utility (Fénelon who is so superior to the maid that she herself must acquiesce to her own death). Nor does he find any serious inconsistencies in a utilitarianism that deplores self-interest and places the highest value on altruism; or an altruism so suspicious of anything short of disinterested, universal benevolence that it would abolish the family itself; or a hedonism that contemns sensuality and sexuality; or a mechanistic philosophy that is also rationalistic and voluntaristic; or a conception of truth so punctilious as to make sincerity preferable to humaneness or even self-preservation (a dying woman should be told the news of her husband's death, and the "whitest" of lies is unjustified even to save one's life); or an absolute freedom of action associated with a total denial of free will (there can be no punishment because there is no free will, hence no personal responsibility, hence no crime or guilt—"the assassin cannot help the murder he commits any more than the dagger");[15] or a communism that eschews all forms of voluntary cooperation, let alone any institutional mechanisms to ensure the equal distribution and sharing of property; or a libertarianism that makes each individual the "ingenuous censor" of his neighbor (legal sanctions would be replaced by a moral suasion that is "not less irresistible than whips and chains");[16] or a concept of "political justice" that is totally incompatible with any kind of polity or any administration of justice; or a humanism that would extirpate much of human nature as we know it, including sex, emotion, parental love, even parental identity. (In the perfect society it may not be known who the father of a child is, but "such knowledge will be of no importance.")[17]

To Marshall none of this is a serious problem, certainly not serious enough to detract from the claim that Godwin was a metaphysician, psychologist, political theorist, and moral philosopher of the first order. Godwin's vision of a "free and equal society," we are told, derived from the "Greek notion of individual self-fulfilment"[18]—and was presumably superior to the Greek notion because it did not require anything so oppressive as the *polis*. He was a better utilitarian than Bentham, because he had a more subtle idea of pleasure, and a better liberal than Mill, because he carried liberalism to the point of libertarianism and anarchism. Like Rousseau, he was a humanist who wanted to produce "the whole person who would make the ideal society."[19] That "whole person" would be unencumbered by sex or "personal affections"; and that "ideal society" would happily do without government, laws, churches, or families—a society, Godwin said, that would be nothing more than an "aggregation of individuals."[20] It is this Godwin who is recommended to us as peculiarly appropriate and admirable today. "Above all, he speaks directly to the new radicalism which has emerged in the last decade which seeks a libertarian way between the bureaucratic centralism of communist states and the organized lovelessness of the capitalist world."[21]*

---

*There is no doubt that Godwin has attracted much attention in recent years, although perhaps not entirely for the reasons Marshall suggests. Since 1980 there have been six full-length books on him; of these, four have been on a subject that once merited only passing mention, his novels. This compares with the single work on him in the whole of the nineteenth century. There have also been reprints of Godwin's own work. *Political Justice* was issued in a three-volume critical edition in 1946, and three other editions appeared in the 1970s (one in French, another in the Pelican paperback series, and an abridged

One of the difficulties in this glowing account is the fact that in some measure it would seem to be belied by Godwin himself, who felt it necessary to make numerous changes in his work in later editions. These changes, he insisted, did not alter the basic thesis but only clarified and improved it. Yet they inevitably call attention to some of the more dubious aspects of that thesis. Thus in the revised edition of 1796, he reaffirmed the principle of perfectibility while stopping short of predicting, as part of that movement toward perfection, the elimination of sleep, disease, and death. He also qualified, in the third edition of 1798 even more than in the second, the condemnation of feelings, private affections, and sensual and sexual pleasures, even conceding that marriage, while still the "worst" (no longer "most odious") of all monopolies, could be a "salutary and respectable institution" on condition that it allowed for liberty and "repentance" (presumably divorce).[22] If these changes make the work seem less extreme, they also weaken and at points even contradict the original thesis. They also make it more difficult to praise the first edition so fulsomely while approving of all the emendations in the later editions.

Godwin was thirty-seven when *Political Justice* was first published—thirty-seven, as we now say, going on seventeen. However wary one may be of the kind of reductionism that accounts

---

version together with selections from his other writings). Two volumes of his tracts have been reprinted, two editions of his best known novel, *Caleb Williams,* and new editions of several deservedly little known novels. Currently, apart from his own writings, there are no fewer than seventeen books on him in print in English. Part of the explanation for this revival of interest is, as Marshall suggests, the attraction of utopianism and anarchism to a generation of radicals disaffected from Marxism. It also reflects the interest in feminism, his association with Mary Wollstonecraft making him one of the heroes of that cause. And not least is the growing number of Ph.D. candidates desperate for dissertation subjects; this must surely account for so many books on so many third-rate novels. (None of these explanations accounts for another intriguing publishing statistic: five books on Godwin were published in Germany in a single three-year period before the First World War.)

for ideas in terms of personal experiences or interests, one can hardly avoid noting that it was a celibate who wrote so contemptuously of sex; a loner and drifter who had so little respect for social associations; a man with no love for his own family who was prepared to abolish the family; a former member of a sect that made reason the source of religious salvation who later made reason the *fons et origo* of human and social redemption.

The religious passion in atheism, the messianic zeal in radicalism, are familiar enough, but rarely are they so demonstrable as in the case of Godwin. He himself later explained the depreciation of feeling in *Political Justice* as the lingering effect of "Sandemanianism," a form of Calvinism that located salvation neither in good works nor in faith but rather in a rational understanding of divine truth.* "After Calvin had damned ninety-nine in a hundred of mankind," Godwin later wrote, Sandeman "contrived a scheme for damning ninety-nine in a hundred of the followers of Calvin."[23] It was this doctrine that dominated much of Godwin's early life. Although his own father was an orthodox Calvinist minister, the boy was sent at the age of eleven to live and study with a disciple of Sandeman. During those six years he became indoctrinated in a creed that was at once intensely religious and highly rationalistic. And this religious mode of rationalism (like the secular variety later espoused by Godwin) carried with it a distrust of emotions and affections and a disposition toward egalitarianism and communism. (Although Sandemanians were permitted to engage in trade with those outside the sect, their property was, in theory at least, at the disposal of the congregation and they were enjoined from "laying up treasures on earth.")

This faith persisted even after Godwin, at the age of seventeen, entered a liberal Dissenting academy to prepare for the ministry. His principal tutor was an active political reformer and an

---

*Another name for the sect, which existed in America as well as England, was Glassites, John Glas and Robert Sandeman being the eighteenth-century Scottish co-founders.

avowed Socinian, who, in the name of "rational religion," denied
not only the Trinity but the divinity of Christ and original sin;
another tutor was a Unitarian with a still more enlightened and
less orthodox conception of religion. Yet during his five years at
the academy Godwin continued to regard himself as a San-
demanian and a Tory—perhaps because he was so intensely unhappy at school that he rejected the views of his teachers and
fellow students, as he himself felt rejected by them. Later he
recalled that despite his "calm and dispassionate" temper and the
"intrepidity" of his opinions, the other students "almost with one
voice, pronounced me to be the most self-conceited, self-sufficient
animal that ever lived."[24]

Within a year after leaving the academy, Godwin rapidly
moved from Toryism to republicanism and from Sandemanianism to deism. Yet for five years he tried to establish himself as
a minister, going from one congregation to another and being
dismissed by one after the other, his congregants evincing as little
liking for him as had his fellow students. Finally, in 1783, at the
age of twenty-seven, he settled in London to make a career as a
writer. He wrote short stories and novels, articles, political pam-
phlets, brief histories, and whatever other assignments came his
way. By 1791 he had been sufficiently productive to receive an
advance of one thousand guineas for a book on "Political Principles." Two years later the two volumes of *Political Justice* appeared, and Godwin suddenly found himself famous.

It is impossible to think of *Political Justice,* certainly it is
impossible to account for its success, apart from the French Enlightenment and the French Revolution. One winces now at
those all too familiar lines from Wordsworth's *Prelude:* "Bliss
was it in that dawn to be alive,/ But to be young was very
Heaven!" But they do express the powerful attraction of the
French Revolution—"the attraction of a country in romance!"
—and of a philosophy like Godwin's which was eminently at-
tuned to that Revolution, a philosophy in romance. The prospect
of being liberated from "the meagre, stale, forbidding ways/ Of

custom, law, and statute," of being free to follow Reason, that "prime enchantress," was especially appealing to the young. Of the triad of poets who were enraptured by *Political Justice* when it first appeared, Wordsworth was twenty-three, Southey nineteen, and Coleridge twenty-one.

What is remarkable is not that Godwin's "Fantasy of Reason" (the title of another recent biography of him)[25] appealed to those for whom the French Revolution gave promise of a new heavenly city on earth, but that it did so at a time when the Revolution itself was beginning to lose its glamor. By February 1793, when *Political Justice* was published, the Revolution was becoming an embarrassment even for some of its more zealous English defenders. Earlier unfortunate episodes could be explained as the birth pangs of a new world, but the execution of the king in January and the declaration of war against England the following month put English Jacobins in a difficult position; and they became harder-pressed in the course of the year with the extension of the war, the creation of the Revolutionary Tribunal and Committee of Public Safety, and the execution of the queen and of the Girondins. If enlightened opinion did not immediately respond to these events, it was because the romance of revolution, of social rejuvenation, dies hard. And the romance of reason, of a "human nature seeming born again" (Wordsworth once more), dies harder still.

So it was that Godwin's book was at first hailed as a masterpiece. Three thousand copies of the two volumes were sold at the considerable price of three guineas. The price may have saved it from being proscribed; Pitt is reputed to have said that it could do no harm to those "who had not three shillings to spare."[26] Although it did reach some of the poor in cheap pirated editions and in extracts in collections of radical writings, it had its greatest success among intellectuals. By 1796, however, when the second edition was published, and still more by the time of the third edition in 1798, the shift in the climate of opinion caught up with

Godwin, and some of his most ardent admirers became his most bitter critics.

By then another kind of reality had caught up with Godwin. When he fell in love with Mary Wollstonecraft in 1796, he was forty and she thirty-seven. He was unattractive, ungainly, socially ill at ease, and sexually inexperienced (this was his first affair and possibly his first sexual experience). She was handsome, buxom, gregarious, and, by reputation, promiscuous. She was also as celebrated a writer as he was. Her *Vindication of the Rights of Man,* a reply to Burke's *Reflections on the French Revolution,* established her credentials as a radical; and her *Vindication of the Rights of Woman* made her the first serious feminist. Her most recent affair had left her with an illegitimate child, and it was after she was abandoned by her lover and had tried (for the second time) to commit suicide that she became involved with Godwin. Godwin himself, having just published the second edition of his book deploring the irrationality of emotions, the immorality of private affections, and the puerility of sex, took to writing love letters that are almost a parody of the form, and he carefully recorded the consummation of his love in his diary: "Chez moi, toute."[27]

Since both of them had made such a large point of condemning that "most odious of all monopolies," marriage, they carried on their affair openly while maintaining separate lodgings. The scandal was not their liaison but their marriage the following year, decided upon after she became pregnant and apparently at her urging.* To his friends Godwin explained (what he had not said in his book) that morality was "nothing but a balance between opposite Evils," and that he himself had had to choose "between the Evils social and personal, of compliance and non-compliance."[28] Perhaps it was to assert his independence that

---

*Wollstonecraft had earlier shown herself to be more conventional in practice than in theory. When her first child was born, she called herself "Mrs. Imlay," this without benefit of clergy or law.

he kept separate rooms for himself in addition to their common establishment, and went off on a trip while she stayed home to await the birth of their child. In spite of her occasional complaints that he was lacking in affection, the marriage was apparently happy for both of them. And there is no question but that he was genuinely desolate when she died soon after giving birth to their daughter, Mary. Their celebrated relationship (which feminists regard as his principal claim to fame) lasted all of one year.

A few years after Wollstonecraft's death, having discovered the pleasures of sex and of the domestic affections—and having revised *Political Justice* accordingly—Godwin entered into another marriage with another Mary. This was far less happy and much longer-lived. In addition to an uncongenial wife, he acquired two new stepchildren (also, apparently, illegitimate), a son William, and endless financial obligations which required him to write profusely and to engage in several unsuccessful publishing ventures.

His greatest satisfaction came from his strikingly pretty and precocious daughter Mary. But she was also the cause of his greatest distress. She was sixteen when Shelley, then twenty-two, married and a father, and already cutting a romantic figure as a poet, novelist, atheist, and radical, moved into the Godwin household to escape his debtors. He promptly fell in love with her, as she did with him. Godwin denounced their "licentious love," his outrage compounded by the fear that people might accuse him of having sold his daughter (and perhaps stepdaughter as well) to Shelley.[29] (Although Shelley was in debt at the time, he was heir to a substantial fortune and had given Godwin large sums of money.) Shelley promised at first to give up Mary, then reneged and suggested to his wife (about to have their second child) a *ménage à trois,* then came to Godwin's house brandishing a pistol and a bottle of laudanum and threatening to commit suicide together with Mary. A few days later Shelley and Mary eloped—accompanied by Jane (Mary's stepsister and Mrs. Godwin's daughter).

This was the beginning of a bizarre saga in which money figured almost as prominently as sex. While Godwin refused to see either Mary or Shelley and resolutely ignored the births of their three children (one of whom was named after him), he continued to badger Shelley for money, which Shelley, at first obligingly and then grudgingly, gave him. In the meantime Shelley, Mary, and Jane continued to travel and live together. It is not clear whether Shelley was also having an affair with Jane (who, to complicate matters, decided to change her name to Claire), when she became involved with Byron and bore his child. About the same time Fanny (Wollstonecraft's first daughter) committed suicide, apparently out of unrequited love for Shelley. A month later Harriet, Shelley's wife, also committed suicide in an advanced state of pregnancy, having been abandoned by her lover, a groom. A month after that Shelley and Mary were married, and Godwin was finally reconciled to them. It was a good match, he informed his brother—not that he himself cared about money or title, he said (carefully identifying Shelley as "the eldest son of Sir Timothy Shelley, of Field Place, in the county of Sussex, Baronet"), but only because he wanted his daughter to be "respectable, virtuous, and contented."[30] He was also pleased to attend the christening in church of his grandchildren.

That was not, however, the end of the tale. Two years after the marriage, Jane (Claire as she now was) gave birth to Shelley's child, who was registered as Mary's. The following year Mary wrote a short novel about incest (with obvious autobiographical intimations), which she sent to Godwin for his opinion. He told her that while he thought parts of it were well done, he found the subject "disgusting and detestable," and he refused to return the manuscript in spite of her repeated requests.[31] (The book was only published posthumously.) After Shelley's death in 1822, Mary continued to write novels and became increasingly conservative as she grew older. When a friend advised her to send her only surviving son to a school where they would teach him to think for himself, she replied, "For heaven's sake, let him learn to think like everyone else!"[32] Thus the son of Shelley and the grandson of Godwin (his last descendant) went to Harrow and Trinity College, became a lawyer, a Member of Parliament, and a respectable patron of letters—achieving the respectability Godwin had wanted for his own daughter.

This would make for a dramatic enough story even if the protagonists were not who they were. But it is all the more dramatic with this cast of characters, and all the more in conjunction with Godwin's ideas. For his life—first his marriage with Wollstonecraft, than his second unhappy marriage, then the Shelley saga—was a cruel commentary on his theories. It was said at the time that Shelley was only carrying out the teachings of Godwin, that libertinism was the consequence of libertarianism and promiscuity of free love. Shelley, no doubt, would have carried on as he did without the inspiration of *Political Justice*. But the fact is that he did profess, publicly as well as privately, the greatest admiration for that book, which was why he so generously subsidized its author.

What makes the situation even more ironic is the fact that Godwin himself, long before Shelley entered his life, had begun to modify or discard one after another of his original doctrines (without, to be sure, repudiating *Political Justice* itself). By the time they met, in 1812, he had gone so far as to criticize a pamphlet in which Shelley, echoing *Political Justice*— "when all men are good and wise, government will of itself decay"—called upon the Irish to repeal the Union with England and form political associations that would prepare them to be emancipated from government itself. Reminding Shelley that he was against all associations, including radical ones, Godwin went on to praise some notably conservative ones:

Every institution and form of society is good in its place and the period of time to which it belongs. How many beautiful and admirable effects grew out of Popery and the monastic institutions in the period when they were in their genuine health and vigour. To them we owe almost all our logic and literature. What excellent effects do we reap, even at this day, from the feudal system and from chivalry! In this point of view nothing perhaps can be more worthy of our applause than the English Constitution.[33]

To another would-be disciple Godwin described the Whigs as the party to which a "liberal-minded and enlightened man would adhere," and defended religion as one of the sentiments that distinguish men from reasoning machines. "So far as we are employed in heaping up facts and in reasoning upon them merely, we are a species of machine; it is our impulses and our sentiments that are the glory of our nature."[34] Finally, in his last major work, *History of the Commonwealth,* he came close to refuting the very premise of *Political Justice,* the idea of perfectibility. It was easy, he said, for "the philosopher in his closet to invent imaginary schemes of policy, and to shew how mankind, if they were without passions and without prejudices, might best be united in the form of a political community." Unfortunately, however, men are always "creatures of passions," defying the "dictates of sobriety and speculation."[35]

To Marshall these departures from the original doctrine represent the familiar phenomenon of youthful idealism yielding to the mundane and ignominious pressures of life. Godwin, he ruefully comments, "remarried and put on his slippers."[36] A kindly biographer, Marshall treats the last half of Godwin's life with sympathy rather than contempt. But his final words pay tribute to the early Godwin, the author of *Political Justice:* "an authentic human being, a truly creative writer, and one of the great humanists in the Western tradition."[37] It is an equivocal compliment, for it exalts the "humanist" who had so little respect for the "infirmities" of human nature and human society, and it belittles the human being whose mature experiences and reflections are deemed to be of so little merit.

A very different Godwin emerges if *Political Justice* is read not as a humanist tract but as a utopian one. The humanist, accepting human nature with all its infirmities, recognizing (as Godwin finally did) that men are always "creatures of passion," seeks to reform social institutions so as to make men more rational and more virtuous, although not unduly or unnaturally so. It is the utopian who is so dissatisfied with human nature, so obsessed with a vision of perfection, that he can only seek to transform both human nature and social institutions—or, in Godwin's case, to transform human nature so radically as to make social institutions obsolete. This is the meaning of Godwin's anarchism.* Perfect (or near-perfect) men do not require perfect (or near-perfect) institutions; they do not require any institutions.

This Godwin belongs in the utopian tradition of More, Campanella, Condorcet, and Comte, rather than in the philosophical tradition of Hobbes, Locke, Rousseau, and Mill. Thomas More is mentioned in Marshall's biography once in passing, referring to Godwin's own citation of him; the other utopians appear not at all. Condorcet is the most extraordinary omission, since his

---

*In the first edition, Godwin accepted the term "anarchy" with some reservations. "It has something in it that suggests the likeness, a distorted and tremendous likeness, of true liberty. . . . It disengages men from prejudice and implicit faith, and in a certain degree incites them to an impartial scrutiny into the reason of their actions." But it could not be expected to do the work of philosophy, for while it loosens the hold of some prejudices, others it "arms with fury, and converts into instruments of vengeance."[38] In the revised edition, Godwin was more careful to distinguish anarchy from a "well conceived form of society without government." But even then he insisted that the mischiefs of anarchy were probably no worse than the mischiefs of government and preferable to those of despotism, anarchy being "transitory" and despotism "perennial." Moreover, anarchy "awakens thought, and diffuses energy and enterprise through the community," whereas under despotism "mind is trampled into an equality of the most odious sort."[39]

work was closest in time and spirit to Godwin's. (Godwin himself cited him as one of the writers who contemplated a prolongation of life.)[40] Condorcet's *Sketch of the Progress of the Human Spirit* was written while he was hiding from the Revolutionary police (he was under indictment for having opposed the execution of the king) and was published in 1795 after he had died in prison. It was remarkably similar to *Political Justice* in anticipating not only the infinite extension of life but the infinite progress of mankind toward perfectibility—intellectual, moral, and physical. This is not to say that Condorcet influenced Godwin; his book came out after Godwin's (although before the second edition, hence the footnote citing it). Nor was the *Sketch* like *Political Justice* in every respect; it was more historical, less libertarian and anarchistic. (Condorcet allowed for laws to promote the general welfare and for voluntary associations to promote science.) But the essential ingredients were the same: reason, virtue, freedom, equality, utility, benevolence—all infinitely expandable and perfectible.

Beyond the modern tradition of utopianism was an ancient one, the tradition of Gnosticism, which saw the world—the physical, biological, social, human world—as alien and evil, and sought salvation in *gnosis,* absolute knowledge or reason. Gnosticism was antinomian, anti-orthodox, anti-social, anti-institutional, and above all anti-humanistic, for redemption consisted in man's transcending his flawed and finite human nature by coming to know the "hidden" God. Gnosticism was an esoteric cult because it believed that only a few could attain that knowledge. Modern utopianism democratized and secularized that cult. It made available to all of mankind what had been reserved for a very few; it made public what had been most carefully held in secret; and it sought to establish in this world the perfection of body and spirit that Gnosticism had assigned to another world.

To place Godwin in this tradition is not to belittle or demean him. On the contrary, it puts him in some very distinguished company. And it permits us to understand his most extravagant ideas without embarrassment or evasion, to understand them as the expression of the perennial yearning for perfection, for union with the absolute, for a final state of grace. Robert Sandeman would have been proud of his most famous disciple. But he would not have recognized in him a "humanist" whose ideas may be taken as the basis of a political or social philosophy appropriate for real human beings in a real society. The desire to transcend the human condition is, in most religious traditions, an invitation to heresy. In politics it is an invitation to tyranny, as we seek a perfection that inevitably eludes us and as we redouble our efforts to attain the unattainable.

8

Who Now Reads Macaulay?

"Who now reads Bolingbroke?" Burke asked, thus casually, irrevocably, consigning him to the ash-heap of history.[1] So the modern historian may be tempted to ask: "Who now reads Macaulay?" Who, that is, except those who have a professional interest in him—and professional in a special sense: not historians who might be expected to take pride in one of their most illustrious ancestors, but only those who happen to be writing treatises about him. In fact, most professional historians have long since given up reading Macaulay, as they have given up writing the kind of history he wrote and thinking about history as he did.

Yet there was a time when anyone with any pretension to cultivation read Macaulay. It is often said that he was so widely read because he was so brilliant a stylist, so readable. This should not be taken to mean that he was easy to read, a "good read," as the English say. Even his essays were formidable—fifty-page disquisitions on the *Diary and Letters of Madame D'Arblay* or Lord Mahon's *History of the War of the Succession in Spain,* or the controversial hundred-and-twenty-page essay on Bacon. More popular, and more formidable still, were the five volumes of the *History of England from the Succession of James II* (1848–62). Had Macaulay never written the *History,* he would have been remembered as a brilliant essayist. But the *History* is so impressive that it quite properly overshadows the *Essays,* and it did so in his time as in ours. Its success is all the more remarkable because its scope is so narrow. Originally Macaulay had intended to carry the story "down to a time which is within the memory of men still living"[2]—that is, through the reign of George IV, a century and a half overall. In fact the fifth volume (uncompleted and posthumously published) ends with the death of William III, a mere seventeen years after the accession of James II.*

It is this work, five substantial volumes each of five to six hundred pages, covering seventeen years of English history (with two long introductory chapters surveying the history of England before 1685), that became a best seller in mid-Victorian England and continued to be reprinted throughout the century. The first two volumes sold 22,000 copies within a year, and by 1875 the first volume alone had sold over 133,000 copies. It was bought and read not only by the leisured classes (and not only, as one might suspect, to be bound and displayed). The lending libraries did a thriving trade in it. Mudie's, the largest of the libraries, bought over two thousand copies of the volumes as they appeared, and business was so brisk that they had to set aside a special room to handle them. A gentleman living on the outskirts of Manchester invited his poorer neighbors to his house every evening after work and read the entire *History* aloud to them. At the end of the last reading, one of them rose and moved a vote of thanks to the author "for having written a history which working men can understand," a motion the gentleman dutifully reported to Macaulay.[4]

Today it is all one can do to get a graduate student in history

---

*It has been estimated that on the scale of the existing volumes, the complete work would have required something like fifty volumes; and at the speed at which he wrote—three years a volume, which, considering the density and originality of the work, is no mean feat—would have taken 150 years, almost exactly the same time for the writing as for the unfolding of those historic events. (He had planned on a faster pace: five volumes bringing him to the beginning of Walpole's administration, a period of thirty-five years. But even at that rate, he would have had to live to a ripe old age.)[3]

to read, let alone appreciate, Macaulay. If the *History* is, as is commonly thought, a paean to progress, the history of the *History* is a sad testimonial to the cultural regression of our own times. Macaulay was pleased to think of his work as in a direct line of descent from Thucydides' *History of the Peloponnesian War*; he admitted that his was far inferior to that greatest of all histories, but it aspired to the same standard of greatness. He also privately confessed that he had been sustained, through all his years of research and writing, by the hope that his work would be remembered in the year 2000 or even 3000[5]—not as arrogant a thought as it might seem, considering the fact that Thucydides has survived considerably longer than that. That remark was quoted in 1959, the centenary of his death, by a commentator who thought it safe to predict that Macaulay would indeed be read half a century hence, "if there are any readers left."[6] It is not clear whether that ominous proviso referred to a nuclear catastrophe or simply to the death of the written word as the result of television or a debased mass culture. What was not anticipated was that professional historians would turn against Macaulay, making him seem as unreadable and unmemorable as Bolingbroke.

A notable exception is John Burrow, who has made a valiant attempt to revive our interest in Macaulay, together with three historians of a later generation: William Stubbs, Edward Freeman, and James Anthony Froude. *A Liberal Descent: Victorian Historians and the English Past* is a subtle, sympathetic, thoughtful account; if it has a fault, it is that it makes too modest a claim on our attention. For we are invited to consider these historians not so much as historians recording momentous events in England's past—Macaulay on the Revolution, Stubbs on the "ancient constitution," Freeman on the Norman Conquest, Froude on the Reformation—but as Victorians reflecting in their histories ideas and attitudes peculiar to their own times. Thus Macaulay and his successors are assimilated into Victorian culture "on the premise that one of the ways in which a society reveals itself, and its assumptions and beliefs about its own character and destiny, is by its attitudes to and uses of the past."[7] This is surely not what Macaulay had in mind when he hoped to be read in centuries to come—as a specimen of Victorian society rather than as a historian of the Glorious Revolution. Yet he and the others could hardly complain, since they themselves insisted on the continuity of past and present, the relevance of their subjects and their works to their own times.

The break in continuity comes in our time. Ruefully, almost elegiacally, Burrow describes the kind of history, and the kind of culture producing that history, which is over and done with, which we can understand and enjoy only in its "remoteness." Macaulay, possibly even Stubbs, may continue to be read. But for the most part the great Victorian histories are the "triumphal arches of a past empire, their vaunting inscriptions unintelligible to the modern inhabitants"—monuments occasionally visited, Burrow comments in an uncharacteristically brutal expression, "as a *pissoir,* a species of visit naturally brief."[8] Yet he does not explain why this has happened, what it is in our idea of history and in our own culture that would account for our remoteness from these great Victorian monuments.

The decline of Victorian history is the decline of "Whig history." For professional historians this can be dated from 1931, with the publication of Herbert Butterfield's *Whig Interpretation of History.* The Whig historian, Butterfield argued, distorted the past by interpreting it in terms of the present. He judged the past by standards appropriate to the present; he made of the past a battleground between the forces of light and darkness; he sought in the past the origins and development of those institutions and ideas which he valued in the present. Thus Whig history became the story of the gradual, natural, inevitable progress of political liberty, religious tolerance, and representative government. More recently the "Whig interpretation" has been understood generically, as applicable not only to the classic Whig historian but also to the radical or Marxist historian, for whom history is the progress of democracy, equality, collectivism, and socialism. In either case the integrity of the past is violated by the imposition of a specious pattern of progress and an anachronistic set of ideas.

Butterfield's book was (and is, since it has been reprinted and is still widely read and often cited) a valuable corrective to any reductivist or deterministic mode of history which obscures the complexities, contingencies, and discontinuities of the past—all those aspects of the past which were unique to it, which made it distinctively different from, even if vaguely reminiscent of, the present. But the attempt to dissociate the past completely from the present, to counter a too intrusive present-mindedness with a too austere past-mindedness, also has its perils, as Butterfield was well aware. For it tends to encourage antiquarian and monographic history at the expense of the dramatic, narrative kind of history that Macaulay himself wrote. It also tends to belittle the ideas that were the moving force of that history, the ideas the Whig historians attributed to the past and celebrated in the present.*

A Liberal Descent, the title of Burrow's book, is meant to encapsulate the essential principles of Whig history, the idea of liberty and the idea of continuity. The expression is Burke's: "This idea of a liberal descent inspires us with a sense of habitual native dignity, which prevents that upstart insolence almost inevitably adhering to and disgracing those who are the first acquirers of any distinction."[10] Burke's idea of liberty derived from and depended upon the idea of descent. This was his quarrel with Paine, who believed that liberty inhered in man as a natural right, thus was an attribute of each individual and of each generation *de novo.* For Paine the idea of descent was not only unnecessary; it was pernicious, for it implied the "usurpation" of a right

---

*In *The Englishman and His History,* written during the Second World War, Butterfield paid tribute to the Whig interpretation of history, which was itself part of the "English mind" and the "English tradition," and which had served so well to perpetuate English liberties.[9]

that was innate and natural and that could only be diminished and distorted through descent. For Burke the only real, reliable, worthy liberty—or better yet, liberties—came by way of descent. The historic liberties of Englishmen were in the form of a "patrimony," a "hereditary title," an "entailed inheritance," a "pedigree" from their "canonized forefathers."[11] Such liberties were not only legitimized by the past; they were secured and extended by the same process of inheritance that brought them into the present.

> The idea of inheritance furnishes a sure principle of conservation, and a sure principle of transmission; without at all excluding a principle of improvement. It leaves acquisition free; but it secures what it acquires. . . . By a constitutional policy, working after the pattern of nature, we receive, we hold, we transmit our government and privileges, in the same manner in which we enjoy and transmit our property and our lives.[12]

The Burkean idea of the "inheritance" of liberty is very different from the familiar idea of the "progress" of liberty. "Progress" says nothing about the mechanism by which liberty advances, nothing about the means by which the past evolves into the present. It only asserts that there is such an evolution, as if it were foreordained, inherent in the nature of man and history. In this sense progress resembles the kind of "metaphysical" principle Burke so abhorred. The "inheritance" of liberty, on the analogy of the inheritance of property, is more concrete and substantive. It suggests the several stages through which liberty, like property, passes: the original act of acquisition, the protection of that acquisition, the acquisition of additional liberty (or liberties—the plural is more appropriate to this metaphor), and the transmission of those liberties which have been so laboriously acquired and preserved. It also suggests, as the idea of progress does not, that what has been acquired can be lost or taken away, in whole or in part (again the plural form is more fitting). Far from being assured by some providential order, liberty in this image is seen as vulnerable and precarious, in need of all the laws, institutions, conventions, and principles which encourage its acquisition, preservation, and transmission.

It might have been Burke writing that magnificent passage in the *History:*

> As our Revolution was a vindication of ancient rights, so it was conducted with strict attention to ancient formalities. In almost every word and act may be discerned a profound reverence for the past. The Estates of the Realm deliberated in the old halls and according to the old rules. . . . Both the English parties agreed in treating with solemn respect the ancient constitutional traditions of the state. The only question was, in what sense those traditions were to be understood. The assertors of liberty said not a word about the natural equality of men and the inalienable sovereignty of the people. . . . When at length the dispute had been accommodated, the new sovereigns were proclaimed with the old pageantry. . . . To us, who have lived in the year 1848, it may seem almost an abuse of terms to call a proceeding, conducted with so much deliberation, with so much sobriety, and with such minute attention to prescriptive etiquette, by the terrible name of Revolution.[13]

Yet Macaulay, as Joseph Hamburger has shown, was an imperfect Burkean, more of a "trimmer," a compromiser and conciliator, than was proper for a true Whig.[14]* Burke's reverence for tradition, history, established institutions, and conventions was rooted in a theory of natural law: "the great primeval contract of eternal society, linking the lower with the higher natures, connecting the visible and invisible world, according to a fixed compact sanctioned by the inviolable oath which holds all physical and moral natures, each in their appointed place."[15] For Burke, expediency, compromise, prudence, and the pragmatic accommodation to "circumstances" were the means, not the ends,

---

*It is revealing that Macaulay twice contemplated writing about Burke and twice abandoned the project, once after being well into it. That missing essay is a conspicuous and tantalizing gap in his corpus.

of policy. For Macaulay, lacking any such commitment to natural law, they were the ends, the only principles of government.

Macaulay was not even comfortable, Burrow points out, with the idea of the "ancient constitution," although he sometimes invoked it for rhetorical and polemical purposes.[16] The ancient constitution had for him the double liability of being reactionary and revolutionary: reactionary in not acknowledging the debt liberty owed to modernity, revolutionary in threatening to subvert the distinctive institutions of modernity—the monarchy, most notably—by appealing to the ancient ideal of a republic. In the battle of the ancients and moderns, Macaulay was unequivocally on the side of the moderns. (His *Lays of Ancient Rome,* in this view, was a *jeu d'esprit.*) Liberty, he insisted, was not ancient; it was peculiarly modern. "In almost all the little commonwealths of antiquity, liberty was used as a pretext for measures directed against everything which makes liberty valuable."[17] It was England, not Greece or Rome, that gave birth to the traditions he cherished.

> Senate has not to our ears a sound so venerable as Parliament. We respect the Great Charter more than the laws of Solon. The Capitol and the Forum impress us with less awe than our own Westminster Hall and Westminster Abbey. . . . Our liberty is neither Greek nor Roman; but essentially English. It has a character of its own—a character which has taken a tinge from the sentiments of the chivalrous ages, and which accords with the peculiarities of our manners and of our insular situation. It has a language, too, of its own, and a language so singularly idiomatic, full of meaning to ourselves, scarcely intelligible to strangers.[18]

For all their differences, however, Macaulay and Burke belonged to a common tradition, that "liberal descent" which both took to be the glory of England. And so, too, Burrow maintains, for all their more considerable differences, did those later Victorian historians, Stubbs, Freeman, and Froude. On the surface "liberal" hardly seems an apt label for any of them, least of all for the Tory High Churchman William Stubbs, who resigned the Regius Professorship of Modern History at Oxford in 1884 to become Bishop of Chester (and, later, Bishop of Oxford). While Stubbs's own political views were decidedly conservative, his *Constitutional History of England* (1873–78) was generally acknowledged to be fair and judicious. Yet it did have political implications, even Whiggish implications.

The "ancient constitution" described by Stubbs, with its local assemblies, legal institutions such as the jury, and a property system favoring the independent freeholder, was designed to secure those principles of personal freedom and political rights which were an essential part of the Whig tradition. Later developments, to be sure—the Norman Conquest, feudalism, and the rise of the nation-state—altered that ancient heritage, but enough survived to preserve some continuity with the past and to give promise of some continuity with the future. Stubbs, no less than Macaulay, looked forward to that "truer and brighter day, the season of more general conscious life, higher longings, more forbearing, more sympathetic, purer, riper liberty," indeed "unto the perfect day."[19] If his was not quite the Whig view of history, it was a Tory view that made conservatism itself, the appeal to the past, the guarantor of progress and freedom.

When Edward Freeman, in his *History of the Norman Conquest* (1867–79), extolled the ancient constitution, it was from the point of view not of a Whig or Tory but of a radical and democrat. Having coined the epigram, "History is past politics, and politics is present history,"[20] he was suspected by some of his contemporaries of making of history not so much past politics as present politics. Burrow reverses this judgment, arguing that it was not his politics that determined his history but his history that

determined his politics.* His enthusiasm for the national liberation movements of his own day derived from his reading of the
early history of those nations. "Every stage that has been taken
towards the unity of Germany and Italy is not a step towards
something new but a step back towards something old."[22] Unlike
Macaulay and like Stubbs, Freeman believed liberty to be ancient
rather than modern. "As far at least as our race is concerned,
freedom is everywhere older than bondage. . . . Our ancient
history is the possession of the liberal."[23] This was a distinctly
un-Macaulayite kind of progress, a progress toward the restoration of the past. And it was an un-Macaulayite kind of liberalism
—not pluralistic, pragmatic, latitudinarian, but homogeneous,
doctrinaire, restrictive. This great proponent of democracy and
freedom, of republicanism and national self-determination, was
also an avowed racist and xenophobe; only the Aryan race, he
insisted, and only special breeds of Aryans at that, could aspire
to the ancient liberties and privileges of the ancient constitution.

In this odd company of historians, James Anthony Froude is
the odd man out. He and Freeman were bitter enemies, his
contempt for Freeman's politics being matched by Freeman's
contempt for his scholarship.† In fact, Froude's *History of England
from the Fall of Wolsey to the Defeat of the Spanish Armada* (1856–
70) was not as inaccurate as Freeman made it out to be. Froude's

---

*This was also the view of William Lecky, yet another Victorian historian:
"We are Cavaliers or Roundheads before we are Conservatives or Liberals."[21]

†The Victorians, for all their reputation for civility, were no mean polemicists.
"Mr. Froude," Freeman wrote in the *Saturday Review,* "is not an historian. His
work consists of four volumes of ingenious paradox and eight of ecclesiastical
pamphlet. The blemishes which cut it off from any title to the name of history
are utter carelessness as to facts and utter incapacity to distinguish right from
wrong."[24] It is ironic that a favorable review of Froude should have generated
one of the most memorable controversies of the century. Almost in passing,
Charles Kingsley made the comment that was to provoke John Henry Newman to write his *Apologia Pro Vita Sua:* "Truth for its own sake had never
been a virtue with the Roman clergy. Father Newman informs us that it need
not, and on the whole ought not to be."[25]

reputation, however, was such that it seemed plausible to attribute to him the sentence that was said to have concluded his contribution to Newman's series of *Lives of the Saints:* "This is all, and perhaps more than all, that is known of the life of the blessed St. Neot." That sentence did not actually appear in Froude's book, but a variant of it did appear in one of the other *Lives* co-authored by Newman himself: "And this is all that is known, and more than all—yet nothing to what the angels know —of the life of a servant of God."[26]

More controversial than Froude's scholarship was the interpretation that colored his *History*. Where Stubbs and Freeman exalted the ancient constitution and Macaulay the modern, Froude, like his mentor Carlyle, despised constitutionalism itself—"constitution-mongering," Carlyle called it. And where the others exalted some idea of liberty, Froude proudly traced England's descent from the Tudors, whom he saw as benevolent despots, strong, natural, paternal rulers presiding over a strong, confident, imperial nation. It was a romantic history he wrote and a heroic past he celebrated, a past that threw into sharp relief everything he disliked in Victorian England: industrialism, liberalism, materialism, laissez-faireism. But while he did not share the Whigs' enthusiasm for liberty and representative government, he did share their admiration for Protestantism, and in this respect he contributed a vital ingredient to the Whig interpretation of history. As Macaulay legitimized the Revolution, so Froude legitimized the Reformation, a Reformation that was Whiggishly undoctrinaire and unsectarian, more moral than theological and more national than ecclesiastical.

Today it is not only the "Whig interpretation" that is in disrepute, not only the idea of a "liberal descent," but the idea of any "descent." If the Victorian historian could take for granted the continuity of the past, it was because he took for granted the political nature of that continuity, which is to say, the essentially political nature of history. Whatever period he chose to trace his descent from—medieval England, or the Reformation, or the Revolution—he identified that period with political principles, and he saw those principles transmitted (and in the process altered) by way of political institutions and traditions. Only now, with the displacement of political history by social history, can we appreciate how crucial that political dimension was both to Victorian history and to Victorian culture—and to the continuity between history and culture, the past and the present.

Historians have always written social history, in some form and to some degree. Macaulay himself did so. The famous third chapter of his *History,* on England in 1685, deals with social classes, standards of living, the condition of the poor, the state of agriculture and industry, the growth of population and of towns, child labor, pauperism, science, art, travel, newspapers, and books. But, as Jacques Barzun has pointed out, this is only one of six chapters of the first volume; appearing in the middle of the volume, it is a static interlude in an otherwise political narrative.[27] This is very different from the current mode of social history, which, if it does not lay claim to all of history, "total history," at the very least professes to be the dominant, determinant part of history. In the "new history," political events appear as the "epiphenomena" or "superstructure" of history, while the essential reality, or "infrastructure," is found in the relations of social classes and the lives of the "anonymous masses." Historians now vie with one another in plumbing the lower depths of this "history from below," and in rescuing from oblivion one submerged group after another: women, children, racial and ethnic minorities, sexual deviants, criminals, the insane. When Macaulay prepared his readers for his chapter on the "history of the people," he said that he would "cheerfully bear the reproach of having descended below the dignity of history."[28] But it never occurred to him to descend so far below the dignity of history as to make these subjects the whole or even the major part of his work.

Another Victorian historian, J. R. Green, wrote an entire history of the "people"—indeed, two such histories, *A Short*

History of the English People (1874) and a four-volume *History of the English People* (1877–80). But while he himself was something of a radical, he was well within the Whig tradition of history. A good friend of Freeman, he criticized him for having too narrow a view of history. "He passes silently by religion, intellect, society. He admires the people gathered in its Witan, but he never takes us to the thegn's hall or the peasant's hut. Of the actual life of our forefathers the book tells us nothing."[29] Yet Green himself, on the very first page of his book, admitted that "of the temper and life of these English folk in this Old England we know little."[30] And the reader of his book was never shown the inside of the thane's hall or peasant's hut, for the good reason that Green had no more evidence than Freeman to warrant such domestic intrusions.

In fact Green's enormously popular *Short History* (the best selling work of history since Macaulay) was not nearly as populist as he made out. "It is a history," his preface announced, "not of English Kings or English Conquests, but of the English People," which was why he proposed to devote more space "to Chaucer than to Cressy, to Caxton than to the petty strife of Yorkist and Lancastrian, to the Poor Law of Elizabeth than to her victory at Cadiz, to the Methodist revival than to the escape of the Young Pretender."[31] The statement is somewhat misleading; while he did make room for other subjects, royalty and war continue to dominate the book as a whole.* Moreover, the

---

*Chaucer does occupy more space than Cressy, but not than the Hundred Years' War, in which the Battle of Cressy was only one incident. The three pages on the printer Caxton are notable, but they are half the number devoted to the "petty strife" of the Wars of the Roses. The half-page on the Elizabethan Poor Law compares favorably with the few sentences on Cadiz, but not with the three pages on the Spanish Armada. And while the actual escape of the Young Pretender is given short shrift, the Jacobite revolts take up about as much space as the Methodist revival, and both are enmeshed in a lengthier account of the wars of the period. Oddly enough, social history becomes more scanty as Green approaches his own time. The agricultural and industrial developments of the late-eighteenth and early-nineteenth centuries—"revolu-

subjects he prided himself on including—and criticized Freeman for neglecting—were not social issues as we now use that term, but religious and intellectual ones. Of the four examples he gave, only one (the Poor Law) belongs to social history proper; the others are intellectual (Chaucer and Caxton) and religious (Methodism). "I dare say you would stare," he wrote to Freeman, "to see seven pages devoted to the Wars of the Roses and fifteen to Colet, Erasmus and More."[32] Today such a "history of the people" would be deplored as "elitist."

Nor did Green belittle political history. He gave so much space to Colet, Erasmus, and More, he explained, because these were formative influences on English political life. And he sacrificed the colorful details of court intrigues in order to dwell at greater length on the "constitutional, intellectual, and social advance in which we read the history of the nation itself."[33] Even social conditions were often less important in themselves than in relation to the polity. The economic and social changes of the "New Monarchy," for example (which he dated from the reign of Edward IV), were important because they sapped "the social organization from which our political constitution had hitherto sprung and on which it still rested."[34] As much as Freeman (indeed, Freeman was a major source for much of the early part of his book), Green admired the primitive democracy of old England, "the people gathered in its Witan." And as much as any Whig, he sought to discover the sources of modern parliamentary government.

> Here, too, the "witan," the Wise Men of the village, met to settle questions of peace and war, to judge just judgment, and frame wise laws, as their descendants, the Wise men of a later England, meet in Parliament at Westminster, to frame laws and do justice for the great empire which has sprung from this little body of farmer-commonwealths in Sleswick.[35]

tions," as they were already being called by his contemporaries—occupy little more than two pages, while the wars with France take almost twenty.

Compared with their modern counterparts, Victorian historians, even when they were writing social history, were insistently political. In this respect too they maintained their continuity with the past, and not only with the history of their country but with the history of their discipline. Like Herodotus and Thucydides, they assumed that the polity—some kind of polity, ancient or modern, folk or state, Whig, Tory, or Radical—was the bearer of that "entailed inheritance" which ensured the continuity of the past and the present, and of the present and the future. They had different conceptions of the past, different views of the present, different hopes for the future. But they shared this essential ingredient of Whig history and of the English political tradition.

❧ 9 ❧
Disraeli: The Tory Imagination

〰〰〰〰〰〰〰〰〰〰

More than a century after Disraeli's death, a conference on current British politics was diverted by an animated discussion about the rival claims of Margaret Thatcher, leader of the Conservative Party, and Michael Foot, then leader of the Labour Party, to the label "Disraelian." (Foot had something of an edge by virtue of his dog named "Dizzy.")* In the United States some years earlier, Senator Moynihan, then Counsellor to the President, urged President Nixon to assume the mantle of Disraeli by adopting the Family Assistance Plan. More recently, when the human rights issue was being debated, an article in the *Wall Street Journal* recalled the "Bulgarian Massacres" of 1876 and held up Disraeli's policy as a model for similar cases in our own day.[2]

Historians are made acutely uncomfortable by such invocations of the spirit of Disraeli; they have difficulty enough with the real Disraeli in his own time and place. Yet the allusions tell us something important about the historical Disraeli, something many historians have yet to learn. However inconsistent and

---

*Foot makes no secret of his admiration for Disraeli. Indeed, he delights in pointing out that he is more of an admirer than some Conservatives—Lord Butler, for example, who wrote a rather dismissive introduction to a new edition of Disraeli's *Sybil*. He has also criticized the author of a book on Disraeli's novels for not being sufficiently appreciative of Disraeli's "revolutionary mind."[1]

inconstant he may have been, however opportunistic and eccentric, he did represent a distinctive political mode, a disposition and sensibility that did not quite qualify as a philosophy and policy—hence the vacillations on his part and the disagreements about him on ours—but which were recognized as unique and significant in his own time and still command attention today. He speaks to us as his great antagonist does not; it is a long time since anyone invoked the name of Gladstone to lend authority to a political figure or cause.*

A recent spate of books by and about Disraeli might suggest a Disraeli "revival," were it not for the fact that such books have been coming out with fair regularity since his death in 1881. It is a tribute to him that biographers continue to take on the daunting task of competing with the great Monypenny and Buckle *Life*—six fascinating volumes published between 1910 and 1920, which give the lie to Carlyle's comment on that genre: "How delicate, decent, is English biography, bless its mealy mouth!"[3] Robert Blake's biography of 1966 is perhaps as good as a one-volume biography can be, but it cannot and does not presume to replace Monypenny and Buckle. Nor does the latest briefer biography by Sarah Bradford, which gives greater weight to Disraeli's private life, supersede Blake's.[4] And no biography can begin to compare with Disraeli's own writings, which is why the really important publication of recent years is the definitive edition of his letters.† The true Disraeli enthusiast will also welcome so minor a work as *A Year at Hartlebury,* a novel originally published anonymously and only recently revealed to have been written by Disraeli and his sister.

*The Primrose League, founded by Lord Randolph Churchill in 1883 in honor of Disraeli (the primrose was supposedly his favorite flower), today has some two or three million members. While its functions are more social than political, it testifies to the popular appeal of a mode of conservatism that is still identified with Disraeli.

†It is a commentary on the present state of "little England" that this edition of the *Letters,* like the collected works of John Stuart Mill, should have been

As with all the eminent Victorians, one is astonished by the sheer quantity of written matter: almost seven hundred letters (and how many others that have not been recovered?), newspaper articles, political tracts (one running to three hundred pages), and seven novels (not counting the new one which was largely written by his sister)—this in the first thirty-two years of Disraeli's life, the period covered by the initial two volumes of letters. The first part of *Vivian Grey*, which achieved a *succès de scandale*, was published in 1826 when he was twenty-one, the second part the following year. Four other novels were written before 1834 when *A Year at Hartlebury* appeared. This novel, about a parliamentary election, drew upon his own electoral experiences, for by then he had twice been defeated at the polls and on two other occasions had unsuccessfully sought nomination. (In the novel the hero is elected by one vote.)

It was at this time, fresh from these defeats, that Disraeli informed Lord Melbourne, then Home Secretary and shortly to become Prime Minister, that he himself intended one day to be Prime Minister, to which a startled Melbourne replied: "No chance of that in our time. It is all arranged and settled. Nobody can compete with Stanley [the future Earl of Derby]."[6] Disraeli was to lose two other elections, publish two more novels, two political works, and an epic poem, before finally winning a seat in Parliament in 1837, at the age of thirty-two. It was to be another thirty-one years before he succeeded Derby as Prime Minister. But long before that, in spite of a series of rebuffs and near-disasters, Disraeli had reason to be confirmed in his self-confidence and self-esteem.

Electioneering and writing were not Disraeli's only occupations in these early years. Indeed, they seem to have been minor distractions in an endless round of parties and travels (including

undertaken by Canadian scholars, subsidized by Canadian foundations, and published by a Canadian university press.[5] (What is still lacking is a complete edition of Disraeli's works.)

a grand tour of the Middle East in 1830–31), flirtations and amours, entrepreneurial schemes and financial speculations, and stratagems to pacify creditors and avoid bankruptcy and arrest. Had Disraeli gone to debtor's prison, as he very nearly did in the spring of 1837, his parliamentary career might well have been thwarted even before it began.

Much else in his mode of life was equally perilous. Writing novels—and such novels: *romans à clef* caricaturing politicians who were important to his career, "silver fork" novels romanticizing (and ridiculing) high society, a historical novel fantasizing and eulogizing the Hebrew "race"—was hardly a prescription for political success. His father, in some ways more worldly than he, once asked him: "How will the Fictionist assort with the Politician?"[7] The problem was less the particular kinds of fiction he wrote than the fact that he wrote them at all. And this objection told as much against him in the social world as in the political; his inveterate, unregenerate "fictionizing" was apparently the main reason he was blackballed from the Athenaeum. (He was finally elected thirty years later.)

And so too his dandyism. After walking up crowded Regent Street arrayed in a blue frock coat, light blue trousers, black stockings with red stripes, and low shoes (most men wore boots), he reported to his friend, "The people quite made way for me as I passed. It was like the opening of the Red Sea which I now perfectly believe from experience." Upon which his friend commented in his diary, "I should think so!"[8] Dandyism, to be sure, was itself a convention in a small circle, as was being in debt—indeed the two went hand in hand—but not in the circle of aspiring prime ministers and not in the brazen spirit displayed by Disraeli.

There was something wanton about all this, a deliberate courting of danger. Disraeli flaunted his debts as he flaunted his attire. They were part of his romantic persona, the same persona that emerged in his novels and in his relations with women. He was not only calling attention to himself by defying bourgeois conventions, not only elevating himself socially by taking on the airs and manners of a bohemian aristocrat, not only narcissistically preening and indulging himself. He was also, like any good romantic hero, making things hard for himself, stimulating himself to greater exertion, testing and proving himself, to himself as well as to others. Several years later, in *Tancred,* the third novel in his famous trilogy, he said of one of his characters: "Fakredeen was fond of his debts; they were the source indeed of his only real excitement, and he was grateful to them for their stirring powers." Even more revealing was Fakredeen's own confession: "I am actually so indolent, that if I did not remember in the morning that I was ruined, I should never be able to distinguish myself."[9]

What made Disraeli's appearance and behavior even more egregious was his Jewishness. He was not, in fact, Jewish in religion, having been baptized, on the instructions of his father, at the age of twelve, a few months before he would have qualified for the Bar Mitzvah rite. But he prided himself on being of the Jewish "race" (his word, not his enemies'). "All is race, not religion—remember that," he told Lady Rothschild.[10] And he never permitted anyone to forget it. He exaggerated his racial features by having his black hair set in elaborate ringlets (it was dyed in his later years by his wife), and by an unconventional attire that made him seem even more exotic and foreign. (The hero of *A Year at Hartlebury* is hated by the local magnates because "he had not a snub nose, because he was suspiciously curious in his linen, because his coat was not cut after their fashion.")[11] He made not the least effort to dissociate himself from his Jewish friends and relations even while he was assiduously climbing the social ladder. (His father, remaining a Jew after the children were baptized, retained the old spelling of the name, D'Israeli.) And he deliberately drew attention to his Jewishness, in his personal life, in his novels, even in his biography of Lord Bentinck, where he used the pretext of the controversy over Jewish emancipation to insert an entire chapter celebrating the history of the Jews.

If Disraeli gave himself a more romantic and exalted ancestry than he actually had, he also romanticized and exalted the Jewish "race" as a whole. Psychologists may explain all this as "compensation" or "overcompensation," testifying to his shame at having been a Jew and guilt at having ceased to be so. But this is to permit a psychological theory to prevail over the facts. On any straightforward reading of the evidence, there is not the slightest intimation of shame, guilt, even unease. On the contrary, Disraeli seems genuinely to have believed in his superiority by virtue of his ancient and honorable lineage. There is a ring of authenticity in his comment: "Fancy calling a fellow an adventurer when his ancestors were probably on intimate terms with the Queen of Sheba."[12]

People did call him an adventurer, however, and worse. Although anti-Semitism in Victorian England was not the virulent disease it has been at other times and places, it was chronic and often enough exceedingly disagreeable. Until 1829 Jews, like Catholics and Dissenters, were excluded from public office and Parliament by the Test Acts. After the repeal of these acts, until the passage of the Jewish Disabilities Bill in 1858, Jews continued to be excluded if they refused to take the oath "on the true faith of a Christian." Religion, not "race," was the legal barrier; even before 1829, converted Jews (Ricardo, most notably) sat in Parliament. And socially, in London literary circles, for example, the barrier was not as great as might be supposed. Disraeli's father was a Reform Jew who did not observe the dietary laws, but his children were circumcised and taught Hebrew, and he himself belonged to a synagogue. It was only when the synagogue required him, against his wishes, to serve as warden that he left the congregation and had his children, although not himself, baptized. Yet he was a member of the Athenaeum and counted among his friends such literary lights as Lord Byron, Robert Southey, Walter Scott, the editor John Lockhart, and the publisher John Murray.

Had Disraeli been content to be, like his father, "a quiet member of a tolerated minority," Blake says, he too could have enjoyed the amenities of the Athenaeum.[13] But he would not condescend to be quiet and tolerated. He wanted nothing less than the highest public office, and he wanted it on his terms, as the most conspicuous member of the most "superior race." When he appeared on the hustings in his customary attire and demeanor, he brought upon himself the familiar gibes: "Shylock," "Old Clothes," "Judas," "Bring a bit of pork for the Jew."[14] Daniel O'Connell, the Irish Radical leader, responding to an attack by Disraeli, said that while there were "respectable Jews," Disraeli was not one of them: "He has just the qualities of the impenitent thief on the Cross"; this was his genealogy and this his "infamous distinction."[15] With even less provocation Carlyle railed against this "Pinchbeck-Hebrew, almost professedly a Son of Belial," a "cursed old Jew, not worth his weight in cold bacon."[16] If England was spared the more vicious kind of anti-Semitism, it had a plenitude of the more mundane kind, of which Disraeli endured more than his share.

The subject raises a host of intriguing questions—social, political, even theological. How did Disraeli reconcile his conversion with his religious and racial pride? What classes and groups were most overtly anti-Semitic in relation to him? How did he, in spite of the prevailing anti-Semitism, manage to climb that "greasy pole," and in the Tory Party, home of the landed aristocracy and country squires? How serious was he in propounding the theory that Christianity was only Judaism "completed," Judaism for the "multitude," and that the Jews deserved to be venerated, not vilified, for making possible the Crucifixion and hence the salvation of humanity?[17] What part did his dictum "All is race" play in his ideology, and how did it bear upon his idea of "Tory Democracy," that peculiar amalgam of paternalistic benevolence and national assertiveness? Can Disraeli be said to be a Zionist, a precursor of Zionism, or perhaps a premature Zionist, or is any association of him with Zionism "anachronistic and not plausible," as Isaiah Berlin has claimed?[18]

No biography, obliged to deal with a life and mind as complicated as Disraeli's, can be expected to treat adequately all the implications of his Jewishness. It may be the very genre that is at fault. The biographer, having to keep some distance from his subject, to be objective and dispassionate, even skeptical and critical—having, in short, to behave like a biographer rather than an autobiographer—finds it difficult to convey the play of mind, the boldness of affirmation, the unashamed passion one finds in Disraeli himself. Blake, for example, had been even more dubious than Bradford about this aspect of Disraeli's life. It is all the more interesting, therefore, to find him reconsidering his earlier views in a recent book on Disraeli's grand tour. In his introduction Blake explains that it was only after he himself saw Jerusalem for the first time and then reread Disraeli that he came to appreciate the importance of Disraeli's own visit to Jerusalem and to credit the seriousness of his ideas about race and religion. This new impression was confirmed by a passage in the recently published diary of Lord Stanley (son of the Earl of Derby, who was then leader of the Tories). Stanley recorded a conversation in 1851 in which Disraeli spoke movingly of the restoration of the Jews to their homeland and even worked out the means of financing it: the Rothschilds and other Jewish capitalists were to provide funds for the purchase of land, and the Turkish government, desperate for money, would agree to the sale. Such plans, Disraeli assured Stanley, were widespread among the Jews, and the man who carried them out would be "the next Messiah, the true Saviour of his people." Recalling this conversation, Stanley observed that Disraeli seemed to be in utter earnestness and that it was the only time he ever appeared to "show signs of any higher emotion."[19] Blake, for his part, has no doubt that Disraeli genuinely meant what he said, that if he did nothing it was because nothing could realistically be done, and that he would undoubtedly have welcomed the Balfour Declaration. In the light of this account, the final sentence of *Tancred* takes on a new significance: "The Duke and Duchess of Bellamont had arrived in Jerusalem."[20]

If one may now take more seriously Disraeli's ideas about the "Hebrew race," perhaps it is also time to take more seriously his ideas about society and politics. It is easy to mock the "Young England" party with which Disraeli identified himself—which, indeed, he invented. That "party" consisted of all of four young men, newly elected to Parliament, whose alliance, such as it was, lasted for exactly two sessions in 1843 and 1844. By the time *Sybil* was published in the spring of 1845, this novel, in effect the manifesto of Young England, was a memorial to a movement that never existed, except as an idea in Disraeli's mind. But as an idea it was potent enough to persuade both the press and Parliament of its existence and importance. By the device of a "party," Tory Democracy entered the public domain and acquired a political status and a legitimacy it might not otherwise have had.

One of the Young Englanders referred to the group as "we esoterics."[21] Their esoteric doctrine was nothing more abstruse than the idea that the Tory Party was, or rather should be, the party that would bind together the "two nations," promoting the welfare and happiness of the people even if the people themselves were not part of the political process. This idea had been enunciated by Disraeli as early as 1835 in his *Vindication of the English Constitution,* in his election address the same year, and in a most interesting letter addressed to a prominent resident of the district and distributed as a pamphlet. In the letter Disraeli distinguished between his own brand of Toryism and the corrupt form he attributed to one of the leaders of the party, Robert Peel:

> I still am of opinion that the Tory party is the real democratic party of this country. I hold one of the first principles of Toryism to be that Government is instituted for the welfare of the many.

This is why the Tories maintain national institutions, the objects of which are the protection, the maintenance, the moral, civil, and religious education of the great mass of the English people: institutions which whether they assume the form of churches, or universities, or societies of men to protect the helpless and to support the needy, to execute justice and to maintain truth, alike originated, and alike flourish for the advantage and happiness of the multitude. I deny that the Tories have ever opposed the genuine democratic or national spirit of the country; on the contrary they have always headed it. It was the Tories who increased the constituency by the £50 tenancy clause; *a most democratic measure,* but one, in my opinion, that has eminently tended to the salvation of the State. I deny that the Tories oppose short parliaments or the ballot, because they will give too much power to *the people:* it is because they will give too much power to *the constituency;* a shrewd and vast difference.[22]

In this same letter Disraeli anticipated one of the most celebrated coups of his career: "dishing the Whigs" by sponsoring the Reform Act of 1867 which enfranchised the urban working classes. His Whig opponent, he wrote in 1835, "is extremely annoyed that being a Tory, I should have pledged myself at Wycombe to promote the cause of Reform. Why to be sure, are the Whigs to have all the Reform to themselves!"[23] Whether in 1835 or 1867, the tactic of preempting the cause of reform was not the Machiavellian maneuver, the triumph of expediency over principle, it has been made out to be. Disraeli never thought of the Whigs (or, later, the Liberals) as the natural party of reform —of political reform, still less of social reform—because he thought of the Tory Party, his kind of Tory Party, as the "natural" leaders of the people. And because he never subscribed to the "do-nothing" doctrine of laissez-faire liberalism, he had no difficulty supporting whatever reforms he believed to be in the interests of the people. Nor did he have any difficulty in giving the largest possible extension to the term "people"—a word, as he said, that was vastly different from "constituency" or "electorate." The people were the whole of the nation, whether represented in Parliament or not, and it was their "happiness" that was the purpose of government. Long before *Coningsby* and *Sybil,* he had enunciated the doctrine of Tory Democracy that was the theme of those novels.

There was no small measure of political opportunism in Disraeli's espousal of reform or in his identification of the Tory Party as the "national" party, the "real democratic" party, the party of "Labour" in alliance with a "natural" aristocracy (natural, because it was an aristocracy of merit as well as birth). But it was an opportunism entirely consistent with his principles. And on occasion principle prevailed over expediency. He had nothing to gain—from his own constituency, from his party or any faction within the party, from the landed or manufacturing classes, or even from the working classes (who at the time were disfranchised and in no position to further his career)—by publicly defending Chartism, the most militant working-class movement in early Victorian England. In July 1839, at the height of that movement, Disraeli made a speech in Parliament warning the government that it was confronting not a "mere temporary ebullition" but a "social insurrection." "I am not ashamed to say," he declared, "however much I disapprove of the Charter, I sympathize with Chartists."[24] He disapproved, that is, of the means, the demand for political equality; but he sympathized with the end, the elimination of such inequities as the New Poor Law and the excessive rigors of laissez-faire. He was also one of the very few in Parliament to oppose the severe punitive measures taken against the Chartists. When a prominent radical praised him for his courageous action, he replied that a union between the Tories and the masses offered the only means by which the Empire could be preserved. "Their interests are identical; united they form the nation."[25]

The nation and the Empire, a united nation at home and a strong nation abroad: the two were of a piece. When Disraeli did finally become Prime Minister, these were the main planks of his platform and the rationale of his administration. His solicitude for the Empire, however, did not entail imperial aggrandizement —indeed, he generally counseled against annexation. And he had none of the "white man's burden" ethic that was used later to justify imperialism. What he did have was a passionate concern for Britain's strength, prestige, and influence, and a determination to pursue a vigorous foreign policy to promote the national interest. This theme too appears in his earliest writings, in his electoral address in 1833 when he urged a Tory-Radical alliance under the name of the "National Party," which would undertake "to maintain the glory of the Empire and to secure the happiness of the People"; or in *A Year at Hartlebury,* when the hero castigated the Whigs as an "anti-national" party and predicted that their victory would lead to the "dismemberment of the Empire."[26] Almost half-a-century later he had Lady Montfort rebuke Endymion for thinking too much of trade and finance. Trade would always revive and finance never ruined a country. What was important was "real politics: foreign affairs; maintaining our power in Europe."[27]

Whether or not Disraeli's handling of the "Bulgarian Massacres" issue—the "Eastern Question," as it was known at the time—commends itself, as has been suggested, as a model for American policy today, it was a triumph for Disraeli personally and for Britain as a European power. The issue flared up in 1876 when Gladstone published an enormously successful pamphlet— 40,000 copies were sold within a week, 200,000 by the end of the month—denouncing the massacre by the Turks of thousands of Bulgarians following the outbreak of a widespread revolt; the deaths were reported to range from 10,000 to 25,000. Religious as well as humanitarian passions were inflamed, and the affair became a major international event when Russia threatened to invade Turkey (and finally did so) under the pretext of a crusade on behalf of oppressed Balkan Christians. In England the "atrocitarians," who believed the worst of the Turks, were opposed by the "jingoists," who believed the worst of the Russians and were prepared to go to war against them if necessary. (The term "jingo" was popularized in a music-hall ditty at this time.) Disraeli had no illusions about the Turks; during his grand tour almost half-a-century earlier, he had written home flippantly about dining with the Bey in Albania, who was "daily decapitating half the province."[28] But he had still fewer about Russia, either about Russia's capacity for atrocities or about her designs on Constantinople. While Gladstone whipped up a frenzy of anti-Turkish, pro-Russian sentiment (and anti-Semitic as well, accusing Disraeli of being indifferent to the sufferings of Christians because of his "crypto-Judaism" and "race antipathy"),[29] Disraeli insisted that however deplorable the atrocities, British policy must be based on British national interests. And those interests dictated that Russia be prevented at all costs from realizing her imperial dream of gaining control of the Dardanelles and the Mediterranean.

Disraeli had not only to convince the country of its national interests; he had to convince his own Foreign Office and cabinet. At the height of the crisis he wrote to the queen, who was his staunchest supporter: "This morning a torturing hour with Lord Derby [the Foreign Secretary] who was for doing nothing and this afternoon with Lord Salisbury [Secretary of State for India] who evidently is thinking more of raising the Cross on the cupola of St. Sophia than of the power of England."[30] In fact, as Disraeli discovered, Derby was not quite for "doing nothing"; he was deliberately leaking cabinet secrets to the Russian ambassador in London. Later Salisbury proved to be a loyal and able Foreign Secretary, but it was Disraeli who was the architect of foreign policy and, at the age of seventy-three, the leading figure at the Congress of Berlin. By being bold and determined, threatening to break up the Congress and even declare war, he succeeded in depriving Russia of the crucial gains she had achieved after her victory over Turkey and in bringing about a settlement of the crisis that was more to the liking of the European powers than of either Turkey or Russia. He returned home from Berlin a conquering hero. Historians may speculate about what might have happened had Gladstone presided over Britain at that particular moment and Russia been permitted to expand, possibly to Constantinople. In the event, Bismarck may have the last word on this affair: *"Der alte Jude, das ist der Mann."*[31]

How did *der alte Jude* climb that "greasy pole" to power? This is the question that haunts the opening chapters of any biography of Disraeli, as one reads of all the obstacles (some self-imposed) that stood in his way. But the question disappears as his character and ideas emerge from behind the trappings of dress and rhetoric. A truly discerning reader might have found the clues to Disraeli's success early in the story, in a diary entry in 1833: "The Utilitarians in Politics are like the Unitarians in Religion. Both omit Imagination in their systems, and Imagination governs Mankind."[32] Disraeli's political career, as much as his personal life, was a triumph of imagination. And it is a tribute to the boldness and complexity of that imagination that, a century later, biographers and historians still debate the meaning of his ideas and commentators argue about his political bequest and succession.

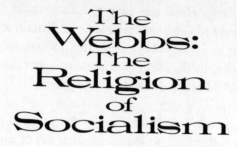

10

The Webbs: The Religion of Socialism

The term "Fabianism" conjures up, if it still conjures up anything whatever, an image of the most moderate, prudent form of socialism, so moderate and prudent as hardly to be socialistic at all. Founded exactly a century ago and still in existence today, the Fabian Society took its name from the Roman general who kept Hannibal's troops at bay by harassing them without ever engaging them in battle. (His replacement by a more forthright commander led to the rout at Cannae.) For the Fabians that strategy translated itself into the doctrines of "gradualism" and "permeation." Socialism—or "collectivism," as the early Fabians more often put it—would come about as it was already coming about, gradually, incrementally, inevitably, by the extension of collectivist controls over one institution after another. And it would come about, again as it was already coming about, not by the direct action of the working class but by a small group of knowledgeable, capable, well-placed people who would permeate the institutions that were the source of power and who would initiate the necessary reforms. Compared with other forms of socialism familiar at the time, Marxism and the several varieties of utopianism, Fabianism appears to be eminently modest and meliorist, pragmatic and pluralist, non-ideological and non-utopian, a gentle, decent, safe prescription for a better society.

That benign image has not gone unchallenged. Fabianism has been criticized for being insufficiently socialist, insufficiently democratic, even insufficiently progressive. In one history of Fabianism the chapter on the early twentieth century is entitled "Fabian 'Aberrances,' " a reference to the predilections of some leading Fabians for imperialism, protectionism, and church-controlled education.[1] The term might also have been applied to their opposition at that time to women's suffrage, their aloofness from the trade union movement and the Independent Labour Party, their preference for Conservative rather than Liberal (still less Labour) politicians, and other policies that comport oddly with the popular image of the movement. The recent spate of books by and about the Fabians, and the Webbs in particular who were their most prominent leaders, obliges us to take more seriously these and other "aberrances" which, it now appears, were not momentary lapses from grace, perhaps not aberrances at all, but significant aspects of their creed.[2]

In the vast literature of Fabianism, Beatrice Webb's diaries take pride of place. A biographer, even a "psychobiographer," is in the unenviable position of having to compete with Beatrice Webb herself; one can add to her account or correct it, but one cannot reproduce the drama and passion of her diaries. When she attributed her "duplex" personality to the conflicting heritage of her parents, one may doubt that they were quite as she portrayed them. But one can have little doubt that they represented for her the source of her own tragically "divided" nature.[3]

Her father, Richard Potter, was what would now be called a "venture capitalist," a director and promoter of railway companies and other more speculative enterprises. He was not a self-made man; his own father, having made the transition from small-town draper to prosperous Manchester businessman, became a Member of Parliament after the Reform Act of 1832 and was one of the founders of the *Manchester Guardian*. But much of the family fortune was lost in the late 1840s, and Richard, trained as a barrister but well on his way to becoming a gentleman of leisure, took to business with energy, skill, and notable success. Scientific-minded, rationalistic, cultivated, sociable, enjoying the luxuries of wealth but sufficiently rooted in the Puritan ethic to indulge them only in moderation, devoted to his wife and nine daughters, he was a model Victorian paterfamilias—although not, perhaps, a typical one. Beatrice later said that he was the only man she knew (presumably she was not excepting her husband) who genuinely believed women to be superior to men. He encouraged his daughters to converse candidly and intelligently about business, politics, religion, literature, even sex. The result, Beatrice noted, was that all nine of them, at least in their younger years, were anti-feminist, feeling no need of the franchise or any other tokens of equality.[4]

If her father was preeminently a Yea-sayer, her mother was of the classic Nay-saying type. The daughter of a prosperous Liverpool merchant, the only girl in a family of boys, the darling of her widowed father (his name was Lawrence, hers Laurencina), she had intellectual and social ambitions beyond her talents. Dismayed at finding herself the wife of an active businessman and feeling superior to most of their acquaintances, including the philosopher Herbert Spencer, she became a distant and forbidding figure to her children. When her only literary effort, a novel, was poorly received, she retreated to a less challenging form of mental exercise, the study of languages, which she made more arduous by learning the grammar of one language in a primer written in another foreign language. Deeply religious but also imbued with the utilitarian faith of her father, she imposed upon the household an austere and impersonal regimen. It was unfortunate, Beatrice remarked, that a woman having so little liking for other women "was destined to have nine daughters and to lose her only son" —and daughters none of whom was, as she fancied herself, "a scholar and a gentlewoman." It was especially unfortunate for Beatrice, who was her least favorite daughter, "the only one," her mother wrote in her diary (a comment Beatrice quoted in her own autobiography), "who is below the average in intelligence."[5]

"My mother was cursed with a divided personality; she was not at peace with herself."[6] But in Beatrice's own diary it was she herself who was thus cursed, torn between the conflicting natures bequeathed her by her parents. She identified her mother with her own "nethermost being"—despondent, vain, grasping, doomed to failure, guilty of the "sin of self-consciousness," finding consolation only in a gloomy, ascetic, superstitious religion. "Left under the dominion of this personality my natural vocation and destiny was the convent; for in this life the phantom [of her mother] would have been strengthened by religious exaltation, and the nethermost being soothed and deluded with hopes of another world where merit would be regarded by its true worth." But she was also, in aspiration at least, her father's daughter, confident, unegotistical, pursuing truth and thought without regard for self—"a *realist* in intellectual questions, a rationalist in metaphysics and therefore a sceptic of religion."[7] This she believed to be the happiest and highest part of her Ego. Unfortunately it was not, for much of her early life, the dominant part. Until her marriage at the age of thirty-four, her alter ego prevailed, a creature of exacerbated sensibility, tormented by doubt and guilt, painfully self-conscious, self-critical, and self-absorbed, the victim of a "suicidal constitution."[8] The paternal side of her nature was, "alas," suppressed because it had "its life and origin in my sensual nature: it springs from vigorous senses and keen perceptions." And that "sensual nature" was doomed to be unfulfilled.

If I were a man, this creature would be free, though not dissolute, in its morals, a lover of women. These feelings would be subordinated to the intellectual and practical interests, but still the strong physical nature upon which the intellectual nature is based would be satisfied. And as I am a woman: these feelings, unless fulfilled in marriage, which would mean destruction of the intellectual being, must remain controlled and unsatisfied, finding their only vent in one quality of the phantom companion of the nethermost personality, religious exaltation.[9]

That *cri de coeur* was uttered in December 1886, after the end of the one great love affair of her life, an unconsummated but nonetheless passionate affair. Her published autobiography alludes to the "black thread of personal unhappiness" running through these years, the "slough of despond" that engulfed her as a result of her mother's death, her father's invalidism, her anxieties about her work, and the "divided" nature that made her suspect her "egotistical" motives even as she devoted herself to good works.[10] But all of this was incidental, her private diary makes clear, to the main cause of her despair, her unrequited love for Joseph Chamberlain. When Beatrice met him in 1883, he was in Gladstone's cabinet, having earlier made his reputation as the mayor of Birmingham, a vigorous proponent of "municipal socialism," a leading light of the Radical wing of the Liberal Party, and perhaps the most effective and popular speaker of the time. He was also a twice-widowed, eminently marriageable man of forty-seven, who saw in Beatrice a good-looking, intelligent, young, but not too young, woman of twenty-five who would make a suitable wife, political hostess, and mother to his six children. (His oldest daughter, Beatrice, was only a few years younger than our Beatrice.)

Chamberlain was, we would now say, a sexy politician: bold, arrogant, unabashedly ambitious—"the master and the darling of his town," Beatrice discovered when she attended a meeting he addressed in Birmingham.[11] She soon found that he was as domineering in private relations as in public, that his political passions left little room for any other kind of passion, that he required of women what he called "intelligent sympathy" but what she rightly interpreted as "servility." (He informed her that he would not tolerate a wife who "controverted" him, even in private.) She also came to see him as a manipulating, self-serving politician, who shamelessly exploited his role as "the people's tribune."[12] Knowing all this about him, she was nevertheless deeply in love with him—and in love too, she confessed, with the aura of power that emanated from him. She rejected his proposal of marriage, then reconsidered it, although he did not actually proffer it again. Neither his marriage nor hers a few years later diminished the memory of her passion or the pain of her loss. For years to come her diary continued to record the "relapses" occasioned by every thought of him, every chance encounter; and there were many such, since their circles overlapped.[13]

All of this is only vaguely alluded to in her autobiography. Appropriately entitled *My Apprenticeship,* that first volume emphasizes the public aspect of her life, her search for a "craft" and a "creed": a craft first as social worker and then as social researcher and writer; and a creed appropriate to that craft, a "Religion of Humanity" that would unite science and religion in the service of mankind. The parallel volume of her diary, by contrast, is preoccupied with her private life.

> There is glitter all around me and darkness within, the darkness of blind desire yearning for the light of love. All sympathy is shut from me. I stand alone with my own nature now too strong for me. I clutch desperately at *my duty* to those around me, that last hope for the soul despairing of its own happiness.[14]

With her marriage to Sidney Webb in 1892, Beatrice entered that period commemorated in the second volume of her autobiography as *Our Partnership,* and in the second volume of her diary, in the quotation serving as the subtitle, as *"All the Good Things of Life."* That subtitle should be taken with a touch of irony, for her life with Sidney was not without its equivocations and complications. When she agreed to marry him, after much dithering, it was almost as if she was clutching at that "duty" that was the "last hope for the soul despairing of its own happiness." She did not conceal from herself—or from him—the fact that she found him physically unattractive (she spoke of his "tiny tadpole body" and "Jewish nose") and socially déclassé. His "H's were shaky," he had no *"savoir-faire,"* he wore a "most bourgeois black coat shiny with wear," and he was so unacceptable to her father that they delayed marriage until after his death. She could quite understand her cousin's objections to this "undersized, underbred, and 'underendowed' little socialist."[15] When he sent her a photograph of himself, she told him that it was "too hideous for anything," and requested one of "your *head only*—it is the head only that I am marrying!" She made it clear to him that she did not love him, that the wound of an old love was still open, and that she was marrying him "simply because you are a Socialist and I am a Socialist." "That other man I loved but did not believe in, you I believe in but do not love."[16] In her diary she described her contemplated marriage as "an act of renunciation of self and not of indulgence of self as it would have been in the other case." In her autobiography it appeared as a "working comradeship founded in a common faith." To Sidney she spoke of it as a "partnership" and "fellowship."[17]

Sidney accepted, perhaps welcomed, marriage on those terms. Only a month before he met Beatrice, he had occasion to congratulate a friend, a member of the Fabian Society, on her engagement to another comrade, and he took the opportunity to give them some unsolicited advice. As individualists or "anarchists," they had to be wary of indulging their anarchistic impulses in those small private matters that make up four-fifths of life, lest they find it difficult to deal with the larger public matters, the other fifth of life, on properly "collectivist lines." Marriage should be a "mere partnership," with the partners acting "in and for the partnership—except in such spheres as they may severally act in and for larger Committees." He himself, in his unmarried state, was preeminently a committee man:

Now my theory of life is to feel at every moment that I am acting as a member of a committee, and for that committee—in some affairs a committee of my own family merely, in others again a committee as wide as the Aryan race. But I aspire *never* to act alone, or for myself. This theoretically combined action involves rules, deliberation, discussion, concert, the disregard of one's own impulses, and in fact is Collectivism or Communism. The contrary habit is logically Anarchism.[18]

This may be taken as the manifesto of their marriage, a long and happy one, as it turned out. One can see now why she was attracted to him, in spite of his physical and social deficiencies. He represented that other side of her nature, the paternal side, that she so much admired in her youth but could never attain. By character as much as conviction, Sidney was the complete rationalist and utilitarian. He once confessed to a friend that he had "no inside" and that he had never experienced any "physical or spiritual indigestion."[19] Beatrice enviously noted the fact that he never had a headache, never dreamed or brooded, and was totally unself-conscious. He could not even think without reading or writing, and when he happened to be without book or pen in hand, he found that idleness so intolerable that he counted the lines or spots on whatever object was before him.[20]

Beatrice could never achieve that blissfully unconscious, self-effacing state which she associated with virtue. But Sidney did help her mute her private doubts and musings, so that the second volume of her diary, covering the first dozen years or so of their marriage, shows her spending far less time "brooding"—her besetting sin, as she saw it—and far more time writing, researching, lecturing, hectoring, socializing, intriguing. She repeatedly spoke of her love for "my boy," as she called him.[21] But, as that term suggests, it was almost a maternal love, with little sexual connotation. The character modeled on her in H. G. Wells's novel *The New Machiavelli* was said to regard "sexual passion as being hardly more legitimate in a civilized person than—let us say—homicidal mania."[22] That, of course, was a parody; but she lent herself to such parodies, giving her friends to believe that she looked upon sexual passion as an irresponsible, antisocial force to be exercised, at most, within the confines of marriage. "Marriage," she was fond of saying (and Sidney fondly quoted her) "is the waste-paper-basket of the emotions."[23] Her decision not to have children was based on a simple utilitarian calculation: "I had laboriously and with many sacrifices transformed my intellect into an instrument for research. Child-bearing would destroy it, at any rate for a time, probably altogether." As a good utilitarian, she sometimes wondered whether she had been "dutiful to the community in shirking motherhood," or whether she had lost a valuable "safety valve" for herself. But on the whole she did not regret the decision.[24]

The "Webb firm," as Beatrice called it, was less a family in the conventional sense than a collectivist society in miniature.[25] She used to describe themselves as belonging to the "B's" of this world—"bourgeois, bureaucratic, and benevolent"—as opposed to the "A's"—"aristocratic, anarchist, and artistic."[26] Their personal circumstances were eminently suited to that "B" status. Without family to occupy them, without artistic, aesthetic, or private interests to distract them, without the need to earn a living (Beatrice's income of £1,000 a year supplemented by Sidney's free-lance earnings made it possible for him to resign his position in the Colonial Office), they were free to pursue their common aims, so that in their case it was at least four-fifths of their lives that were conducted on "collectivist lines." The second volume of her diary opens with a brief reference to the marriage ceremony, describes the day or two spent sight-seeing and reading Amiel's *Journals*—"by way of relieving the preoccupation of the first hours of married life"—and then has them in Dublin getting on with the real work of their honeymoon, which was research on *The History of Trade Unionism.*[27]

This book set the pattern of their intellectual partnership: two "second-rate minds," as Beatrice put it, perfectly complementary, producing together what they could not have produced apart.

She saw herself as the "investigator," Sidney as the "executor"; in fact he proved to be the more efficient researcher, she the bolder thinker.[28] And as they themselves were complementary, so were their scholarly and political pursuits. Although they prided themselves on the objectivity of their scholarship, their subjects and purposes were avowedly political. Their massive tomes on the institutions of local government were meant to provide the scientific analysis necessary for the reorganization of those institutions, just as their multi-volumed history of the Poor Law was an integral part of their campaign for the reform of that law. These works are a tribute to the intellectual resourcefulness and energy of the Webbs, and they remain a useful compendium of primary sources and historical information. But they are hardly the "scientific" history the Webbs professed to write.

"Nothing in England," Sidney wrote shortly before joining the Fabian Society, "is done without the consent of a small intellectual yet practical class in London not 2,000 in number. We alone could get at that class."[29] At that time, before he had met Beatrice, he thought of the Fabians as the vanguard of that class. After their marriage the Webbs became the vanguard of the vanguard, as it were, permeating not only that intellectual class but also the political class. Parliament would have been an obvious base of permeation for Sidney, but Beatrice early decided, and candidly told him, that he had not the qualities of a "really big man," and that his talents as a committee man and "wire-puller" better qualified him for the London County Council.[30] He remained in the LCC for almost twenty years, with Beatrice resisting any suggestion that he stand for Parliament; when he did become a Member of Parliament in 1922, he proved more effective in committee than on the floor of the House.

Their real influence was exercised indirectly, through their work in Royal Commissions and their strenuous efforts to "educate" party leaders and government officials. In the early years they worked harder at permeating the Conservative Party than the Liberal, partly because the former was in power and they miscalculated the length of time it would remain in power, and partly because it was ideologically congenial, being less individualistic and more imperialistic than the Liberal Party. (They did, however, cultivate the small group of Liberal Imperialists, the "Limps," as they were called.) And they kept their distance from the newly formed Independent Labour Party, which tried to organize the working class rather than, as they preferred, to convert the ruling class.

"I could insinuate myself," Beatrice boasted, "into smoking-rooms, business offices, private and public conferences, without rousing suspicion."[31] In fact, her tactics were so obvious that "permeation" became a euphemism for manipulation, machination, and downright deception—hence the title of Wells's novel *The New Machiavelli.* She was occasionally troubled by the distrust they aroused and by her own enjoyment of political intrigue as if it were a "sport," but she consoled herself with the thought that this was the only way anything could get done. "There is no such thing as spontaneous public opinion; it all has to be manufactured from a Centre of Conviction and Energy radiating through persons."[32]

She was more successful in "insinuating" herself at dinner parties, although even here she overestimated her deftness. Bertrand Russell, himself not unduly diffident, was so impressed by her self-confidence that he once asked her whether she had ever felt shy. "Oh no," she assured him. "If I ever felt inclined to be timid as I was going into a room full of people, I would say to myself, 'You're the cleverest member of one of the cleverest families in the cleverest class of the cleverest nation in the world, why should you be frightened?' "[33] She was, perhaps, too clever by half. One wonders whether Prime Minister Arthur Balfour, who was also a distinguished philosopher and an eminently urbane and cultivated man, was as amused and interested as she thought him to be when, seated next to him at a dinner party, she "seized every opportunity to insinuate sound doctrine and information as to the position of London education."[34] Her own dinner parties were so contrived, the guests so obviously invited for a purpose, the conversation so deliberately directed, that Wells described her dining room as a "chamber of representatives." Others were reminded, on entering her parlor, of the parable of the spider and the fly.[35]

These dinner parties were also notable for their austerity. Beatrice was pleased to think that the setting she provided for Sidney, of "simple fare and distinguished friends," was suitable both to his reputation and to his taste, that it adhered to a "democratic standard of expenditure" while bringing him within the "inner circle" of the political and scientific world.[36] It is not clear that Sidney himself was quite so appreciative; friends noticed that he helped himself to more food when she was otherwise occupied. Nor were their guests pleased to be spared a surfeit of food and drink. Not a few complained of the meager fare and the haste with which the table was cleared so that serious conversation could resume. (Habitués, knowing of Beatrice's displeasure when guests absented themselves to go to the lavatory, exchanged ideas on how best to cope with their needs.)[37]

In *The New Machiavelli,* the Baileys, Wells's fictional Webbs, had the initials "P.B.P." engraved inside their wedding rings— *Pro Bono Publico.*[38] The real Webbs might well have done the same. Like the Baileys, the Webbs were confident that they were the custodians of the public good because they were only seeking for the public what they knew to be good for themselves. Thus the regimen Beatrice imposed upon her dinner guests was a very mild version of that which she imposed upon herself. Before her marriage her diary has her wrestling with her soul, the "sin of self-consciousness"; afterward it shows her in mortal combat with her body, obsessively trying to curb her appetites. She found it easy to abstain from alcohol and meat, far more difficult to give up coffee and cigarettes. By eliminating breakfast and literally weighing every bite she took, she succeeded in reducing her intake to no more than six ounces a day.

She started the diet to cure her indigestion, but she soon became convinced that overeating caused most diseases, including pneumonia and cancer, and, more important, that it was psychologically and intellectually debilitating. "Until I took to the rigid diet, the sensual side of my nature seemed to be growing at the expense of the intellectual." She felt herself becoming emotional and sentimental, yearning for music, and otherwise lapsing into a "subjective state." The diet was meant to subdue these unwholesome impulses so as to attain "the lowest level in abstemiousness and the highest in efficiency."[39] It was a new utilitarian version of that ancient adage *Mens sana in corpore sano.* It was also a way of exercising the spiritual virtues and exorcising the demons of corporeality. "Physical appetites are to me the devil: they are signs of the disease that ends in death, the root of the hatred, malice and greed that make the life of man a futility."[40] Again and again her diaries read like the confessions of a religious penitent. Refusing breakfast after an overnight visit with a friend, she described herself, only half in jest, as leaving in "an odour of 'personal abstemiousness' akin to an odour of sanctity!" On another occasion she confided: "Abstinence and prayer may prove to be the narrow way to salvation in this world—at least for such as me."[41]

"For such as me"—and, in varying degrees, for everyone who sought salvation, and for whom she sought salvation. *"Renunciation,"* she had written many years earlier, "that is the great fact we all, individuals and classes, have to learn."[42] At that time it was Comte's "Religion of Humanity" that demanded renunciation, asceticism being a corollary of altruism. Now it was Fabianism that required the same self-sacrifice. The genre of ascetic socialism is familiar enough, quite as familiar as that of hedonistic socialism; the classic exemplars of the two types are Comtism and St. Simonianism. What makes the ascetic Fabian a more curious phenomenon is the contrast it offers to the conventional image of the Fabian: the realistic, pragmatic reformer seeking no radical transformation of mankind, not even a radical transformation of society, but only a series of gradual, moderate, melioratory changes. Beatrice's diary belies that image, at least as it applies to the Webbs and such other leading Fabians as George Bernard Shaw. Their socialism was evidently closer to Comtism, and thus to utopianism, than one might suspect.

Beatrice distrusted "the average sensual man"—a phrase that appears repeatedly in her diary and autobiography—as much as she distrusted her own "sensual" nature.[43] When after the Boer War a campaign for "National Efficiency" was launched to improve the health and efficiency of the people and thus make them a more powerful "imperial race," she insisted that the control of consumption was far more important than an increase of production or a greater equality of distribution—certainly too important to be left to "the appetites of each individual." It would not be long, she was pleased to think, before "a whole system of sumptuary laws, at any rate as regards non-adults, will come into force." And "non-adults" was to be interpreted loosely; she liked Wells's "brilliant suggestion" that the world be divided into adults and non-adults, with the "age of consent" raised to fifty or so.[44]

A more "audacious" subject, she recognized, was the new study of eugenics, the control of "human breeding." At first she felt that it was not a subject the Webbs could raise, because it was "not ripe for the mere industry of induction." She was delighted, however, when Shaw, in *Man and Superman,* dealt with this "most important of all questions, this breeding of the right sort of man."[45] And it was not long before she decided that it was, after all, ripe for the Webbs, that it was time to make people aware of the urgency of the problem and of the need for a policy that would bring about the "compulsory raising of the standard of health and conduct."[46] "Health and conduct"—this was not the way most eugenicists saw the issue. But it was characteristic of the Webbs, who believed a Republic of Virtue to be the necessary precondition for a Republic of Efficiency.

Another feature of their ideal republic was the dominance of the "expert" over the common man. Beatrice conceded that in this respect she and Sidney were not very good democrats, "for we have little faith in the 'average sensual man,' we do not believe that he can do much more than describe his grievances, we do not think that he can prescribe the remedies."[47] Nor did they have much more faith in the average Member of Parliament, who, like his constituents, might understand the problems that came his way but was unable to prescribe the solutions. The Webbs sought not only to permeate the institutions of power but also to alter those institutions, "to introduce into politics the professional expert—to extend the sphere of government by adding to its enormous advantages of wholesale and compulsory management, the advantage of the most skilled entrepreneur."[48]

The "science" of society and the "religion" of humanity: this was the duality that corresponded to Beatrice's "duplex personality." In the introduction to *My Apprenticeship,* she described the persistent controversy in her life between "an Ego that affirms and an Ego that denies." The affirmative Ego believed that there was a "science of society" which could determine the proper organization of society. The negative Ego believed that science could determine the means, the processes, by which society was organized to achieve a particular end, but that the end itself, the purpose, belonged to another domain, that of religion, emotion, and faith.[49]

Beatrice Webb as *religieuse*—it is impossible to make too much of this aspect of her life. Although she was unhappy with some tenets of the official doctrine, she was a believing and practicing Anglican, regularly praying at home and less regularly, but often enough, attending services and taking communion at St. Paul's. And religion was as much a part of her public creed as of her private. She had no sympathy with demands for the disestablishment of the Church; on the contrary, she (and Sidney, she insisted) wanted to see a rejuvenated and strengthened Church, less "superstitious" but no less "sacerdotal and ritualistic."[50] When she defended the Education Act of 1902, which provided public funds for Anglican schools and was hotly criticized on that account, she did so not only for the pragmatic reason that some act was better than none, but because she approved in principle of religious education. The secularist alternative, she argued, would have the unfortunate effect of establishing "pure materialism as the national metaphysic." And the "lie of materialism" was "far more pernicious and more utterly false" than whatever "untruths" might be found in Christianity.[51] "I do not believe that the ordinary man is capable of prescribing for the diseases of the soul any more than they are for the diseases of the body. We need the expert here as elsewhere. Religion, to my mind, should consist in the highest metaphysic, music and ritual and mental hygiene."[52]

Religion and science made for a formidable conflict in Beatrice's early years, and for a formidable—lethal, one might say—combination in her later years. In 1926, she was still agonizing over the problem: "I am perpetually brooding over my inability to make clear even to myself, let alone to others, why I believe in religious mysticism, why I hanker after a Church—with its communion of the faithful, with its religious rites, and its religious discipline, and above all with its definite code of conduct."[53] Five years later she discovered the solution to that problem in the Soviet Union.

In the Soviet Union, she found, science and religion were perfectly complementary. The Soviets had a scientific economy of "planned production for community consumption"; they had a scientific government with "administrators" in the Kremlin whose "professed faith" is science;[54] and they had a scientific constitution which was remarkably similar, Beatrice claimed, to the *Constitution for the Socialist Commonwealth of Great Britain* that the Webbs had devised a few years earlier.* But whereas their

---

*That *Constitution* is a more remarkable and revolutionary document than is commonly supposed. It provided for the nationalization of industry, the elimination of privately owned newspapers and journals, the centralized direc-

own constitution, she now realized, was a "paper-constitution" without "soul," the Soviets had given theirs soul in the shape of the Communist Party, which was a "religious order" complete with "strict disciplines" and "vows of obedience and poverty."[56]

Just before visiting the Soviet Union in 1932, she anticipated what she would find there: "It is the invention of the religious order, as the determining factor of a great nation, that is the magnet which attracts me to Russia. Practically, that religion is Comtism—the religion of Humanity."[57] And like Comtism it was an ascetic religion. When she returned from that visit, she was pleased to report that unlike the "average sensual man" of the West, who judged success by such material standards as housing, food, and motorcars, the Soviet people measured success in terms of "moral uplift," "intellectual advancement," and the "reformation of manners and morals." From personal observation she could testify that there was "no spooning in the Parks of Recreation and Rest" and that Soviet officials were model "Puritans." She quoted approvingly Stalin's warning to an errant commissar: "I do not want to inquire into your private affairs, but if there is any more nonsense about women, you go to a place where there are no women."[58]

The Webbs' passion for the Soviet Union remained undiminished by purges, trials, the Nazi-Soviet pact, and the other disagreeable revelations of the thirties and forties. (Beatrice died in 1943, Sidney in 1947, by which time there were all too many such revelations.) And that passion, there is now good reason to think, was not the "aberrance" some would make of it. One could not deduce, from Beatrice's early diaries, that the resolution of the conflict of Egos would take just this form: she might have been

---

tion and allocation of labor, the discouragement of permanent political parties, the abolition of the House of Lords, and the establishment of two independent and co-equal parliaments. A Political Parliament was to preside over foreign affairs, justice, and other matters involving "power over persons"; and a Social Parliament was to control all economic and social activities—the "administration of things," as they (following Saint-Simon) put it.[55] This was no mere "reform."

satisfied to live out her life with the conflict unresolved; or she might have submitted to the dominion of one or the other Ego. (One can imagine her, as she saw herself in 1886, finding her "natural vocation and destiny" in a convent.)[59] But the diaries do suggest that there was nothing anomalous in the path she did choose. Communism exerted the powerful appeal it did in large part because it was in accord with long-held ideas and beliefs, ideas and beliefs which had originally drawn her to Fabianism and which permitted her to end her life as both a Fabian in good standing and an ardent admirer of Stalinism.

Not all Fabians took that route; Fabianism was neither a doctrinaire ideology nor a monolithic movement. But a good many Fabians did. For them, as for George Bernard Shaw, the Soviet Union represented a form of "applied Fabianism." And many of them, including the Webbs, could well have said, as Shaw did: "Stalin is a good Fabian, and that's the best that can be said about anyone."[60]

11

Michael Oakeshott: The Conservative Disposition

In the title of his first volume of essays, published in 1950, Lionel Trilling perfectly captured the spirit of the time. *The Liberal Imagination*—not "The Liberal Philosophy," or "The Liberal Creed," or "The Liberal Doctrine"—implied a mode of thought that was more cultural than political (although it did have political consequences), that depended more upon sentiments and attitudes than upon ideas (although it did have intellectual implications), and that was unquestionably the dominant force in American life. So dominant was it that Trilling could find no "conservative imagination" to set beside it, nothing but occasional, erratic, conservative impulses, "irritable gestures which seek to resemble ideas."[1]

Trilling was right about America circa 1950. But in England at that time there was one thinker who enjoyed a somewhat subterranean reputation and who perfectly exemplified the "conservative imagination." Michael Oakeshott preferred the term "conservative disposition," but he used it in the sense of "imagination," to convey a temper of mind rather than a set of ideas, a spirit and attitude rather than a philosophy or political creed.[2] Although Oakeshott was the author of a major philosophical work, his reputation derived rather from his occasional essays and his personal influence upon generations of students—which may be fitting for one who valued "disposition" and "conversation" more than system and organization.

From any conventional point of view, Oakeshott's career seems to have been full of anomalies. For over two decades he was a lecturer in history at Cambridge University. But while he reviewed historical books and wrote a provocative essay on the "activity" of being a historian, he never wrote a work of history, not even a historical essay.[3] When he was appointed to a chair at the London School of Economics in 1951, it was neither the chair of history nor of philosophy but of political science. In his inaugural lecture, he paid tribute to the previous occupants of that chair, Graham Wallas and Harold Laski. He did not have to dwell on the obvious irony of the situation: that a self-avowed conservative should be taking the place of two notable socialists in an institution generally regarded as the citadel of socialism. He did delicately allude to the fact that while his two predecessors were great teachers, firmly confident of the truth of their teachings, he was as thoroughgoing a skeptic. But he did not follow through on the paradox that a skeptic about political "science" should hold the professorship of political science.

One might be inclined to give him the title of political philosopher instead of political scientist, were it not that he is equally skeptical of the usual claims of political philosophy, skeptical, indeed, of the possibility of any legitimate relationship between philosophy and politics. The philosopher, he insists, has no practical lessons for the politician or the student of politics—except, perhaps, the lesson that politics is and should be totally independent of philosophy. "Political philosophy," he said—again ironically, in his inaugural lecture, addressing the most highly politicized university in the country—"cannot be expected to increase our ability to be successful in political activity. It will not help us to distinguish between good and bad political projects; it has no power to guide or to direct us in the enterprise of pursuing the intimations of our tradition."⁴

Abjuring both political science and political philosophy as these are normally understood, Oakeshott nevertheless has acquired a distinguished body of admirers, and not only in the academy but among journalists, writers, and men of affairs. In this respect, to be sure, he cannot compete with Harold Laski, who had an enormous influence over an entire generation at home and abroad. Oakeshott's appeal is to a much more limited circle. But he is unquestionably the best known and most respected intellectual spokesman for British conservatism.

He has achieved this eminence, moreover, with what might seem to be a modest body of work. Unlike Laski, who wrote voluminously and encyclopedically, Oakeshott's oeuvre is relatively slight. *Experience and Its Modes,* published in 1933, a systematic, comprehensive philosophical treatise, was a remarkable accomplishment for a man of thirty-one, presaging an illustrious and productive career. No less remarkable is the fact that for over forty years, until the publication of *On Human Conduct* in 1975, he wrote nothing else remotely like it. During the thirties he published an essay a year and an undistinguished volume of selections, apparently intended as a textbook, *The Social and Political Doctrines of Contemporary Europe.* He was somewhat more prolific after the war (he spent the war years in the army), editing an edition of Hobbes's *Leviathan* with a substantial introduction, and averaging an essay or two a year for the following decade and a half. It was not until the reprinting of ten of these essays in 1962, in *Rationalism in Politics,* that he finally attracted the attention of a larger public. The republication since then of his earlier books attests to the high regard in which he has come to be held. (It was typical of him that he had these books reprinted in their original form, generally without so much as a new introduction or preface.) His later works—*On Human Conduct* in 1975 and a small volume of essays, *On History,* in 1983

—were respectfully received but did not generate the excitement of *Rationalism in Politics.* In any case his reputation by then was as firmly established as his mode of thought.*

These apparent anomalies—the political philosopher who has so limited a view of the task of political philosophy, the intellectual who is so reluctant a producer of intellectual goods, the master who does so little to acquire or cultivate disciples—these are, of course, no anomalies at all. They are perfectly in character, entirely consistent with the conservative disposition as Oakeshott himself understands it. In the case of anyone else, it might be thought odd that a political philosopher should have written so little about the classics of political thought (with the notable exception of Hobbes). As if in mockery of the traditional function of political philosophy, he entitled one book co-authored by him *A Guide to the Classics;* but the kind of classics he had in mind was revealed in the subtitle, "How to Pick the Derby Winner."†
If the title was facetious, the contents were serious enough—or at least as serious, in Oakeshott's scheme of values, as any other subject occupying a civilized man. His admirers take delight in his being a racing man, in his having owned a racing horse (at least so it has been rumored), and in other evidence of his disdain for academic solemnities and proprieties. They take this as existential confirmation, so to speak, of his philosophy, his conviction that all activities, politics as much as racing, are to be understood

---

*His reputation, that is, among the cognoscenti. The first printing of *Experience and Its Modes* was 1,000 copies, and was sold out only after thirty-one years. A second edition of 1,000 copies in 1966 went out of print after three years and was reissued in 1978. Even *Rationalism in Politics* had a modest sale, with a first printing of 5,000 copies; a small paperback edition appeared in 1967, and a library edition of 1,000 copies in 1974.[5]

†It somehow seems appropriate that his co-author, Guy Griffith, should have been a Byzantine scholar. It is also fitting that this was the only book he revised when it was reissued in 1957. Even the title was changed, to the dismay of the aficionados who enjoyed the pun. *A New Guide to the Derby* may have sold more books, but it lacked the zest of *A Guide to the Classics.*

in their own terms and enjoyed for their own sakes rather than subsumed under rationalist categories and made to serve utilitarian ends.

For Oakeshott, Rationalism is the great heresy of modern times. (He generally capitalizes "Rationalism" and lower-cases "conservatism," which is itself a commentary on his use of those terms.) The Rationalist, taking "reason" as his only authority, is necessarily hostile to any other authority: tradition, habit, custom, prejudice, common sense. It is the nature of the Rationalist to be at the same time skeptical and optimistic: skeptical because "there is no opinion, no habit, no belief, nothing so firmly rooted or so widely held that he hesitates to question it and to judge it by what he calls his 'reason' "; optimistic because he "never doubts the power of his 'reason' (when properly applied) to determine the worth of a thing, the truth of an opinion or the propriety of an action." The Rationalist has no respect for the seemingly irrational vestiges of the past, and little patience with the transitory arrangements of the present. He has only an overwhelming yearning for a future in which all will be made orderly, reasonable, of maximum utility and efficiency. And he would like this future to be realized as soon as possible. His is the politics of "destruction and creation" rather than of "acceptance or reform."[6] He wants no patch-up jobs, no tinkering with this or that, still less the kinds of changes that come about without the direct, conscious, rational intervention of men. He sees life (social and political affairs as well as the life of the individual) as a series of problems to be solved, of felt needs which have to be instantly satisfied. And they can be solved and satisfied only by a set of rationally devised techniques that are of immediate, universal, and certain application.

Although Oakeshott puts the Rationalist's "reason" in quotes, as if it were a special, spurious kind of reason, he does not elucidate any other kind of reason to which the non-Rationalist can lay claim. But he does so implicitly in identifying the Rationalist's "reason" with technical knowledge, in contrast to practical knowledge. "The sovereignty of 'reason,' for the Rationalist, means the sovereignty of technique." The Rationalist does not credit the kind of practical knowledge which "can neither be taught nor learned, but only imparted and acquired,"[7] which cannot be laid down in rules and precepts because it involves a sensitivity, artistry, and intelligence that come only from long exposure to traditions and habits that have proved themselves in practice.

Oakeshott is often accused of being "elitist." But there is nothing precious or recondite in his notion of practical knowledge. His metaphors and analogies are thoroughly commonplace. They come from cooking, racing, gambling, carpentry, sports, love—activities common to all people, although not all people excel in all of them. He concedes that there is some degree of technical knowledge involved in these activities; this is why there can be manuals of cooking, gambling, even lovemaking. But to think that such manuals are any substitute for practical knowledge is the modern fallacy. The author of one such manual, he recalls—he coyly refrains from identifying himself—had gone to some pains to point out that there were no precise rules for picking a Derby winner, no shortcuts for the firsthand familiarity with horses which was once more common than it is today and which made for a kind of intelligence that no amount of rules could supply. Yet some readers of the manual—"greedy, rationalistic readers, on the look-out for an infallible method"— thought they had been "sold a pup" because the book did not bring them up to the level of men of genuine knowledge who had long and intimate experience of racing and betting.[8]

Oakeshott rarely speaks of liberals or liberalism, probably because he himself has too high a regard for liberty to apply those honorific labels to his antagonists. But it is obvious that in describing rationalism, and in characterizing it as the prevalent mode of thought in our time, he has in mind what would normally be called liberalism. Moreover, he has no hesitation in speaking of himself as a conservative and in praising the virtues of the conservative disposition. The most explicit statement of this disposition is the essay "On Being Conservative," written in 1956, a counterpart to "Rationalism in Politics" written almost a decade before. After his uncompromising indictment of the Rationalist mentality, he may have felt it necessary to provide a positive statement of an alternative mode of thought and behavior. Yet even without this essay, the alternative is abundantly clear in everything he has written. And that alternative is always in the form of a disposition rather than a creed—a distinction Oakeshott properly insists upon and that many of his critics perversely choose to ignore. He does not defend philosophical doctrines or even take political positions in the usual fashion. Instead he defines the conservative in terms of attitudes and habits of mind and conduct which pervade all aspects of life. That disposition is exhibited in personal more than public affairs, in the intimate, daily activities of life more than in the large political decisions. It has, to be sure, political implications, and Oakeshott does not hesitate to spell these out. But it is precisely his point that politics is only a small part of life and not the most important part, that it is only the Rationalist, wanting to effect large social changes, who inflates politics and thus deflates man's humanity.

The key word describing the conservative disposition is "enjoyment." Where the Rationalist, pursuing reason, is always lusting after something that is not, the conservative prefers to enjoy whatever is. He enjoys family and friends, as he also enjoys his liberties; he is loyal to them as they are, and is not discontented because they are no better than they are. The popular conception of the conservative is of a person who idolizes the past. For Oakeshott, the conservative is one who esteems the present and therefore values whatever the past has bequeathed to the present. He esteems the present not because it is more admirable than any conceivable alternative but because it is familiar and for that reason enjoyable. And enjoying the present, he realizes how much he would lose if it were gone. Oakeshott admits that if the present were arid, if there were little or nothing in it to enjoy, the conservative disposition would be inappropriate. But the present is rarely, he finds, intolerable, except to those who are ignorant of the resources of their world and of the opportunities for enjoyment, or to those who are so captivated by the Rationalist impulse, the desire to make the world conform to their ideal, that they see the present only as a "residue of inopportunities."[9] If the old are more apt to be conservative than the young, it is not, as the young are inclined to think, because the old are more fearful of what they might lose by change, but because time and maturity have taught them the value of what they have.

Nor is the conservative, as Oakeshott describes him, averse to change as such. He recognizes both the need and the inevitability of change. The question is how to accommodate change. The conservative proposes to do so by small doses rather than large, out of necessity rather than ideology, gradually, slowly, incrementally, naturally, with a minimum disruption of life. Where the Rationalist thinks innovation to be a good thing in itself, the conservative regards it as a deprivation, a loss of something familiar, regrettable even when necessary. To him all innovations are inherently equivocal, a compound of gain and loss—and not only because of their unanticipated consequences but also because of their predictable effects, the fact that a change in any part of life inevitably brings with it a change in the whole texture of life. Thus the true conservative resists unnecessary changes and suffers necessary ones.

> The disposition to be conservative is, then, warm and positive in respect of enjoyment, and correspondingly cool and critical in respect of change and innovation: these two inclinations support and elucidate one another. The man of conservative temperament believes that a known good is not lightly to be surrendered for an unknown better. He is not in love with what is dangerous and difficult; he is unadventurous; he has no impulse to sail uncharted seas; for him there is no magic in being lost, bewildered or

shipwrecked. If he is forced to navigate the unknown, he sees virtue in heaving the lead every inch of the way. What others plausibly identify as timidity, he recognizes in himself as rational prudence; what others interpret as inactivity, he recognizes as a disposition to enjoy rather than to exploit. He is cautious, and he is disposed to indicate his assent or dissent, not in absolute, but in graduated terms. He eyes the situation in terms of its propensity to disrupt the familiarity of the features of his world.[10]

It is typical of Oakeshott that he should introduce the subject of politics only midway in his essay "On Being Conservative." But this is entirely fitting in his own scheme of things. The conservative disposition is an attitude toward life rather than a particular mode of politics, and politics itself is defined and limited by that disposition. Like everything else in life, politics is a matter of experience and habituation. "Political education" is not an indoctrination or even elucidation of political principles, but rather the elucidation of the traditional practices and activities characterizing a nation's actual political life. Similarly, government is an activity rather than a system, and a narrowly conceived activity at that: "the provision and custody of general rules of conduct, which are understood, not as plans for imposing substantive activities, but as instruments enabling people to pursue the activities of their own choice with the minimum frustration."[11]

The purpose of government is not to bring order out of the disorder that is the essential condition of society—society consisting of a multitude of people engaged in a great variety of activities, acting out of a multiplicity of motives, interests, passions, reasons. Government is not intended to direct these activities to a more coherent, rational end, or to instruct or edify the people, or to make them happier or better. The function of government is nothing more nor less than the function of ruling, in the sense in which an umpire may be said to rule, by administering the agreed-upon rules of the game without himself playing in the game; or in which a chairman presiding over a debate rules, by seeing to it that the disputants observe the rules of order without himself participating in the debate.

This idea of government commends itself to Oakeshott not because it derives from some philosophical or political principle —the principle, for example, that freedom of choice is an absolute value, or that truth and goodness emerge only from the complete and unfettered diversity of activity and opinion. (Oakeshott does not mention Mill by name, but it is quite clear that he is dissociating himself from the argument of *On Liberty*.) The conservative assigns a minimal role to government simply because he accepts the "current condition of human circumstances."[12] He accepts the fact that most people are inclined to make their own choices and find their happiness in doing so, that they pursue a variety of enterprises and hold to a variety of beliefs, and that life reveals no large design but only an incessant, changeful, multitudinous activity. The function of government is simply to make and enforce those rules of conduct that are themselves part of these facts of life. With such rules (as distinct from the Rationalist's contrived rules), the conservative is comfortable, both because they are familiar and because they leave him free to do what he wants to do. These are the rules "it is appropriate to be conservative about."[13]

If this modest conception of government—government as umpire or chairman—distinguishes Oakeshott from most modern liberals, it also distinguishes him, and quite as sharply, from many conservatives. Oakeshott is well aware of alternative modes of conservatism, but reading the modern situation as he does, he pays less attention to them than to the Rationalists of the liberal variety. He makes short shrift of those conservatives who rely not upon a disposition but upon a principle or creed: the idea of God, or original sin, or natural law, or organic society, or the absolute value of the human personality. To Oakeshott, these or any other principles intended to legitimize the social order are "highfalutin

metaphysical beliefs."[14] They are not only unnecessary; they are
potentially dangerous since, like any other Rationalist ideal, they
tempt government to do more than it should do, "to turn a
private dream into a public and compulsory manner of living."[15]
Oakeshott's warning applies as much to the conservative Rationalist as to the liberal Rationalist: "The conjunction of dreaming
and ruling generates tyranny."[16]

That Oakeshott is as far removed from these rationalistic
conservatives as he is from the most rationalistic liberals is evident
in his attitude toward religion. One might expect him to be
personally skeptical about the existence of God, of a providential
social order, or of a divinely ordained morality; and at the same
time sensible of the power of these beliefs, their deep roots in the
habits, institutions, and activities of ordinary life. Other thinkers
have managed to combine private disbelief with a sensitive regard
for the public dimensions of belief—and not as a Machiavellian
strategy for social control but out of a proper deference to the
opinions and behavior that have long characterized civilized life.
Oakeshott especially, one might think, would be respectful of
religious sensibilities and would take a disrespect for those sensibilities as the mark of the Rationalist mentality. The last sentence of his essay, "On Being Conservative," sums up the conservative disposition in the expression "coming to be at home in
this commonplace world."[17] One might read this as an invitation
to be at home in the religious beliefs, rituals, and establishments
which, however attenuated, are still part of this commonplace
world—not, perhaps, as important a part as the horseracing,
betting, cooking, fishing, and other homely activities that he
dwells on so lovingly, but still, for many people in many places,
a not insignificant part of their world.

Yet in that essay, when Oakeshott briefly alludes to religion,
he does so begrudgingly. He tolerates religious institutions not
as a means of giving expression and actuality to religious faith
but rather as a means of restraining that faith: "They [conserva-
tives] might even be prepared to suffer a legally established

ecclesiastical order; but it would not be because they believed it to represent some unassailable religious truth, but merely because it restrained the indecent competition of sects and (as Hume said) moderated 'the plague of a too diligent clergy.' " And when he mentions specific religious beliefs—God, divine law, a providential order—it is only to dismiss them together with all other "highfalutin metaphysical beliefs."[18] In effect, religion is made to share the odium that attaches to any presumption of truth. And it is to mitigate religious belief, as much as any other kind of excess, that he calls for a "mood of indifference" which will permit society to tolerate, among other things, "what is abominable."[19] Such a mood, he explains, is not suited to the young; it can be sustained only by the mature—and, he might have added, by those of little faith, or, better yet, of no faith.

Experience and Its Modes has a very brief discussion of religion —four pages in a 350-page work, which suggests the relative weight Oakeshott gives it in the totality of human experience. At one point he credits religion with being "practical experience at its fullest." But he goes on to say that religion, unlike other forms of practical experience, is "characterized everywhere by intensity and strength of devotion and by singleness of purpose."[20] Several pages later, distinguishing between "practical truth" which is conducive to freedom, and "errors of practice" which "enslave, which mislead our conduct and endanger our lives," he makes it clear that religion belongs to the latter category. A footnote quotes Hume: "Generally speaking, the errors of religion are dangerous; those of philosophy only ridiculous."[21]

One can understand Hume's fear of the dangers of religion. He was close enough to the Puritan experience, and a witness in his own day to the Methodist revival (*A Treatise on Human Nature* was published the very year of that revival), to feel a lively sense of the practical, even political, power of religion, of the passion it might evoke and its divisive social and political effects. But Oakeshott, priding himself on his practical common sense, can hardly share that fear—not, at any rate, for the England of his own time. One would like to credit him with foreseeing the religious passions that were to be unleashed in other parts of the world. But he never intended to legislate, or even philosophize, for the whole world. It is only in his world, his kind of civilization, that the conservative disposition is appropriate.

More recently, in *On Human Conduct,* Oakeshott has exhibited a greater tolerance, even sympathy, for religion. It is now seen as providing the kind of faith that reconciles us to the "unavoidable dissonances" of the human condition. And not only the familiar contingencies of life—the infirmities and miseries, disasters and frustrations, culminating in death itself—but the inevitable wrongs that we ourselves perpetrate. By substituting the sense of sin for that of guilt, religion deprives wrongdoing of its fatality without diminishing its enormity; it creates "a refuge from the destroying *Angst* of guilt." And it reconciles us to a still greater "dissonance" of the human condition: the haunting sense of hollowness and futility, of nothingness. Each religion reflects, in its own "idiom of faith" and in the "poetic quality" of its images, rites, and observances, the "civilization of the believer." And each invites us, in its own way, to live "so far as is possible, as an immortal."[22]

It is a sensitive and moving account of religious faith that Oakeshott has now given us, and one in keeping with the conservative "disposition" that he has described elsewhere. But again, the account is all too brief, six pages in all, and introduced almost as an afterthought: "To this consideration of moral conduct I will add a brief recognition of religious belief: not to do so, however inadequately, would be to leave this account of human conduct inexcusably incomplete."[23] As an account of "human conduct," it is still, inexplicably if not inexcusably, incomplete, for it dwells almost entirely on religious "faith" in the existential sense—the religious impulse, or sensibility, or simple feeling of religiosity —rather than the creeds and practices that constitute religious "conduct." Still less is there any recognition of the institutions which form and sanction that conduct, which make of religion a communal and historical reality instead of merely a personal, private, emotive one.*

In morality, as in religion, Oakeshott is chary of anything that might suggest a conscious, deliberate system of principles and practices—of anything reminiscent of Rationalism. Just as the polity, he believed, is ill advised to pursue conscious social ideals, so the individual is ill advised to pursue conscious moral ideals, the Rationalist fallacy lying in both the consciousness and the pursuit of those ideals. And just as the polity does not depend on any idea of divine or natural law, so morality does not depend on moral sense, intuition, conscience, or the "habit of reflective *thought.*" All it does depend on is the "habit of *affection* and *conduct.*" "We acquire habits of conduct, not by constructing a way of living upon rules or precepts learned by heart and subsequently practised, but by living with people who habitually behave in a certain manner: we acquire habits of conduct in the same way as we acquire our native language."[25]

The parallel between morality and politics falters at one point. In politics a reliance on habit, as Oakeshott understands it, tends to limit the role of government and give greater latitude to the individual. In morality a reliance on habit is apt to enhance the role of society (although not of government) and to restrict that of the individual. Moral habituation is a training in social conformity. To the extent to which it succeeds, it would seem to belie the variety and individuality Oakeshott attributes to conservatism. Oakeshott denies that this is a necessary consequence of his position. The "moral eccentric," he insists, is in no way

*Oakeshott's first publication, in 1927, was a ten-page pamphlet originally given as a talk, "Religion and the Moral Life." After reviewing and disputing the commonly held views of the relationship of religion and morality, he concluded that there was at least a historical relationship between "our moral life today" and "what we understand the Christian view of life to be." He never reprinted this pamphlet. Nor did he choose to reprint his only other essay on religion, written the following year: "The Importance of the Historical Element in Christianity."[24]

excluded from the framework of the "moral life." On the contrary, the impulse to dissent derives from the moral tradition itself: "There is a freedom and inventiveness at the heart of every traditional way of life, and deviation may be an expression of that freedom, springing from a sensitiveness to the tradition itself and remaining faithful to the traditional form."[26] The deviant, even while he is protected in his deviancy, does not constitute a threat to the moral life, any more than a change in moral habits is a threat. Since the moral life is not conceived of as a system, since it does not depend upon any set of rational principles, the abandonment of any part of it does not entail a collapse of the whole. The moral life goes on, with all its deviations, anomalies, irrationalities.

Oakeshott's image of the moral life is attractive and even persuasive—until one considers the experience of recent decades (and of many earlier periods of history, but the latest period will do in illustration). When *Rationalism in Politics* was first published in 1962, some critics said that it reflected the temper of the fifties but was inappropriate to the sixties. The critique of Rationalism—so this argument went—was congenial to those who had been disenchanted by the postwar Labour government, with its blundering attempts at social engineering, its irritating paternalism, its mean-spirited austerity. But to the generation of the sixties, imbued with the spirit of reform and seeking to rectify social inequities, Oakeshott sounded negative and querulous, committed to an outmoded and unjust *status quo,* hopelessly out of tune with the new social sensibility.

There is something in this identification of Oakeshott with the fifties and his dissociation from the sixties, but it is not quite what his critics were then saying. It was not the advent of a new social consciousness that made Oakeshott seem irrelevant; on the contrary, that turn of affairs made his admonitions all the more timely and urgent. What gave even a sympathetic reader pause, however, was the experience of the late sixties when it became apparent that something like a moral revolution was taking place, that moral deviancy was being popularized and democratized, so that it was not the occasional eccentric who was rejecting the traditional values, morals, and habits of thought and behavior, but an entire generation.

Where, one might ask Oakeshott, were those traditional habits of mind and conduct that should have prevented the excesses of the decade—and not only the sporadic excesses of violence but the more pervasive and conscious disrespect for law, authority, tradition, and the very "rules of conduct" that supposedly sustain society as well as government? Where, in this age of "alienation," was the disposition to prefer the familiar, to enjoy the present for what it is, to accept the facts of life and make the best of them? And where, once this revolution had taken place, once the old habits were no longer habits, could one look for guidance? For the new generation, what is the source of that "civility" and "rule of law" which permit people to live peacefully together without formal constitutions, fixed rules, or rational precepts?

The logic of Oakeshott's position might suggest that the conservative should acquiesce in the new modes of mind and conduct, adapt to the present realities whatever they might be, on the assumption that they now constitute the prevailing form of "practical knowledge." But what if these new modes are essentially anarchical, if they so illegitimize social authority that they constitute, in effect, a "permanent revolution"? What basis is there, in this state of affairs, for a conservative disposition—or, indeed, for any stable society to which the conservative can be well disposed? What happens, in short, when the "adversary culture," to use Trilling's apt phrase, has become the dominant culture?

One can hardly fault Oakeshott for not having anticipated the cultural revolution of the sixties; few people did. Yet the conservative more than the liberal (and the student of Hobbes still more) might have been expected to do so, since he has traditionally been sensitive to the precariousness of social arrangements, the fragility of the social fabric. The French Revolution had hardly started before Burke had taken its full measure. Long before a republic was seriously contemplated, he spoke as if it were an accomplished fact. While Wordsworth and Paine were blissfully celebrating the dawn of a new age, Burke was delineating the shape of the Terror that was to come. But Oakeshott, as he often reminds us, is no Burke—not even a Burkean. In his scheme of things Burke belongs, together with Bentham, at the opposite pole from his own heroes: Montaigne, Pascal, Hobbes, and Hume.[27] For Burke is only another variety of Rationalist, a believer in religion and religious institutions, in natural law, in an organic society held together not only by the bonds of habit but also by the bonds of the natural order, that "great primeval contract of eternal society."[28] From Oakeshott's perspective, these metaphysical beliefs are the ideological props of weak minds. Yet it may be that these beliefs give Burke a purchase on reality that Oakeshott does not have, a means of understanding reality and judging it—and resisting it, if need be.

Oakeshott's distaste for Rationalism makes him properly distrustful of ideology, the commitment to a structure of belief that is presumed to be adequate to every occasion, that serves both as theory and "praxis," that professes to be scientific even while it evokes all the passion associated with religion. What is disturbing, however, is his tendency to equate ideology with ideas, to be equally suspicious of both, to be impatient with the rigorous exercise of mind. In one of his most eloquent essays, he describes the kind of "conversation" that constitutes civilized discourse—and that has its analogue in all civilized intercourse.[29] Conversation, he says, may have intervals of reasoned argument, but it cannot be that entirely or even largely. It must be hospitable to plays of fancy, flights of speculation, irrelevancies, and inconsequentialities. It speaks in many voices, recognizes no authority, requires no credentials. It asks of its participants only that they have the ability to converse and the good manners to listen, not that they reason cogently, make discoveries about the world, or try to improve it.

Oakeshott's essay is as elegant, urbane, gracious, and civilized as the ideal of conversation that is conjured up in it. One feels churlish in finding fault with it. Indeed, any criticism exposes one to the charge of being unduly earnest, hence insufficiently civilized. Yet if one attends to Oakeshott's argument—and for all his debonair tone he obviously intends us to do so—there is cause for disquiet. Consider, for example, a typical sentence: "As with children, who are great conversationalists, the playfulness is serious and the seriousness in the end is only play."[30] Were it not for passages such as this, one might be tempted to think that what he means by civilized conversation, indeed by civilization, is what Matthew Arnold meant by Hellenism: a free play of mind and imagination, in contrast to the Hebraism that is excessively moralistic, utilitarian, and philistine. But when Arnold praised Hellenism, it was not "play" he was praising but precisely play of *mind,* a high seriousness in the service of rationality and intellectuality. Nor would Arnold have lapsed into the romantic conceit of supposing children to be great conversationalists. We seem to have come a long way from the Oakeshott who confuted the Rationalist by appealing to maturity, sophistication, experience in the ways of the world. And yet, perhaps not so far as one might think.

Matthew Arnold's name may embolden us to a thought that verges on the presumptuous. It may suggest that Oakeshott's animus against Rationalism issues in a radical skepticism which stops just short of the "anarchy" that Arnold counterposed to "culture." "Anarchy" is surely an odd word to apply to a man as cultivated and civilized as Oakeshott. Yet it is not entirely inappropriate in regard to a "disposition" that resolutely refuses to be anything more than that, and cannot allow itself to embrace any idea, principle, or belief lest that imply a commitment to some absolute truth.

Skepticism is innocent enough, even attractive, in an age suffering from a surfeit of principles and enjoying a plenitude of good habits. One can then rely happily enough on those habits without inquiring into their source, their substance, or the reason for their perpetuation. But when those habits become insecure or fall into disuse, the conservative must look elsewhere for the civilized values he has come to enjoy. Oakeshott is right to criticize the Rationalists for subverting all habits, the good together with the bad. But so long as he provides us with no means for distinguishing between good and bad, let alone for cultivating a disposition to do good rather than bad, we are obliged to look elsewhere for guidance—to invoke mind, principle, belief, religion, or whatever else may be required to sustain civilization.

Notes
and
Index

Notes

1. Marriage and Morals Among the Victorians

1. Michael Holroyd, *Lytton Strachey: A Critical Biography* (New York, 1967–8), II, 261.
2. Lytton Strachey, *Eminent Victorians* (London, 1918), pp. 210, 264, 39.
3. Phyllis Rose, *Parallel Lives: Five Victorian Marriages* (New York, 1983), p. 5.
4. Ibid., pp. 7–8.
5. Ibid., pp. 17–18.
6. Ibid., pp. 266, 17.
7. Ibid., p. 12.
8. Ibid., p. 55.
9. Ibid., p. 56.
10. Ibid., pp. 57, 60.
11. Ibid., p. 288, n. 11.
12. Ibid., p. 18.
13. Ibid., pp. 189, 191.
14. Gertrude Himmelfarb, *On Liberty and Liberalism: The Case of John Stuart Mill* (New York, 1974), pp. 218–19.
15. Ibid., pp. 230–1.
16. Rose, p. 137.
17. Ibid., pp. 135–6.
18. Ibid., p. 264.
19. Ibid., p. 265.
20. Ibid., p. 263.
21. Ibid., p. 270.
22. Ibid., p. 269.
23. The reviewer in the *New York Times Book Review* (Oct. 13, 1983) took Rose to task for ignoring the "familiar gossip" that Lewes was unfaithful. If that was the gossip at the time, Eliot's most authoritative biographer, Gilbert S. Haight, finds no evidence for it as a fact. See *George Eliot: A Biography* (New York, 1968), p. 393.
24. Rose, p. 226.
25. Ibid., p. 221.
26. Ibid.
27. Haight, p. 404.
28. Rose, p. 220.

29. Himmelfarb, p. 212.
30. Rose, p. 220.
31. Ibid., p. 213.
32. Ibid.
33. *George Eliot's Life as Related in Her Letters and Journals,* ed. J. W. Cross (Boston, n.d.), III, 179.
34. John Stuart Mill, "Theism," in *Essays on Politics and Culture,* ed. Gertrude Himmelfarb (New York, 1962), p. 487.
35. Thomas Carlyle, *Past and Present* (Everyman ed., n.d.), p. 193.
36. John Forster, *The Life of Charles Dickens* (London, 2-vol. ed., n.d.), I, 6.
37. Gertrude Himmelfarb, *Victorian Minds* (New York, 1968), p. 291.
38. *The Autobiography of Bertrand Russell, 1872–1914* (Boston, 1967), p. 120. On Myers, see page 60.

2. A Genealogy of Morals

1. Friedrich Nietzsche, *Twilight of the Gods,* trans. R. J. Hollingdale (Penguin ed., Baltimore, 1968), p. 70.
2. Nietzsche, *The Genealogy of Morals,* trans. Francis Golffing (New York, 1956), 165; John Stuart Mill, "Coleridge" (1840), in *Essays on Politics and Culture,* ed. Gertrude Himmelfarb (New York, 1962), p. 166; Noel Annan, "The Intellectual Aristocracy," in *Studies in Social History: A Tribute to G. M. Trevelyan,* ed. J. H. Plumb (London, 1955), pp. 243ff.; Annan, *Leslie Stephen: His Thought and Character in Relation to His Time* (Cambridge, Mass., 1952), pp. 1ff; Annan, *Leslie Stephen: The Godless Victorian* (New York, 1984), pp. 3ff.
3. Annan, *Social History,* passim.
4. E. M. Forster, "Mrs. Hannah More" (1928), in *Abinger Harvest* (London, 1936), p. 234.
5. Ibid., pp. 236–7.
6. Forster, "Henry Thornton" (1939), in *Two Cheers for Democracy* (London, 1951), pp. 197–8.
7. Ibid., p. 201.
8. Forster, *Marianne Thornton: A Domestic Biography, 1797–1887* (New York, 1956).
9. Forster, "Mrs. Hannah More," in *Abinger Harvest,* p. 234.
10. Michael Holroyd, *Lytton Strachey: A Critical Biography* (New York, 1967–8), I, 131.
11. T. B. Macaulay, "Westminster Reviewer's Defence of Mill" (1829), in *Works,* ed. Lady Trevelyan (London, 1875), V, 298.
12. F. W. Maitland, *Life and Letters of Leslie Stephen* (London, 1906), pp. 144–5.
13. Virginia Woolf, "Old Bloomsbury" (1921–2), in *Moments of Being: Unpublished Autobiographical Writings,* ed.

Jeanne Schulkind (New York, 1976), p. 163.

14. Among those who reject the appellation are Clive Bell, *Old Friends* (London, 1956), p. 126; Quentin Bell, *Bloomsbury* (London, 1968), p. 12; and Phyllis Rose, *Woman of Letters: A Life of Virginia Woolf* (New York, 1978), p. 76. Those who use it matter-of-factly or defend its use include Virginia Woolf, "Old Bloomsbury"; Leonard Woolf, *Beginning Again: An Autobiography of the Years 1911 to 1918* (New York, 1963), pp. 21–2; J. K. Johnstone, *The Bloomsbury Group: A Study of E. M. Forster, Lytton Strachey, Virginia Woolf, and Their Circle* (New York, 1954); Annan, *Leslie Stephen: His Thought and Character,* pp. 123ff.; Leon Edel, *Bloomsbury: A House of Lions* (Philadelphia, 1979), pp. 11ff.; and Robert Skidelsky, *John Maynard Keynes* (London, 1983), pp. 242ff.

15. Edel, pp. 256–7.

16. Annan, *Leslie Stephen: Godless Victorian,* p. 336.

17. Gertrude Himmelfarb, "Leslie Stephen: The Victorian as Intellectual," in *Victorian Minds* (New York, 1968), p. 215.

18. Forster, "Virginia Woolf" (1941), in *Two Cheers for Democracy,* p. 259.

19. Johnstone, p. 36.

20. Ibid., p. 49.

21. Virginia Woolf, "Mr. Bennett and Mrs. Brown" (1924), in *Collected Essays* (New York, 1967), I, 320.

22. Virginia Woolf, "Montaigne" (1925), ibid., III, 22.

23. Nietzsche, *Genealogy of Morals,* p. 286.

24. Skidelsky, p. 118.

25. Holroyd, I, 180.

26. John Maynard Keynes, "My Early Beliefs," in *Two Memoirs* (New York, 1949), p. 82.

27. Edel, p. 189.

28. G. E. Moore, *Principia Ethica* (Cambridge, Eng., 1965), pp. 188–9.

29. Keynes, *Memoirs,* p. 82.

30. Ibid., pp. 97–8.

31. Ibid., p. 96.

32. Ibid., pp. 97–8.

33. Ibid., pp. 92, 98.

34. *The Letters of Sidney and Beatrice Webb,* ed. Norman Mackenzie (Cambridge, Eng., 1978), II, 372 (Sept. 18, 1911). Paul Levy argues that Bloomsbury was influenced not so much by Moore's book as by his personality, and that Keynes's memoir is confusing and misleading—*G. E. Moore and the Cambridge Apostles* (New York, 1979), pp. 6–7, 240ff. This interpretation is strongly rebutted by Skidelsky, pp. 146, 245. Annan also makes much of Moore's influence ("The Mind of the 'Twenties,' " *The Listener*, Feb. 8, 1951, pp. 211–12).

35. Bertrand Russell, *Autobiography* (Boston, 1967), I, 95.

36. Edel, p. 180.

37. *The Letters of Virginia Woolf,* ed. Nigel Nicolson and Joanne

Trautmann (New York, 1975–80), IV, 195–6 (Aug. 2, 1930). On this occasion she added, "What a snob I was: for they have immense vitality, and I think I like that quality best of all." But having said that, she went on to speak of them with contempt and disgust. For similar remarks, see, for example, *Letters,* I, 184 (April 5, 1905); ibid., IV, 222–3 (Sept. 28, 1930); and *The Diary of Virginia Woolf,* ed. Anne Oliver Bell and Andrew McNellie (New York, 1977–84), III, 320–1 (Sept. 29, 1930).

38. Skidelsky, p. xviii.
39. Keynes, *The Economic Consequences of the Peace* (New York, 1920), p. 20. See also Roberta and David Schaefer, "The Political Philosophy of J. M. Keynes," *Public Interest* (Spring, 1983), p. 52.
40. On the disputed subject of Keynes's application for conscientious-objector status, see Skidelsky, pp. 318ff.
41. Ibid., p. 345.
42. Peter Stansky and William Abrahams, *Journey to the Frontier: Julian Bell and John Cornford, Their Lives and the 1930s* (London, 1966), p. 23.
43. Skidelsky, p. 326.
44. Holroyd, II, 179.
45. Bell, *Bloomsbury,* p. 68.
46. Forster, "What I Believe" (1938), in *Two Cheers for Democracy,* pp. 77–8.
47. Ibid., p. 78.
48. Ibid., p. 79.

49. Ibid., p. 82.
50. Forster, "Liberty in England" (1935), in *Abinger Harvest,* p. 63.
51. Keynes, p. 97.
52. Forster, "Liberty in England," in *Abinger Harvest,* p. 63.
53. Forster, "Post Munich" (1939), in *Two Cheers for Democracy,* p. 35.
54. Hilton Kramer, "Bloomsbury Idols," *New Criterion* (January, 1984), pp. 2ff.
55. See, for example, Rose, *Woman of Letters.*
56. Bell, *Bloomsbury,* p. 9.
57. Charles H. Hession, *John Maynard Keynes: A Personal Biography of the Man Who Revolutionized Capitalism and the Way We Live* (New York, 1984), p. 64.
58. Keynes, *Memoir,* p. 102.
59. Holroyd, I, 413.
60. Edel, p. 77.
61. Francis Spalding, *Vanessa Bell* (New Haven, 1983), p. 177. See also Angelica Garnett, *Deceived with Kindness* (London, 1984), pp. 147, 155.
62. Holroyd, I, 338.
63. Holroyd, I, 185 (April 8, 1906).
64. *A Writer's Diary: Being Extracts from the Diary of Virginia Woolf,* ed. Leonard Woolf (London, 1953), p. 47 (Aug. 16, 1922).
65. Edel, p. 189.
66. Ibid., p. 265.
67. Forster, "English Prose Between 1918 and 1939" (1944), in *Two Cheers for Democracy,* p. 289.

68. Bell, *Bloomsbury*, pp. 117, 106.
69. Johnstone, p. 376.
70. Edel, p. 263.
71. Keynes, *Memoirs,* p. 76.
72. Ibid., p. 103.
73. F. R. Leavis, "Keynes, Lawrence and Cambridge," in *The Common Pursuit* (London, 1952), p. 260.

3. The Victorian Trinity

1. Peter Gay, *Voltaire's Politics: The Poet as Realist* (Princeton, 1959), p. 239.
2. Ludwig Feuerbach, *The Essence of Christianity,* trans. George Eliot (New York, 1957), p. 271.
3. Karl Marx, *Critique of Hegel's Philosophy of Right,* trans. Annette Jolin and Joseph O'Malley (Cambridge, Eng., 1970), p. 132.
4. Friedrich Nietzsche, *The Genealogy of Morals,* trans. Francis Golffing (New York, 1956), pp. 166, 191.
5. Elie Halévy, *England in 1815* (vol. I of *A History of the English People in the Nineteenth Century*), trans. E. I. Watkin and D. A. Barker (London, 1960), p. 387.
6. The use of the "war" metaphor is well documented in James R. Moore, *The Post-Darwinian Controversies: A Study of the Protestant Struggle to Come to Terms with Darwin in Great Britain and America, 1870–1900* (Cambridge, Eng., 1979), pp. 19ff.
7. This is the contemporary report of one member of the audience, the distinguished historian John Richard Green, then an undergraduate at Oxford. See Green, *Letters,* ed. Leslie Stephen (New York, 1901), p. 45 (July 3, 1860).
8. Gertrude Himmelfarb, *Darwin and the Darwinian Revolution* (New York, 1959), p. 276.
9. *The Life and Letters of Charles Darwin,* ed. Francis Darwin (London, 1887), II, 324–5 (July, 1860).
10. Jack Morrell and Arnold Thackray, *Gentlemen of Science: Early Years of the British Association for the Advancement of Science* (Oxford, 1981), p. 21; Samuel Taylor Coleridge, *On the Constitution of the Church and State* (vol. X of *Collected Works*) (Princeton, 1976), pp. 46ff.
11. Coleridge, pp. 70, 44.
12. Ibid., p. 43.
13. Morrell and Thackray, pp. 21ff.
14. *Life and Letters of Darwin,* II, 288 (Nov. 18, 1859).
15. *Essays and Reviews* (London, 1860), p. 139.
16. Himmelfarb, p. 373.
17. Asa Gray, *Letters,* ed. James L. Gray (London, 1893), II, 656 (Aug. 14, 1875).
18. Himmelfarb, p. 374.

19. Moore, p. 303.
20. Frank Miller Turner, *Between Science and Religion: The Reaction to Scientific Naturalism in Late Victorian England* (New Haven, 1974).
21. Ibid., p. 55.
22. Ibid., p. 112.
23. See chapter 1, page 21.
24. L. E. Elliott-Binns, *English Thought, 1860–1900: The Theological Aspect* (London, 1956), p. 59.
25. Turner, p. 51.
26. Ibid., p. 208.
27. Ibid., p. 144.
28. Ibid., p. 164.
29. Ibid., p. 185.
30. Ibid., p. 188.
31. Lewis Feuer, unpublished essay, "The Owenite Communism of Alfred Russel Wallace and the Formation of the Theory of Natural Selection," p. 60, quoting Frank Podmore, *Modern Spiritualism: A History and a Criticism* (London, 1902), I, 209.
32. R. K. Webb, *Harriet Martineau: A Radical Victorian* (New York, 1960), p. 246.
33. Turner, pp. 97–8.
34. Feuer, pp. 51ff.
35. Turner, pp. 3, 9.
36. T. H. Huxley, "The Origin of Species" (1860), in *Darwiniana Essays* (New York, 1893), p. 52.
37. Ibid., p. 74.
38. Huxley, "The Darwinian Hypothesis" (1859), ibid., p. 20.
39. *Life and Letters of Thomas Henry Huxley,* ed. Leonard Huxley (London, 1903), I, 314 (Sept. 23, 1860).
40. Ibid., pp. 347–8 (May 5, 1863).
41. Huxley, "Agnosticism" (1889), in *Science and Christian Tradition* (New York, 1898), p. 239.
42. *Life and Letters of Huxley,* III, 97–8, quoting *Agnostic Annual,* 1884.
43. Turner, p. 29.
44. Huxley, "On the Relations of Man to the Lower Animals" (1862), in *Man's Place in Nature and Other Essays* (London, 1906), pp. 96–7.
45. Ibid., p. 102.
46. *Life and Letters of Huxley,* I, 323–4 (Jan. 6, 1861).
47. Huxley, "Science and Morals" (1886), in *Evolution and Ethics and Other Essays* (New York, 1898), pp. 119, 122, 133.
48. Huxley, *Man's Place in Nature,* p. xv.
49. Turner, p. 85.
50. Huxley, *Evolution and Ethics,* pp. 81ff. See chapter 4, pages 81–2.
51. Huxley, "Prologue," in *Essays upon Some Controverted Questions* (London, 1892), p. 53.
52. Nietzsche, "Expeditions of an Untimely Man" (#5), in *Twilight of the Idols,* trans. R. J. Hollingdale (London, 1968), p. 69.
53. Ibid., p. 70.
54. Hesketh Pearson, *George Bernard Shaw: His Life and Personality* (New York, 1963), p. 224.
55. Nietzsche, *Beyond Good and*

Evil, trans. Walter Kaufmann (New York, 1966), p. 102 (#189).

56. Ibid., p. 190 (#252).
57. Nietzsche, *Genealogy of Morals,* p. 188; *Twilight of the Idols,* pp. 75–6 (#14); *The Gay Science,* in *The Portable Nietzsche,* ed. Walter Kaufmann (New York, 1968), p. 94 (#4); and *The Will to Power,* trans. Walter Kaufmann and R. J. Hollingdale (New York, 1967), p. 364 (#685). Arthur C. Danto belittles Nietzsche's objections to Darwinism, suggesting that they were based on a misreading of Darwin and a pun on the word "existence." (*Nietzsche as Philosopher* [New York, 1965], pp. 186–7, 223–4.) But this seems to me to trivialize and distort Nietzsche's point.

58. Nietzsche, *Beyond Good and Evil,* p. 157 (#228).
59. Ibid., p. 190 (#252).
60. Nietzsche, *Will to Power,* pp. 488–9 (#925–6).
61. Nietzsche, *Twilight of the Gods,* pp. 74–5 (#12).

4. Social Darwinism, Sociobiology, and the Two Cultures

1. Lord Acton, *Letters to Mary Gladstone* (New York, 1905), p. 99.
2. Thomas Robert Malthus, *An Essay on the Principle of Population,* ed. Gertrude Himmelfarb (reprint of 1st ed., New York, 1960), p. 61.
3. Walter E. Houghton, *The Victorian Frame of Mind: 1830–1870* (New Haven, 1957), quoting David Masson, "The Poems of Arthur Hugh Clough," *Macmillan's Magazine,* 1862.
4. George Eliot, "Janet's Repentance," in *Scenes of Clerical Life* (Philadelphia, n.d.), p. 342.
5. Charles Darwin, *The Descent of Man and Selection in Relation to Sex* (rev. ed., London, 1901), p. 146.
6. Alfred Tennyson, "In Memoriam," cxviii.
7. T. H. Huxley, *Life and Letters,* ed. Leonard Huxley (London, 1903), I, 316–17 (Sept. 23, 1860).
8. Huxley, "Science and Morals" (1886), in *Evolution and Ethics and Other Essays* (New York, 1898), p. 146.
9. Huxley, "The Struggle for Existence in Human Society" (1888), ibid., pp. 199–200.
10. Huxley, "Evolution and Ethics" (1893), ibid., p. 58.
11. Ibid., pp. 81, 83.
12. Ibid., p. 82.
13. Huxley, "Evolution and Ethics: Prolegomena" (1894), ibid., pp. 19, 23.
14. Huxley, *Life and Letters,* III, 320.
15. Darwin, *Life and Letters,* ed.

Francis Darwin (London, 1887), II, 197.

16. Arnold C. Brackman, *A Delicate Arrangement: The Strange Case of Charles Darwin and Alfred Russel Wallace* (New York, 1980), p. 23.

17. Matthew Arnold, "In Harmony with Nature," in *The Poems of Matthew Arnold, 1840–1866* (London, 1908), p. 35.

18. Arnold, "Literature and Science" (1882), in *Complete Prose Works of Matthew Arnold* (Ann Arbor, 1974), X, 65–8.

19. C. P. Snow, "The Two Cultures and the Scientific Revolution" (1959), in *Public Affairs* (New York, 1971).

20. Snow, "The Two Cultures: A Second Look" (1963), ibid., p. 59. (Snow did mention Darwin in passing in this second essay.)

21. E. O. Wilson, *Sociobiology: The New Synthesis* (Cambridge, Mass., 1975), p. 4.

22. Wilson, *On Human Nature* (Cambridge, Mass., 1978), pp. x, 10.

23. *New York Review of Books,* Nov. 13, 1975.

24. Ibid., Dec. 11, 1975.

25. Wilson, *On Human Nature,* p. 80.

26. Lionel Trilling, "Freud: Within and Beyond Culture" (1955), in *Beyond Culture: Essays on Literature and Learning* (New York, 1965), p. 115.

27. Wilson, *On Human Nature,* p. 10.

28. Ibid., p. 7; *Sociobiology,* p. 562.

29. *On Human Nature,* p. 167.

30. Albert Rosenfeld, "Sociobiology Stirs a Controversy over Limits of Science," *Smithsonian* (September, 1980), p. 74.

31. Snow, p. 19.

32. See chapter 1, page 21.

33. C. S. Lewis, *The Abolition of Man* (New York, 1973 [1st ed. 1947]).

5. Bentham Versus Blackstone

1. *Works of Jeremy Bentham,* ed. John Bowring (Edinburgh, 1838–43), I, 260.

2. Jeremy Bentham, *A Comment on the Commentaries and A Fragment on Government,* J. H. Burns and H. L. A. Hart (London, 1977), p. 526. (All citations are to this edition, unless otherwise noted.)

3. Ibid., pp. 504, 526, 540.

4. Ibid., pp. 515, 517.

5. Ibid., pp. 545–7.

6. *Correspondence of Jeremy Bentham,* ed. Timothy L. S. Sprigge (London, 1968), II, 103, 148–9 (March 10, 1777).

7. For a more complete account of this episode, see Gertrude Himmelfarb, "Bentham Scholarship and the Bentham 'Problem,'" *Journal of Modern History,* 1969, pp. 200–4. Lind's manuscript (or part

of it) is in the collection of Bentham papers at University College London (Mss. XCV: 1–28).

8. The *Fragment* should not be confused with Bentham's *Comment on the Commentaries,* a more ambitious but incomplete work which was first published almost a century after his death. But even this much larger work dealt almost entirely with two sections of Blackstone's introduction.

9. William Blackstone, *Commentaries on the Laws of England* (Oxford, 1765–9), I, 46–9. This, the first edition, was the one used by Bentham (*Fragment,* p. 401). Unless otherwise noted, all references are to this edition.

10. Ibid., p. 47.

11. Ibid., p. 51.

12. *Fragment,* p. 394.

13. Ibid.

14. "A General View of a Complete Code of Laws" (1802), in *Works,* III, 163.

15. *Fragment,* p. 413.

16. Ibid., pp. 400, 407; Blackstone, *Commentaries,* IV, 49. Bentham quoted this first as "everything as it should be," and then as "everything is as it should be."

17. Ibid., p. 409.

18. Ibid., p. 420.

19. Ibid., pp. 429–31.

20. *Commentaries,* I, 47.

21. *Fragment,* p. 472.

22. *Commentaries,* I, 48.

23. Ibid., IV, 435.

24. *Fragment,* pp. 420, 413.

25. Ibid., p. 473.

26. Ibid., p. 393. Here, as elsewhere, I have eliminated most of the italics. Bentham used italics so indiscriminately that to reproduce them all gives an undue impression of emphasis.

27. Ibid., p. 448.

28. Ibid., p. 440.

29. Ibid., pp. 398–9.

30. Ibid., p. 452.

31. Ibid., p. 481.

32. Ibid., pp. 482–3.

33. William Cobbett, in *Political Register,* 1818. His *Legacy to Labourers* (1834) was also full of quotations from Blackstone.

34. *Fragment,* p. 484.

35. Ibid., pp. 485–6.

36. Ibid., p. 485.

37. *Constitutional Code,* in *Works,* IX, 119.

38. *Fragment,* pp. 502–3.

39. "Memoirs," in *Works,* X, 57, 63.

40. Ibid.

41. Mary P. Mack, *Jeremy Bentham: An Odyssey of Ideas* (New York, 1963), p. 363.

42. Bentham Papers, University College London, Mss. CXLIX.

43. Gertrude Himmelfarb, "The Haunted House of Jeremy Bentham," in *Victorian Minds* (New York, 1968), pp. 39–40.

44. *Commentaries,* I, 172.

45. Ibid., I, 4, 27, 30.

46. John Stuart Mill, "Bentham," in *Essays on Politics and Culture,* ed. Gertrude Himmelfarb (New York, 1962), p. 113.

47. James Fitzjames Stephen, *A History of the Criminal Law of*

England (London, 1883), II, 214–15.

48. Daniel J. Boorstin, *Mysterious Science of the Law* (Boston, 1958), p. ii.

49. Edmund Burke, "Speech on Moving the Resolutions for Conciliation with the Colonies," in *Works* (London,

World's Classics ed., n.d.), II, 185–90.

50. Bentham, *An Introduction to the Principles of Morals and Legislation,* ed. J. H. Burns and H. L. A. Hart (London, 1970), p. 9; *Fragment,* p. 448.

51. *The Federalist,* number 9.

52. Boorstin, p. i.

6. Bentham's Utopia

1. R. H. Tawney, *Religion and the Rise of Capitalism* (New York, 1947), p. 222.

2. Lionel Robbins, *Bentham in the Twentieth Century* (London, 1965), p. 15.

3. *The Works of Jeremy Bentham,* ed. John Bowring (London, 1838–43), VIII, 358. For the substantial differences between this plan and the New Poor Law of 1834, see the original version of this essay in the *Journal of British Studies,* November 1970, pp. 121–2.

4. M. I. Zagday, "Bentham and the Poor Law," in *Jeremy Bentham and the Law,* ed. G. W. Keeton and G. Schwarzenberger (London, 1948), pp. 64–65.

5. Charles W. Everett, "The Constitutional Code of Jeremy Bentham," in *Jeremy Bentham Bicentenary Celebrations* (London, 1948), pp. 14–15.

6. Jacob Viner, "Bentham and John Stuart Mill," in *The Long View and the Short* (Glencoe, Ill., 1958), p. 309 (originally

published in the *American Economic Review,* 1949).

7. Mary Mack, *Jeremy Bentham* (New York, 1963), pp. 315, 212–13.

8. Robert J. Lampman, "The Anti-Poverty Program in Historical Perspective," February 25, 1965.

9. Charles F. Bahmueller, *The National Charity Company: Jeremy Bentham's Silent Revolution* (Berkeley, 1981), p. 103.

10. Bentham originally intended to publish two works: *Pauper Systems Compared* and *Pauper Management Improved.* The first was to have been based on two questionnaires printed in an earlier issue of the *Annals;* it was not written, probably because the replies were inadequate. (Some of the returned questionnaires are in the Bentham Mss. University College London, CXXXIII, 42–6, 48, 51–4, 58.) And he never completed the "Outline" of the second, so that that word appears in the title of all

the later editions, and the text continues to refer to sections that were never written. That "Outline," however, comes to something like 70,000 words, and his manuscripts attest to the considerable labor and thought that went into its composition. The manuscripts also include title pages for a new edition as well as new copies of the text; these date from January 1828 to March 1831, a year before his death. (British Museum Mss. 33550 ff. 372–97.)

Citations here are to the edition printed in Volume VIII of the *Works,* which is identical to the original work as published in the *Annals.* For differences between this text and the editions of 1802 and 1812, see page 140 below. Unless otherwise specified, it is this volume of the *Works* that is cited.

11. *Works,* IV, 39–172. For a detailed account of the Panopticon, see Gertrude Himmelfarb, *Victorian Minds* (New York, 1968), pp. 32–81.

12. *Works,* VIII, 369, 373–4, 397.

13. Univ. Coll. Mss. CLIIIb, 309; CLI, 308. Where Bentham provided alternative words or phrases in his manuscripts, as he often did, I have selected those which seem to represent his final choice, or failing any indication of that, those which most clearly convey his meaning. I have also occasionally simplified his

erratic punctuation. Unless otherwise specified, "Mss." refers to this collection.

14. *Works,* pp. 380–1, 386. In the first years of the enterprise, the governors would be salaried employees, but thereafter they would be on a contractual basis.

15. Mss. CLIIb, 335–6; CLI, 5.

16. Ibid., CLIVb, 547.

17. *Works,* p. 381. The term "headmoney" was commonly used at the time in quite another sense, to refer to child allowances as provided under the Speenhamland system.

18. Ibid.

19. Ibid., p. 392. The expression "pitch of perfection" was used in the *Panopticon* (IV, 63–4) and frequently in the manuscripts (e.g., CLI, 296, 317; CLIVb, 541).

20. *Works,* pp. 371, 386–7, 391, 393–4; Mss. CLIb, 393.

21. *Works,* p. 369.

22. Ibid., p. 383.

23. For details of Pitt's bill and Bentham's critique, see the original version of this essay in the *Journal of British Studies,* 1970, pp. 118ff.

24. Mss. CLIVb, 544–5.

25. *Works,* p. 370.

26. Ibid., p. 401.

27. Ibid., p. 369.

28. Ibid., pp. 401–2.

29. Ibid., p. 403.

30. Ibid., pp. 403–4.

31. Ibid., p. 404.

32. Ibid., pp. 404–5.

33. Mss. CLIVa, 242–3.

34. *Works,* p. 20.

35. Ibid., p. 404.
36. Ibid., pp. 417–19; Mss. CLIVa, 223.
37. *Works*, p. 405; Mss. CLIVa, 223.
38. Mss. CLIVa, 216.
39. Ibid., CXXXIII, 17.
40. Ibid., CLI, 157.
41. Ibid., CLIVa, 238.
42. Ibid., 181.
43. *Works*, pp. 383, 369.
44. Ibid., p. 402.
45. Ibid., p. 384.
46. Ibid., p. 388.
47. Ibid., p. 389.
48. Ibid., pp. 376–7.
49. Mss. CLIIIa, 188.
50. *Works*, pp. 382–4.
51. Ibid., pp. 370, 383, 397, 418.
52. Ibid., p. 383.
53. Ibid., p. 398; Mss. CLIVb, 385.
54. *Works*, p. 370.
55. Ibid., p. 390.
56. Ibid., p. 404.
57. Ibid., p. 374; Mss. CLIIa, 146.
58. *Works*, p. 369.
59. Ibid., pp. 404–5.
60. Mss. CLI, 290.
61. Ibid., 284; *Works*, p. 390.
62. *Works*, p. 390.
63. Mss. CLIIIa, 90.
64. *Works*, p. 390.
65. Mss. CLI, 348, 377.
66. Ibid., CLIIIa, 107. The age of parish apprenticeship was sometimes lower than fourteen, but Bentham seems to have taken that as the norm.
67. Ibid., CLIVb, 317.
68. *Works*, p. 388.
69. Mss. CLIIa, 4; CLI, 397.
70. *Works*, pp. 405, 373.
71. Ibid., p. 372.

72. *Works*, pp. 373, 385; Mss. CLI, 133.
73. *Works*, p. 391; Mss. CXXXIII, 14, 50.
74. *Works*, p. 395.
75. Mss. CXLIX, 92.
76. *Works*, p. 395.
77. Ibid., p. 396.
78. Mss. CLI, 284.
79. *Works*, p. 397.
80. Ibid., p. 437.
81. Mss. CLIVa, 44.
82. Ibid., CXXXIII, 104; *Works*, pp. 396–7.
83. Himmelfarb, *Victorian Minds*, p. 50.
84. Mss. CLIIIa, 85, 111; CXXXIII, 104; CXLIX, 71.
85. Ibid., CXXXIII, 105, 120–3; CLIIIa, 123; CXLIX, 74.
86. Ibid., CLIIIa, 123.
87. Ibid., CXLIX, 54.
88. Ibid., CXXXIII, 104; CXLIX, 62, 64.
89. Ibid., CXXXIII, 100.
90. Ibid., CLIIIa, 139.
91. Ibid., 140.
92. Ibid., 141.
93. *Works*, p. 384.
94. Ibid., pp. 422–3.
95. Ibid., p. 388.
96. Ibid., pp. 430–2.
97. Ibid., pp. 435–6.
98. Mss. CLIIIa, 93.
99. *Works*, p. 437.
100. Ibid.
101. Mss., CXXXIII, 94.
102. For a more complete discussion of Malthusianism in relation to this plan, see the *Journal of British Studies*, 1970, pp. 119–20.
103. *Works*, p. 436.
104. Ibid., pp. 436, 439.

105. Ibid., p. 439.
106. Mss. CLIIIb, 260.
107. *Works*, p. 437.
108. Ibid., p. 362.
109. Mss. CLI, 400.
110. Himmelfarb, *Victorian Minds*, p. 59.
111. Mss. CLI, 102–5.
112. *Works*, XI, 103.
113. Ibid.
114. Ibid., pp. 96–7. See also X, 212, for a slightly different wording of the same complaint.
115. Ibid., XI, 72.
116. Shirley Letwin, *The Pursuit of Certainty* (Cambridge, Eng., 1965), pp. 183, 187–8.

7. Godwin's Utopia

1. William Godwin, *An Enquiry Concerning Political Justice, and its Influence on General Virtue and Happiness* (1st ed., London, 1793), I, 237. (In the second edition, "General Virtue" was changed to "Morals.")
2. Ibid., II, 846–7.
3. Ibid., I, 163.
4. Ibid., p. 80.
5. Ibid., p. 83.
6. Ibid., II, 862.
7. Ibid., pp. 865, 868.
8. Ibid., I, 1–2.
9. Ibid., II, 870–1.
10. Ibid., p. 871.
11. Ibid., pp. 871–2.
12. Ibid., I, 43.
13. Peter H. Marshall, *William Godwin* (New Haven, 1984), p. 117.
14. *Political Justice*, I, 241.
15. Ibid., II, 690.
16. Ibid., p. 565.
17. Ibid., p. 852.
18. Marshall, p. 112.
19. Ibid., p. 5.
20. *Political Justice*, I, 90.
21. Marshall, p. 3.
22. *Political Justice* (3rd ed., 1798), II, 510.
23. William Petersen, "The Malthus–Godwin Debate, Then and Now," *Demography* (February, 1971), p. 14.
24. Marshall, p. 43.
25. Don Locke, *A Fantasy of Reason: The Life and Thought of William Godwin* (London, 1980).
26. C. Kegan Paul, *William Godwin: His Friends and Contemporaries* (London, 1876), I, 80.
27. Marshall, p. 183.
28. Ibid., p. 186.
29. Ibid., p. 306.
30. Ibid., p. 324.
31. Ibid., p. 331.
32. Ibid., p. 388.
33. Ibid., p. 297.
34. Ibid., p. 344.
35. Ibid., p. 359.
36. Ibid., p. 233.
37. Ibid., p. 408.
38. *Political Justice* (1st ed.), II, 738–9.
39. Ibid. (3rd ed.), II, 366–9.
40. Ibid., II, 520.

8. Who Now Reads Macaulay?

1. Edmund Burke, *Reflections on the Revolution in France* (New York, 1961), p. 103. Burke may have been echoing Pope: "Who now reads Cowley?"

2. Thomas Babington Macaulay, *Works,* ed. Lady Trevelyan (London, 1875), I, 1.

3. J. Cotter Morison, *Macaulay* (London, 1902), p. 143.

4. G. Otto Trevelyan, *The Life and Letters of Lord Macaulay* (New York, 1875), II, 207.

5. Ibid., pp. 215–16.

6. Mark A. Thomson, *Macaulay* (Historical Association Pamphlet, London, 1959), p. 25.

7. J. W. Burrow, *A Liberal Descent: Victorian Historians and the English Past* (Cambridge, Eng., 1981), pp. 1–2.

8. Ibid., p. 300.

9. Herbert Butterfield, *The Englishman and his History* (London, 1944), p. 2.

10. Burke, p. 46.

11. Ibid., pp. 44–6.

12. Ibid., p. 46.

13. Macaulay, II, 395–6.

14. Joseph Hamburger, *Macaulay and the Whig Tradition* (Chicago, 1976).

15. Burke, p. 110.

16. Burrow, pp. 55ff.

17. Macaulay, "History" (1828), in *Works,* V, 136.

18. Ibid., p. 138.

19. Robert Brentano, "The Sound of Stubbs," *Journal of British Studies* (May 1967), p. 4.

20. Burrow, p. 164.

21. Ibid., p. 14.

22. Ibid., p. 224.

23. Ibid., p. 102.

24. G. P. Gooch, *History and Historians in the Nineteenth Century* (London, 1952), pp. 313–14.

25. Wilfrid Ward, *The Life of John Henry Cardinal Newman* (London, 1912), II, 1, quoting *Macmillan's Magazine* (December 1863).

26. Gertrude Himmelfarb, *Victorian Minds* (New York, 1968), p. 241.

27. Jacques Barzun, *Clio and the Doctors: Psycho-History, Quanto-History, and History* (Chicago, 1974), p. 110.

28. Macaulay, *Works,* I, 3.

29. Gooch, p. 325.

30. John Richard Green, *A Short History of the English People* (London, 1964), I, 1.

31. Ibid., p. xi.

32. Gooch, p. 330.

33. Green, I, xi.

34. Ibid., p. 274.

35. Ibid., pp. 3–4.

9. *Disraeli*

1. *Times Literary Supplement,* April 18, 1980, p. 434.
2. Paul Seabury, *Wall Street Journal,* June 23, 1981.
3. William Flavelle Monypenny and George Earle Buckle, *The Life of Benjamin Disraeli Earl of Beaconsfield* (3 vols., London, 1910–20); James Anthony Froude, *Thomas Carlyle: A History of the First Forty Years of His Life* (London, 1882), I, ix.
4. Robert Blake, *Disraeli* (London, 1966); Sarah Bradford, *Disraeli* (New York, 1983).
5. Benjamin Disraeli, Vol. I, *Letters: 1815–1834;* Vol. II, *Letters: 1835–1837,* ed. J. A. W. Gunn, John Matthews, Donald M. Schurman, and M. G. Wiebe (Toronto, 1982).
6. Bradford, p. 75.
7. Ibid., p. 88.
8. Robert Blake, *Disraeli's Grand Tour: Benjamin Disraeli and the Holy Land, 1830–31* (New York, 1982), p. 7.
9. Disraeli, *Tancred, or The New Crusade* (1st ed. 1847; London, Longmans, Green ed., n.d.), pp. 370, 294.
10. Bradford, p. 186. The expression appears repeatedly in his works. In *Tancred,* for example, Sidonia says: "All is race; there is no other truth" (p. 149).
11. Benjamin and Sarah Disraeli, *A Year at Hartlebury, or The Election* (Toronto, 1983), p. 103.
12. Cecil Roth, *Benjamin Disraeli: Earl of Beaconsfield* (New York, 1952), p. 60.
13. Blake, *Grand Tour,* p. 129.
14. Bradford, pp. 94, 113.
15. *Letters,* II, 42n (quoting speech, May 2, 1835).
16. Lawrence and Elisabeth Hanson, *Necessary Evil: The Life of Jane Welsh Carlyle* (New York, 1952), p. 413 (quoting Carlyle's notebook, Feb. 28, 1852); Monypenny and Buckle (2-vol. ed., London, 1929), II, 698.
17. *Tancred,* p. 427.
18. Isaiah Berlin, "Benjamin Disraeli, Karl Marx and the Search for Identity," in *Against the Current: Essays in the History of Ideas* (London, 1982), p. 270.
19. Blake, *Grand Tour,* pp. 130–2.
20. *Tancred,* p. 487.
21. Bradford, p. 126.
22. *Letters,* II, 60–1 (July 2, 1835).
23. Ibid., p. 62. See Gertrude Himmelfarb, "Politics and Ideology: The Reform Act of 1867," in *Victorian Minds* (New York, 1968).
24. 3 Hansard 49:246–52 (July 12, 1839).
25. Monypenny and Buckle, I, 486.
26. Bradford, p. 58; *A Year at Hartlebury,* p. 104.

27. *Endymion* (1st ed. 1880;
London, Longmans, Green ed.,
n.d.), p. 286.
28. Bradford, p. 337.

29. Ibid.
30. Blake, *Disraeli,* p. 624.
31. Ibid., p. 646.
32. *Letters,* I, 447.

10. The Webbs

1. Margaret Cole, *The Story of
Fabian Socialism* (New York,
1961), pp. 95ff.
2. Norman and Jeanne MacKenzie
have been the most assiduous
chroniclers of the Webbs. In
addition to their book on the
early history of the movement,
The Fabians (New York,
1977), they have edited *The
Diary of Beatrice Webb:* vol. I,
*1873–1892: "Glitter Around and
Darkness Within";* vol. II,
*1892–1905: "All the Good Things
of Life"* (Cambridge, Mass.,
1982–3). Norman MacKenzie
has also edited *The Letters of
Sidney and Beatrice Webb:* vol.
I, *Apprenticeships, 1873–1892;*
vol. II, *Partnership, 1892–1912;*
vol. III, *Pilgrimage, 1912–1947*
(Cambridge, Eng., 1978). The
two volumes of Beatrice Webb's
autobiography have been
reissued: *My Apprenticeship* and
Our Partnership (Cambridge,
Eng., 1979, 1975). (The
latest edition of the diary
is a substantial abridgment of
the original, but the latter is
available, in manuscript and
typescript, at the London
School of Economics.)
3. *Diary,* I, 189.
4. *My Apprenticeship,* p. 35.
5. Ibid., pp. 36–7.

6. Ibid., p. 38.
7. *Diary,* I, 188–9, 259.
8. Ibid., p. 215.
9. Ibid., p. 189.
10. *My Apprenticeship,* pp. 279,
284.
11. *Diary,* I, 107.
12. Ibid., pp. 102, 115, 108.
13. For example, ibid., II, 93.
14. Ibid., I, 118.
15. Ibid., pp. 324, 329; *Letters,* I,
382; *Diary,* II, 76.
16. *Letters,* I, 281, 201–2.
17. *Diary,* I, 355–6; *My
Apprenticeship,* p. 410; *Letters,*
I, 382.
18. *Letters,* I, 121.
19. Kingsley Martin, "The Webbs
in Retirement," in *The Webbs
and Their Work,* ed. Margaret
Cole (London, 1949), p. 297.
20. *Diary,* I, 324; II, 293, 203.
21. For example, ibid., 95, 126,
204.
22. H. G. Wells, *The New
Machiavelli* (London, 1946),
p. 172.
23. Desmond MacCarthy, "The
Webbs as I Saw Them," in
The Webbs and Their Work,
p. 124.
24. *Diary,* II, 193.
25. *Our Partnership,* p. 433.
26. Margaret Cole, *Beatrice Webb*
(New York, 1946), p. 69;
MacCarthy, p. 126.

27. *Diary,* II, 19.
28. Ibid., I, 358; *Our Partnership,* p. 12.
29. MacKenzie, *Fabians,* p. 62.
30. *Letters,* I, 274; *Our Partnership,* p. 7.
31. *Our Partnership,* p. 12.
32. *Diary,* II, 271; *Our Partnership,* pp. 259–60.
33. Bertrand Russell, *Autobiography, 1872–1914* (Boston, 1967), I, 107.
34. *Diary,* II, 262.
35. Wells, *New Machiavelli,* p. 165; R. C. K. Ensor, "Permeation," in *The Webbs and Their Work,* p. 63.
36. *Diary,* II, 204.
37. Martin, in *The Webbs and Their Work,* p. 287.
38. Wells, p. 160.
39. *Diary,* II, 224–5, 333.
40. *Beatrice Webb's Diaries, 1912–1924,* ed. Margaret Cole (London, 1952), p. 50.
41. *Diary,* II, 295, 217.
42. Ibid., I, 131.
43. Ibid., II, 236, 335, 336; *Our Partnership,* p. 120.
44. *Diary,* II, 212, 298.
45. Ibid., p. 267.
46. *Letters,* II, 204.
47. *Our Partnership,* p. 120.
48. Ibid.
49. *My Apprenticeship,* xliii–iv. (This introduction is inexplicably omitted from the Penguin edition.)
50. *Diary,* II, 199.
51. Ibid., p. 250.
52. Ibid., pp. 199–200.
53. *Our Partnership,* p. li.
54. Sidney and Beatrice Webb, *Soviet Communism: A New Civilization* (London, 1947), pp. 901, 908–9. (In the first edition, the title ended with a question mark.)
55. Sidney and Beatrice Webb, *A Constitution for the Socialist Commonwealth of Great Britain* (1st ed. 1920; Cambridge, Eng., 1975), p. 130.
56. *Diaries, 1924–1932,* ed. Margaret Cole (London, 1956), p. 299.
57. Ibid.
58. Barbara Drake, "The Webbs and Soviet Communism," in *The Webbs and Their Work,* p. 226.
59. *Diary,* I, 188.
60. MacKenzie, *Fabians,* p. 406; Hesketh Pearson, *George Bernard Shaw: His Life and Personality* (New York, 1963), p. 458.

11. Michael Oakeshott

1. Lionel Trilling, *The Liberal Imagination: Essays on Literature and Society* (New York, 1950), p. ix.
2. Michael Oakeshott, "On Being Conservative" (1956), in *Rationalism in Politics and Other Essays* (London, 1962), p. 168.
3. "The Activity of Being an Historian" (1955), ibid., pp. 137ff.
4. "Political Education" (1951), ibid., p. 132.
5. Josiah Lee Auspitz,

"Bibliographical Note," *Political Theory*, August 1976, pp. 295–6.

6. "Rationalism in Politics" (1947), ibid., pp. 1, 6.

7. Ibid., p. 11.

8. Ibid., p. 19.

9. "On Being Conservative" (1956), ibid., p. 169.

10. Ibid., pp. 172–3.

11. Ibid., p. 184.

12. Ibid., p. 186.

13. Ibid., p. 184.

14. Ibid., p. 193.

15. Ibid., p. 186.

16. Ibid., p. 194.

17. Ibid., p. 196.

18. Ibid., pp. 193–4.

19. Ibid., p. 195.

20. *Experience and Its Modes* (Cambridge, Eng., 1978), pp. 294–5.

21. Ibid., p. 308.

22. *On Human Conduct* (Oxford, 1975), pp. 81, 83, 86.

23. Ibid., p. 81.

24. *Religion and the Moral Life* (Cambridge, Eng., 1927), p. 13; "The Importance of the Historical Element in Christianity," *The Modern Churchman*, 1928–9, pp. 360–71.

25. "The Tower of Babel" (1948), in *Rationalism in Politics,* pp. 61–2.

26. Ibid., p. 65.

27. "On Being Conservative," ibid., p. 195.

28. Edmund Burke, *Reflections on the Revolution in France* (New York, 1961), p. 110.

29. "The Voice of Poetry in the Conversation of Mankind" (1959), in *Rationalism in Politics,* pp. 197ff.

30. Ibid., p. 202.

Index

Gertrude Himmelfarb is Distinguished Professor of History at the Graduate School of the City University of New York. She has received
fellowships from the Guggenheim Foundation, the National Endowment
for the Humanities, and the Woodrow Wilson International Center,
among others. Her previous books include *Lord Acton: A Study in Conscience and Politics; Darwin and the Darwinian Revolution; On Liberty and
Liberalism: The Case of John Stuart Mill; Victorian Minds,* which was
nominated for a National Book Award; and *The Idea of Poverty: England
in the Early Industrial Age.* Miss Himmelfarb has also edited works by
Acton, Malthus, and Mill.